ACTIVITIES 1940–1943

The Collected Writings of John Maynard Keynes

Keynes talking to reporters on his arrival in New York in May 1941.
(Business Week, © 1941 by McGraw-Hill, Inc.

THE COLLECTED WRITINGS OF
JOHN MAYNARD KEYNES

VOLUME XXIII

ACTIVITIES 1940-1943
EXTERNAL WAR FINANCE

EDITED BY

DONALD MOGGRIDGE

MACMILLAN

CAMBRIDGE UNIVERSITY PRESS

FOR THE

ROYAL ECONOMIC SOCIETY

Published for the Royal Economic Society
throughout the world, excluding
the U.S.A. and Canada, by

THE MACMILLAN PRESS LTD
London and Basingstoke
Associated companies in Delhi Dublin
Hong Kong Johannesburg Lagos Melbourne
New York Singapore Tokyo
and throughout the U.S.A. and Canada by

THE SYNDICS OF THE CAMBRIDGE UNIVERSITY PRESS
32 East 57th Street, New York, NY 10022, U.S.A.

Macmillan ISBN 0 333 19415 2 (excluding the U.S.A. and Canada)
C.U.P. ISBN 0 521 22016 5 (the U.S.A. and Canada only)

Printed in Great Britain
at the University Press, Cambridge

Library of Congress Cataloguing in Publication Data

Keynes, John Maynard, 1883–1946.
The collected writings of John Maynard Keynes.

Vol. XXIII has imprint: New York, Cambridge University Press,
for the Royal Economic Society.
CONTENTS: v. 1. Indian currency and finance.—
v. 2. The economic consequences of the peace.—
v. 3. A revision of the treaty. [etc.]
1. Economics—Collected works.
I. Royal Economic Society, London.
HB171.K44 330.15′6′08 76-13349

ISBN 0–521–22016–5

CONTENTS

GENERAL INTRODUCTION

This new standard edition of *The Collected Writings of John Maynard Keynes* forms the memorial to him of the Royal Economic Society. He devoted a very large share of his busy life to the Society. In 1911, at the age of twenty-eight, he became editor of the *Economic Journal* in succession to Edgeworth; two years later he was made secretary as well. He held these offices without intermittence until almost the end of his life. Edgeworth, it is true, returned to help him with the editorship from 1919 to 1925; Macgregor took Edgeworth's place until 1934, when Austin Robinson succeeded him and continued to assist Keynes down to 1945. But through all these years Keynes himself carried the major responsibility and made the principal decisions about the articles that were to appear in the *Economic Journal,* without any break save for one or two issues when he was seriously ill in 1937. It was only a few months before his death at Easter 1946 that he was elected president and handed over his editorship to Roy Harrod and the secretaryship to Austin Robinson.

In his dual capacity of editor and secretary Keynes played a major part in framing the policies of the Royal Economic Society. It was very largely due to him that some of the major publishing activities of the Society—Sraffa's edition of Ricardo, Stark's edition of the economic writings of Bentham, and Guillebaud's edition of Marshall, as well as a number of earlier publications in the 1930s—were initiated.

When Keynes died in 1946 it was natural that the Royal Economic Society should wish to commemorate him. It was perhaps equally natural that the Society chose to commemorate him by producing an edition of his collected works. Keynes himself had always taken a joy in fine printing, and the Society, with the help of Messrs Macmillan as publishers and the Cambridge University Press as printers, has been anxious to give Keynes's writings a permanent form that is wholly worthy of him.

The present edition will publish as much as is possible of his work in the field of economics. It will not include any private and personal correspondence or publish many letters in the possession of his family. The edition is concerned, that is to say, with Keynes as an economist.

Keynes's writings fall into five broad categories. First there are the books which he wrote and published as books. Second there are collections of articles and pamphlets which he himself made during his lifetime (*Essays in Persuasion* and *Essays in Biography*). Third, there is a very considerable volume of published but uncollected writings—articles written for newspapers, letters to newspapers, articles in journals that have not been included in his two volumes of collections, and various pamphlets. Fourth, there are a few hitherto unpublished writings. Fifth, there is correspondence with economists and concerned with economics or public affairs. It is the intention of this series to publish almost completely the whole of the first four categories listed above. The only exceptions are a few syndicated articles where Keynes wrote almost the same material for publication in different newspapers or in different countries, with minor and unimportant variations. In these cases, this series will publish one only of the variations, choosing the most interesting.

The publication of Keynes's economic correspondence must inevitably be selective. In the day of the typewriter and the filing cabinet and particularly in the case of so active and busy a man, to publish every scrap of paper that he may have dictated about some unimportant or ephemeral matter is impossible. We are aiming to collect and publish as much as possible, however, of the correspondence in which Keynes developed his own ideas in argument with his fellow economists, as well as the more significant correspondence at times when Keynes was in the middle of public affairs.

Apart from his published books, the main sources available to those preparing this series have been two. First, Keynes in his will made Richard Kahn his executor and responsible for his economic papers. They have been placed in the Marshall Library of the University of Cambridge and have been available for this edition. Until 1914 Keynes did not have a secretary and his earliest papers are in the main limited to drafts of important letters that he made in his own handwriting and retained. At that stage most of the correspondence that we possess is represented by what he received rather than by what he wrote. During the war years of 1914–18 Keynes was serving in the Treasury. With the opening in 1968 of the records under the thirty-year rule, many of the papers that he wrote then and later have become available. From 1919 onwards, throughout the rest of his life, Keynes had the help of a secretary—for many years Mrs Stevens. Thus for the last twenty-five years of his working life we have in most cases the carbon copies of his own letters as well as the originals of the letters that he received.

There were, of course, occasions during this period on which Keynes wrote himself in his own handwriting. In some of these cases, with the help of his correspondents, we have been able to collect the whole of both sides of some important interchange and we have been anxious, in justice to both correspondents, to see that both sides of the correspondence are published in full.

The second main source of information has been a group of scrapbooks kept over a very long period of years by Keynes's mother, Florence Keynes, wife of Neville Keynes. From 1919 onwards these scrapbooks contain almost the whole of Maynard Keynes's more ephemeral writing, his letters to newspapers and a great deal of material which enables one to see not only what he wrote but the reaction of others to his writing. Without these very carefully kept scrapbooks the task of any editor or biographer of Keynes would have been immensely more difficult.

The plan of the edition, as at present intended, is this. It will total thirty volumes. Of these the first eight are Keynes's published books from *Indian Currency and Finance*, in 1913, to the *General Theory* in 1936, with the addition of his *Treatise on Probability*. There next follow, as vols. IX and X, *Essays in Persuasion* and *Essays in Biography*, representing Keynes's own collections of articles. *Essays in Persuasion* differs from the original printing in two respects: it contains the full texts of the articles or pamphlets included in it and not (as in the original printing) abbreviated versions of these articles, and it also contains one or two later articles which are of exactly the same character as those included by Keynes in his original collection. In *Essays in Biography* there have been added a number of biographical studies that Keynes wrote both before and after 1933.

There will follow two volumes, XI–XII, of economic articles and correspondence and a further two volumes, already published, XIII–XIV, covering the development of his thinking as he moved towards the *General Theory*. There are included in these volumes such part of Keynes's economic correspondence as is closely associated with the articles that are printed in them. A supplement to these volumes, XXIX, will print some further material relating to the same issues, which has since been discovered.

The following thirteen volumes deal with Keynes's *Activities* during the years from the beginning of his public life in 1905 until his death. In each of the periods into which we divide this material, the volume concerned publishes his more ephemeral writings, all of it hitherto uncollected, his correspondence relating to these activities, and such other material and correspondence as is necessary to the understanding of Keynes's activities. These volumes are edited by Elizabeth Johnson and Donald Moggridge, and it has been their task to trace and interpret Keynes's activities sufficiently to make the material fully intelligible to a later generation. Elizabeth Johnson has been responsible for vols. XV–XVIII, covering Keynes's earlier years and his activities down to the end of World War I reparations and reconstruction. Donald Moggridge is responsible for all the remaining volumes recording Keynes's other activities from 1924 until his death in 1946.

The present plan of publication is to complete the record of Keynes's activities during World War II with the group of three volumes of which this forms one, and with a further two volumes that will next follow. These five volumes will cover not only the problems of external war finance, but also his contributions both in the Treasury and at Bretton Woods and elsewhere to the shaping of the post-war world. It is planned to publish the new material relating to the evolution of the *Treatise* and the *General Theory* with the last two of these World War II volumes. It will then remain to fill the gap between 1924 and 1939, to print certain of his published articles and the correspondence relating to them which have not appeared elsewhere in this edition, and to publish a volume of his social, political and literary writings.

Those responsible for this edition have been: Lord Kahn, both as Lord Keynes's executor and as a long and intimate friend of Lord Keynes, able to help in the interpreting of much that would be otherwise misunderstood; Sir Roy Harrod as the author of his biography; Austin Robinson as Keynes's co-editor on the *Economic Journal* and successor as Secretary of the Royal Economic Society. Austin Robinson has acted throughout as Managing Editor; Donald Moggridge is now associated with him as Joint Managing Editor.

In the early stages of the work Elizabeth Johnson was assisted by Jane Thistlethwaite, and by Mrs McDonald, who was originally responsible for the systematic ordering of the files of the Keynes papers. Judith Masterman for many years worked with Mrs Johnson on the papers. More recently Susan Wilsher, Margaret Butler and Leonora Woollam have continued the secretarial work. Barbara Lowe has been responsible for the indexing. Susan Howson undertook much of the important final editorial work on the present group of volumes. Judith Allen has been responsible for seeing the present group of volumes through the press.

EDITORIAL NOTE

In this volume, the second of three concerned with Keynes's involvement in the problems of financing Britain's war effort, the concentration is on external financial policy, in particular on lend lease. A later volume will deal with the final stages of lend lease and the transition to peace. A further three volumes will be devoted to Keynes's efforts to shape the post-war world.

The main sources for this volume are Keynes's surviving papers, materials in the Public Record Office and, on occasion, the papers of colleagues and friends. Where the material has come from the Public Record Office, the call numbers for the relevant files appear in the List of Documents Reproduced following page 348.

In this and the succeeding wartime volumes, to aid the reader in keeping track of the various personalities who pass through the pages that follow, we have included brief biographical notes on the first occasion on which they appear. These notes are designed to be cumulative over the whole run of wartime volumes.

In this, as in all the similar volumes, in general all of Keynes's own writings are printed in larger type. Keynes's own footnotes are indicated by asterisks or other symbols, to distinguish them from the editorial footnotes. All introductory matter and all writings by others than Keynes are printed in smaller type. The only exception to this general rule is that occasional short quotations from a letter from Keynes to his parents or to a friend, used in introductory passages to clarify a situation, are treated as introductory matter and are printed in the smaller type.

Most of Keynes's letters included in this and other volumes are reprinted from the carbon copies that remain among his papers. In most cases he has added his initials to the carbon in the familiar fashion in which he signed to all his friends. We have no certain means of knowing whether the top copy, sent to the recipient of the letter, carried a more formal signature.

Chapter 1

PRE-LEND LEASE
EXTERNAL WAR FINANCE

Keynes's arrival at the Treasury in July 1940 coincided with a transformation in Britain's external economic position. Before June 1940 the authorities' use of Britain's gold and dollar reserves plus marketable overseas securities had been based on the assumption that they would have to last three years. The German successes in the West in May and June led to a decision not to let financial considerations stand in the way of Britain's struggle for survival. Almost immediately, the fall of France led the authorities to take over existing French contracts in the United States, thus adding an additional financial burden. As a result, the efficient use of existing foreign resources and the realisation of assets became major short-term concerns of the Treasury, although in the longer term, everyone expected American financial assistance.

At the beginning of August 1940, largely as a result of his previous activities and experience, Keynes became a member of the Chancellor's newly formed Exchange Control Conference. The terms of reference of this advisory body, made up of Treasury and Bank of England officials, were:

(1) to review exchange control policy with a view to its modification or development;

(2) to deal with major administrative questions arising from the policy; and

(3) to consider steps to control the rate of expenditure of foreign exchange.

In the circumstances of August 1940, item (3) was regarded as contingent.

For the first meeting of the Conference, the following memorandum prepared by Keynes for the Chancellor's Consultative Council was the subject of discussion.

FOREIGN EXCHANGE CONTROL AND PAYMENTS
AGREEMENTS

I

The following major questions, which were controversial not long ago, have now been settled in the main one way or another:–

(1) Pre-war balances owing to foreigners have not, even now, been blocked. But the opinion that every steed which wanted to bolt has already done so, and that there is no longer any object in locking the stable door, seems convincing. This is on the assumption that it is possible to distinguish between such balances and balances currently accruing to foreigners from sterling profits and other sterling earnings (as to which see (5) below).

(2) Foreign-owned Stock Exchange securities can no longer be sold in London.

(3) For many months the Treasury undertook to find dollars to pay for imports without taking steps to canalise into their own coffers the proceeds of exports. For visible exports this has now been remedied. As regards invisible exports steps have also been taken, but I do not understand these sufficiently well to know whether or not they are fully effective.

(4) Triangular exchange transactions, as a result of which (for example) we might be involved in paying dollars for imports from non-dollar countries, have been completely, or almost completely, interrupted by the latest regulations.

II

During the long period after the outbreak of war before these steps had been taken our gold and dollar resources were depleted by sums which (in my judgment) were substantial in the aggregate (say £50 million *at least*, though this, I am

2

told, is a doubtful and highly controversial figure), in spite of the fact that the largest losses in respect of foreign balances were suffered in the six months preceding the war. The remaining leakages are on a much smaller scale. Nevertheless they are appreciable and would mount up over a period such as a year to a significant sum. In other connections the Treasury does not regard such amounts as $10 million, $50 million or $100 million as negligible or unworthy of their attention. The most important of these seem to me to be the following, though those who are in close touch with the daily management of exchange control might be able to add to them:-

(5) Sterling profits, interest, royalties and other current income earned by foreigners within the British Empire can be remitted by them into the appropriate foreign currency. In particular, Americans can acquire the dollar equivalent of such sterling income, which includes (for example) the profits of British subsidiaries of American businesses and the income of all American-owned investments within the British Empire. Over a year this adds up to a large sum. The amount of sterling which Americans are allowed to turn into dollars under this arrangement is estimated as being of the order of £20 million per annum.

It needs (I understand) no new regulation to prevent this, but merely a change of administrative practice which could be ordered in five minutes. For it is already necessary to seek permission for such transactions in every case. But at present it is the general practice to grant them.

The object of this practice is, presumably, to oblige the Americans. But the psychological effect of such laxity must be, I should have thought, to cause them great surprise at a policy so contrary to what one would expect in modern total war, and to make them think that we are not taking our financial position seriously.

(6) Whilst foreigners are no longer permitted to sell Stock

Exchange securities in this country, this prohibition does not apply to other forms of property. For example, if an American, owning an estate or a collection of antiques in this country, sells it, he is allowed to remit the proceeds to the U.S.A. Here again it is a case not of altering the regulations which already require an express permission for such remittances, but of stiffening up the administrative practice, so that a refusal, instead of a permission, is the normal rule.

I cannot suppose that the sums involved in such permissions are large even in the aggregate and over a long period. Nevertheless the continuance of the present practice seems inappropriate to our present position and inconsistent with the attitude of the Treasury in other respects to the conservation of our dollar resources.

(7) There is no prohibition against the repatriation into this country of sterling currency notes. This opens a loophole for the evasion of exchange control by British nationals. But— more important than this—it allows foreigners, who have used Treasury and Bank of England notes as a means of hoarding, to withdraw (in effect) the sums which they have thus advanced to us.

World opinion would, in any case, consider it normal in present circumstances for us to prohibit the re-importation of our notes. But the defection of France adds a particular reason for enforcing the prohibition now, even if formerly we preferred not to do so. Owing to the constant fresh supply through British tourists and as a result of the past history of the franc, Treasury and Bank of England notes have long been popular in France as a means of hoarding. It follows that some of these hoards may now be coming into the possession of the enemy, who would enjoy a double satisfaction in employing them since this would increase their own resources and deplete ours.

(8) It is difficult to obtain comprehensive information as to how completely our own exchange regulations apply in theory and are enforced in practice in other parts of the

sterling area. Yet their efficacy depends appreciably upon this. Generally speaking, no doubt, the same sorts of control are supposed to be in operation; and some parts of the sterling area may have been stricter in some respects than we have been. On the other hand, other parts are unquestionably more lax. I have never seen a comparative table (and have never heard of anyone who has) showing, for each administrative unit within the sterling area, exactly how (a) their regulations and (b) their practice conform with ours.

Part of the difficulty of understanding what is happening in other parts of the sterling area (as well as in this country itself) may be due to the present regulations being complicated and not easily intelligible, partly as a result of their having been developed by a slow process of evolution out of a state of affairs which was based, to start with, on widely different ideas of what we were aiming at from those which prevail now. The system has never been codified. Although the substantial effect of the present regulations is fairly simple, I myself find it impossible to understand or to remember how they operate in detail and in particular contexts, and I find that others with whom I discuss these problems are in much the same position.

How our regulations are explained to the numerous authorities throughout the sterling area, many of whom are not highly qualified technicians, so that they can adapt them to local circumstances and assure us that what they are doing has the same effect as what we are doing, I cannot imagine. Moreover even if the banking technicians who are working the regulations in Jamaica, Hongkong, Alexandria, Singapore, Ottawa, Cape Town, etc. are completely *au fait* with what it is all about, the higher and more responsible officials in these places probably have only the foggiest idea of the system and are therefore ill-placed for making sure that incompetence or negligence or corruption is not interfering with its full efficacy.

It is possible, therefore, that a useful purpose might be

served if we were to codify the regulations in simple terms, and then ask for a prompt and comprehensive report from all parts of the sterling area comparing their practices with ours and calling attention to any material differences. (I suppose there is someone who is charged with the duty of securing uniformity of practice throughout the sterling area but I do not know who he is.)

III

There is a further question, closely connected with the problems of exchange control but also raising much wider issues, namely *payments agreements*. The contraction of the neutral world has considerably altered the possible scope of these. But there still remain, apart from the United States, all the countries of South America, Japan, Russia, China, Turkey, Sweden, Portugal, Spain and the Balkans (for what, if anything, the last named are still worth).

I believe that a properly conceived and firmly executed scheme of payments agreements is one of the most important instruments at our disposal for the long-term financing of a long war. But the problem is one of exceptional difficulty, inasmuch as it brings in a great variety of relevant factors, diplomatic, economic and financial, differing considerably from case to case. Thus elasticity of mind and fertility of device is required; and the governing principles can be laid down only in the most general way. No opinion and no advice can be worth much except such as arises out of direct contact with the actual problems. Moreover, I write this in a state of considerable ignorance about the present arrangements. I have never seen the text of a payments agreement, though I have been told the general character of one or two; and what follows is, therefore, the result of thinking at large on the matter and not of an acquaintance with the details:–

(1) Without much further delay payments agreements should become universal between the sterling area as a whole

6

and each particular country outside it. I should even include the United States in due course, but, as that obviously raises special considerations, I shall not attempt to deal with the U.S.A. in this memorandum.

(2) The agreements should be on the basis that henceforward we do not settle adverse balances in gold or its equivalent (I am not here including U.S.A.). What the best use is for our remaining gold reserves raises certain issues which are most conveniently discussed in the context of our financial relations with U.S.A. and I am, therefore, leaving it out of this memorandum.

(3) Where British investors own government or other suitable securities of the country in question, adverse balances up to an appropriate proportion of the total trade should normally be met by the repatriation of such securities. These securities would be requisitioned from their British owners at the market price. But it would not necessarily be right to credit them in the payments agreement at so low a price. The Argentine Government, for example, should be expected to take back its own government bonds at par. The above arrangement would have the advantage of making liquid a large volume of British owned foreign investments which the Treasury cannot now regard in this light.

(4) Where the balance under a payments agreement is in our favour, we should retain the right (without conceding a similar right against ourselves) to transfer this balance to the credit of a third country, should the third country agree to take payment in this form.

(5) Balances in our favour would be regarded as deposits with the Bank of England carrying 5 per cent interest and repayable in sterling a year after the war, unless currently discharged meanwhile in one of the agreed ways; but in no circumstances would gold be ear-marked against them, nor would they be repayable, except over the payments agreements, in any currency other than sterling.

(6) There would be great advantages, diplomatic, econ-

7

omic and financial, in adhering rigidly to this general schematism for every country alike. We should simply say to each of them that we had now reached a stage in our war finance when it is necessary for us to set up arrangements of a kind which we can safely reckon on maintaining so long as the war lasts. There is nothing unreasonable in our laying down the conditions on which we are able to buy. Moreover, the conditions themselves are perfectly fair. There is no compulsion on any country to trade with us on a greater scale than suits them; though if they sell to us at all, they must of course fall in with our ideas as to what we most require. They have the whole of the sterling area from which to import up to the amount of their credits under the agreement; and for a long time to come most of the countries concerned could spend any surplus in their favour in repatriating their own securities and freeing themselves, as U.S.A. did in the last war, from being in the position of debtor countries.

It would be prudent on our part, once we had secured such arrangements as the above, to be liberal in the matter of price policy. By this means we should enlist on our side the farmers and other producers in the neutral country, who would not be in the least interested in the technical means of payment arranged by their government, provided that they were getting a satisfactory price for their products.

(7) Having laid these foundations, we should then proceed to make use in each particular negotiation of the bargaining power which results from our being in many cases the only substantial buyer in sight. This would determine how much we buy and in what proportions we pay for our purchases in exports, in securities and in sterling credits at the Bank of England.

There has been a great increase recently in the strength of our bargaining power, of which so far we have failed to take advantage. The facts that our blockade now embraces almost the whole of continental Europe, that our requirements are for the sterling area alone and no longer include France, and that these requirements themselves are becoming reduced, in some cases as a result of the progress towards civilian economy, have profoundly changed the whole picture.

There is no longer the possibility of scarcity of supply and high prices in the international markets. On the contrary, in commodity after commodity there is a prospect of a hideous unsold surplus and a market collapse. Reasons of internal politics and internal economy will turn most overseas countries, when they have fully tumbled to the new situation, into suppliants for our custom, passionately anxious to find a market on almost any terms for their overwhelmingly burdensome domestic surplus.

It behoves us on every ground to use our strength moderately and justly. Heaven knows that a long war will become sufficiently unpopular anyhow in the neutral world! Mr Cordell Hull has rightly interpreted the clouds on the horizon, as portents of something very big and dangerous to come, in proposing his purchasing cartel to the countries of South America. But apart from him the world seems almost oblivious of the tremendous change-round which is impending in international markets.

But whilst we must not abuse our strength, it would be foolish to overlook it.

(8) There must be a single body to negotiate such payments agreements on behalf of the various departments concerned. The Foreign Office, the Board of Trade, the Ministries of Supply and Food, and the Offices for India, the Dominions and the Colonies, are intimately concerned as well as the Treasury and the Bank of England. The payments agreements should be interwoven, not merely with our technical financial arrangements, but with our diplomatic policy, our export policy and our choice of sources and quantities of supplies. At present there is no convenient machinery for organised, comprehensive negotiation which is in close touch with all the interests of which it is necessary to take account.

(9) Sooner or later arrangements on these lines will surely

become, not only desirable, but necessary and inevitable. If so, we shall only lose time and precious resources by delaying them.

It will be observed that the proposed plan will solve, more or less completely, our external financial problem in respect of countries other than U.S.A. The Chancellor of the Exchequer has invited his Consultative Council to consider the problem of financing a long war. The above might provide a long-term solution to an important section of the problem.

29 July 1940   J. M. KEYNES

Keynes's memorandum served as a basis for discussion for the next few meetings of the Conference. In the end, proposals (6) and (7) were taken up, while (5) was dropped after further discussion.

By the end of August, the American position had come to the centre of Keynes's concerns. In his first intervention he suggested a way of increasing Britain's dollar resources.

To SIR RICHARD HOPKINS, *23 August, 1940*

SCRAPING THE BOTTOM OF THE BOX

(1) By asking American subsidiaries of British businesses to borrow dollars on their own credit; requisitioning prior securities of the British parent businesses from their British owners; and exchanging these securities (with a view to their cancellation) for the dollars.[1]

E.g. Courtaulds have £10 million 5% preference shares worth (say) £12 million. The American Viscose Company is their wholly owned subsidiary and has, I think, no prior obligations outstanding. Thus $50 million might be realised in this way.

---

[1] This resurrected Keynes's proposals to Samuel Courtauld of the previous spring (*JMK*, vol. XXII, pp. 180–4).

Something similar might be arranged in respect of Shell Union and the parent Shell Company though the security here might be not quite so good. The Shell Company has considerable preference shares in issue which could be requisitioned.

There are a number of other cases most of them on a smaller scale than the above.

Perhaps $150 million might be raised in this way given a little time without any serious detriment to the future of these businesses.

(2) By cashing in on our stocks of whisky which normally would be exported to the U.S.A. in the course of the next ten years. If the Distillers Company would ship their stocks to the U.S.A. we might by out-right sale or borrowing against them raise (say) $100 million to $150 million.

(3) By pressing the U.S.A. to buy out-right the stock of wool which is to be stored in the U.S.A.

(4) By drawing on Empire gold stocks against a promise of early replacement out of new gold mined, thus in effect anticipating the South African output.

It might be possible to find $500 million in these ways and in analogous ways which might occur to other people. (I have not included the sale of American insurance interests.)

23 August 1940   [copy initialled] J.M.K.

To SIR RICHARD HOPKINS, *5 September, 1940*

SCRAPING THE BOTTOM OF THE BOX

There are various British-owned balances and securities in U.S.A., amounting altogether to very substantial amounts, which have been allowed hitherto to remain in private owner-ship for various reasons, good or bad. In present circum-stances it might be worth our while to overhaul the list of these. The principal categories of such assets, of which I am aware, are the following:–

(1) *Retained balances in U.S.A.*

Total British balances in U.S.A. are still returned at as much as £36,500,000. I do not know the composition of this total. But I suppose it must consist mainly of 'retained balances', i.e. money which shipping companies, insurance companies, etc., are allowed to retain for the purposes of their businesses. This is a substantial resource which we could take from them, temporarily at least, in case of extremity.

(2) *Insurance assets*

D. H. R[obertson] is writing you a note on this. I fancy that he is right in supposing that there are very large *surplus* British insurance assets in U.S.A. which they are *not* required to retain by American law. At present we seem to be allowing them to retain *all* their American assets.

(3) D.H.R. thinks that the Ministry of Shipping may be retaining in New York unnecessarily large working balances.

5.9.40   [copy initialled] J. M. K.

I am trying to get further particulars about the 'Retained Balances'. It is possible that the £36,500,000 includes the dollar balances of the joint stock banks which, I rather think (I am not sure), have never been requisitioned.
6.9.40   J. M. K.

However, as the autumn progressed, American pressures and the desperate need for foreign resources brought the Treasury to consider all available foreign securities and direct investments in the United States. Readily marketable dollar securities, which using a broad definition were worth £200 million in August 1940, had fallen to £170 million by October. As for other available assets, before Sir Frederick Phillips left for America in November, Keynes contributed a memorandum on general policy prior to a discussion with the Chancellor on 31 October.[2]

[2] Other memoranda were contributed by Lord Catto, Sir Frederick Phillips and Professor Robertson.

NOTES FOR U.S.A.

I

Tin and rubber shares

The U.S. Government may wish British investments in tin and rubber shares to be brought under survey, when considering whether we have further liquid assets which ought to be realised.

1. First of all, as to the practicability of realising these assets. We have to distinguish a proposal to sell them to private U.S. investors from handing them over *en bloc* to some U.S. Government institution. There is good reason to think that they could not be sold to private investors at a price bearing a reasonable relation to their intrinsic value. They have never been popular with American investment institutions, which have been just as free to buy them at any past date as English investors. Even during tin and rubber booms Americans have never held any important amount or for more than very short periods. None of the major investment trusts in U.S.A., so far as we know, have even a single holding of this character at the present time.

A contributory cause of this is, probably, the fact that tin mines and rubber plantations are held by a multitude of small companies and depend for their success on individual management. Taking only those which are quoted on the London Stock Exchange there are about 50 tin companies and between 400 and 500 rubber companies. The nominal capital of the British owned tin shares in Malaya was (at the end of 1936) about £7 million with a present market value of between two and three times that sum. The nominal British capital in rubber plantations, wherever situated, which included many small enterprises not included in the above enumeration, was (in 1938) £35 million (paying in 1938 interest and dividends of £6 million) with a present market value not much above half this sum. There are certain finance houses, such as London Tin or British Tin and Rubber Investment Trust or

Harrisons and Crossfield, which specialise in the management and technical advice of such companies and hold substantial investments in the individual companies in which they are interested. These might be regarded as more suitable investments for outside holders. French and other European investors have, indeed, in the past taken some interest in certain of these, e.g. London Tin. But American investors have never taken up permanent holdings of a significant amount in any of them; partly, perhaps, for the reason that they are out of touch with the managements which are situated in London and in the East, and have no means of gauging their efficiencies.

It should not be overlooked that substantial investments in these companies are held locally in the East; and in Malayan tin there are considerable Chinese interests.

Apart from the above permanent considerations, Malaya is now considered by investors as not free from war risks; and American investors are much more influenced by such considerations than British investors who cannot escape them anyhow. This is so much the case that, in the early months of the war before prohibitions on such transactions were imposed, American investors re-sold on the London market what was probably the greater part of the investments in the sterling area which they previously held. Perhaps we should have interfered with this unloading at an earlier date than we did. In not doing so we were influenced by a reluctance to deprive American investors of what they might have thought a legitimate expectation of a market in case of need.

In any case it would not be common sense for us to embark on a selling-campaign in U.S. for these obscure shares at a time when we have great difficulty, in spite of our utmost efforts, to sell first class investments situated in U.S. itself, of which we still hold a substantial quantity.

2. If the idea has to be rejected, that during the war American investors are likely to be attracted by investments,

such as the above, at a price representing the intrinsic value in vulnerable British possessions under individual British management about which they know nothing, we are left with the alternative of their purchase *en bloc* out of U.S. Government funds. Obviously there is nothing impossible in this. But we have to consider its advisability.

Does the U.S. Administration consider it advisable that they should become the owners of the major part of the natural resources of a British Crown Colony including the anomalously constituted Federal Malay States, under the administration of British officials and native Rajahs, through the medium of a great number of small companies run by British boards of directors and managers and subject to British taxation, with a minority of local and Chinese shareholders? Surely this is not a serious proposition. It cannot be a sound proposal to divorce ownership from responsibility to this extent. Divested from the duties and liabilities of management it would be a project of unadulterated (and, in the end, grossly inefficient) exploitation. For it is a misapprehension to suppose that the British interests in Malaya are those of passive rentiers. They are intensely living and personal enterprises which without the breath of current life would collapse in a very few years. If the United States wish to take over the tin and rubber resources of the British Empire, they must be prepared to take over at the same time the responsibility for the territories in which they are situated. The transfer to the United States of the Crown Colony of Malaya, lock stock and barrel, (including Singapore), as the price of financial assistance during the war, is quite feasible *economically and financially*; and the objections, if any, are of a different character.

If the object of mobilising the above British resources is to delay the date at which American Government assistance becomes necessary, it must be pointed out that the above transfer could not be arranged quickly and would, presumably, require Congressional legislation just as much as any other form of assistance. I may add that a transfer of the whole of British rubber and tin shares would not meet British outgoings in U.S.A. for more than three weeks at the rate of expenditure anticipated for 1941.

II

Much of the same arguments apply *mutatis mutandis* to many other capital assets situated within the British Empire. One can reach the *reductio ad absurdum* of the idea of transferring such assets to the U.S. Administration by suggesting that they should take over the ownership of the railway system of India without interesting themselves in India in any other respect.

But they do *not* apply to certain capital assets owned by British investors outside the British Empire, particularly our assets in South America where, indeed, we ourselves are discovering a similar *reductio ad absurdum* to that indicated above. A transfer to the U.S. of the whole of the British interests in railways and the public utilities in South America would create no greater anomaly than already exists. Indeed, if the natural line of evolution is towards an economic Monroe doctrine, the anomaly of foreign ownership might be diminished.

It is, therefore, proper and reasonable that we should accompany the above arguments, against the present emergency being used as an opportunity for picking the eyes out of the British Empire and seizing its assets without taking over its liabilities, with an offer to transfer at a valuation the whole of our railway, public utility and government bond interests in South America. Moreover the sums involved, measured in terms of the amounts invested, are much larger. Including Government and municipal loans, the total, as shown in the following table, exceeds £500 million.

There is no accurate analysis of British investments in

South America later than Sir Robert Kindersley's survey as at the end of 1936, from which the following particulars are taken. But there have been no important changes since that date.

Total nominal British capital at the end of 1936 invested in	(£million)
Argentina	372
Brazil	160
Chile	50
Rest of South America	85
Mexico and Central America	52
Cuba	27
	£746 million

The total for Mexico would be considerably increased if capital levy in default were included. Moreover the value of British interests in Mexico has, of course, considerably deteriorated since 1936.

We might offer to vest the whole of the above securities, excluding certain commercial interests, and transfer them to a nominee of the U.S. Administration at an agreed valuation in terms of U.S. dollars. It would be fair to point out that the post-war sacrifice involved in this transaction would be considerably greater than the loss of interest and dividends, since the major part of the enterprises concerned are not merely British owned but are British managed. And in addition to the earnings of management there are, as a result of British management, many trade connections of great value, the loss of which would have serious repercussions on the post-war prospects of our exports.

In the case of the Argentine railways it would be necessary to call the attention of the U.S. Administration to our existing negotiations for the ultimate transfer of our interests to the

Argentine Government itself and to the connection between these negotiations and the finance of the Argentine surpluses. If the U.S. Government is inclined to play a part in this negotiation, it is very possible that they could do so usefully. Rather than own a direct interest in the Argentine railway system, they might reasonably prefer to finance the Argentine Government in bringing about a transfer. For example, the U.S. might lend the Argentine $x million with which to buy the railways; and we should then employ the $x million in U.S.A. to diminish our financial calls on the U.S. Government by the same amount. A similar procedure might be suitable in Brazil. Alternatively it might expedite our negotiations with the Argentine, if the U.S. Government were to hint that *they* might be inclined to buy the railways if the Argentines did not do so themselves.

III

It is for the U.S. Administration to decide, whether to press for a large-scale stripping of British enterprise overseas. The upshot of the above argument is that, should something of the kind commend itself to them, our interests in South America are the most suitable for the purpose, since their transfer would lead to less future complications for both of us than an attempt on the part of U.S.A. to take over, as a pure rentier, the raw material resources of the British Empire without assuming the business and administrative responsibilities which the development of those resources should properly carry with it.

But in reaching such a decision the U.S. Administration should not overlook the effect of what they may do on the post-war equilibrium of international trade. According to the official Board of Trade figures Great Britain was slightly over-spending its foreign resources, resulting in a certain amount of foreign disinvestment, in the years immediately preceding the war. It is arguable that these figures are a little too pessimistic and that we were in fact about holding our own. But it is clear that there was no significant current increase in our foreign resources. Thus in any case the loss of pre-war resources and new overseas indebtedness incurred outside the United States, which is to be expected quite apart from the prospective decisions of the U.S. Administration, will set us a severe problem which can only be solved by new methods. If, on the top of this, the assistance we receive from the U.S. Government is on a commercial basis in the sense that it has, directly or indirectly, to be refunded here-after in interest and capital, the severity of our task will be more than doubled on the assumption that the war is continued beyond the end of 1941; and before the end of 1942 we should have become a debtor country on balance after allowing for the whole of our overseas capital assets. Up to the end of 1941 our net adverse balance overseas since the beginning of the war is expected to reach £2,000 million of which we shall be forced to seek about £1,000 million from the U.S.

It is most unlikely that we could meet this situation except by a system of very strict bilateral agreements which would tie up the payment for our imports and our foreign debts with the acceptance of our exports by the other country. In this case the United States would have to choose between an almost entire cessation of her exports to this country, especially of such raw materials as cotton and tobacco which can be obtained elsewhere without undue difficulty, and an acceptance of certain of our exports, especially textiles, on such a large scale as to replace a significant proportion of her domestic industry.

At this point in the discussion it is relevant for us to express our very strong distaste for a 'phoney' loan; that is to say for a financial arrangement between the two Governments which purports to be on a commercial basis requiring repayment of capital and interest, but which by a sort of tacit private understanding we do not in fact honour. This time both countries will be acting with their eyes open and in the light of experience. It is not reasonable to expect this country a second time to accept the dishonour and the reproaches of default whilst allowing to the U.S. all the consequent conveniences to their trade. This time if we are asked to pay, we shall pay; and we should like to make it clear at the outset that it would be exceedingly rash of the U.S. Administration to rely on the contrary in practice. Our only stipulation would be that payment must be taken in the shape of an excess of goods imported into U.S.A., taken at a reasonable valuation, over goods exported by U.S.A. That is to say, we should pay both for the debt and for current U.S. exports in sterling which would be available for no purpose except the purchase of British goods at current prices.

For speaking frankly, it would not be physically impossible for this country to pay to the United States after the war an indemnity of (say) £100 million a year in respect of capital and interest,—a sum which, taking everything into account, is not more than the equivalent of the sum which at the end of the last war I believed Germany could pay. It might not even involve, except over a transitional period, any severe consequences to the standard of life. £100 million per annum is less than 2 per cent of the potential national output of Great Britain (let us look at it as the output of 400,000 men hitherto unemployed); and it is, of course, a sum so small in relation to the American potential output as to have no serious significance to U.S.A. It is the fabric of commercial relations between the two countries—and to a lesser extent between the U.S.A. and the British Empire as a whole—which would suffer severe consequences. For this sum, though small in other contexts, could not be transferred without revolutionary changes in the commercial relations of the two countries. Is the small financial advantage a sufficient recompense for the serious political and social inconvenience?

It is obvious that these reflections are more relevant to the finance of our American purchases taken as a whole than to the particular question of which British foreign-owned assets it is advisable for the U.S. Administration to take over. At the worst such transfers would only aggravate the post-war economic disequilibrium to a modest extent; and are not important compared with the form of the direct assistance, the need for which they would only diminish by a small amount and postpone for a short time. Nor are they intended to detract from the value of an offer on our part to hand over the whole of our South American interests, as a gesture of our sincere readiness for economic sacrifice before American public opinion. They do, however, lead up to certain further considerations which neither government should overlook.

IV

Let us assume that Great Britain will take measures to mobilise sooner or later the whole of the capital resources which can be made liquid at a sacrifice not unreasonably great. Is it advisable that the whole of these resources should be expended before the U.S. Administration comes to the rescue with direct assistance? It is no wonder that an uninstructed public opinion should expect this. But those responsible for the decision must take account of the following:–

(1) It is not in fact possible to mobilise any large sum of money within the time available except by using up to the last ounce our most obvious liquid resource, that is to say literally the *whole* of the reserves of gold which we own and can borrow or steal. I return to the question of gold under (3) below. The immediate point is that it is a plain delusion to suppose that such expedients as the transfer of our South American interests to some organ of the U.S. Administration is a practicable way of postponing the date at which our means of payment in New York will be exhausted.

(2) What would be the consequence of adopting the general principle that Great Britain must exhaust her own resources to the utmost possible extent before she receives direct assistance from the U.S.? I suggest that they would be exceedingly inconvenient to both Governments, without materially reducing the amount of assistance ultimately required.

The point can be illustrated by what happened last time. In December 1916 there was a serious run on British resources in New York which very nearly led to default, so that the British Treasury had to scrape the bottom of the pot and mobilise every item of property which could be liquidated. When the time came for the first loan from the U.S. administration in March 1917, the British Treasury was within the last week of its capacity to pay and had stripped itself of almost every available asset. The result was that all the external financial requirements of Great Britain in excess of currently accruing resources had to be met out of the U.S. dollar loan,—not only the requirements within U.S.A. but, in effect throughout the world, since sterling wherever expended could be converted unrestrictedly into dollars through the sterling exchange in New York being pegged with the proceeds of the borrowed U.S. funds. Naturally this was a source of continual financial friction between the two Associated Powers. It was impossible for the U.S. Government effectively to control the use of the funds they were providing, and the organisation set up for this purpose was, quite inevitably, futile. Moreover the political status of the debt in the view of public opinion was much prejudiced by the fact that its expenditure had not been limited to the purchase of munitions of war, even interpreted in the widest sense. The position arising out of this was my own daily preoccupation for two years, and the surviving members of both Treasuries, of whom Mr Norman Davis is the leading American representative, could testify what great benefits would have ensued if it could have been avoided.

It would, therefore, be worth a great deal if, this time, we could fix a set-up of a different kind. Would it be possible to limit the financial assistance we have to ask from U.S.A. to the programme of the British Purchasing Commission in U.S.A.? If so, it is obvious that great political and administrative advantages would be gained. The U.S. Administration, and also the American public, would know exactly what they were paying for. They could supervise it to the fullest extent, both in itself and in relation to America's own armament programme. The position would be intelligible and defensible. Is such an arrangement financially feasible?

If the British Treasury is stripped of every available asset before American advances are made available, this will scarcely be possible. The experience of the last war would be repeated. But if the U.S. Administration would take over the responsibility of the British Purchasing Commission in U.S.A. as from Jan. 1, 1941, and if, in addition, they would make separate arrangements with Canada so that it would be unnecessary for Great Britain to pay for any part of her Canadian purchases in U.S. dollars, there is a very good chance that Great Britain, with the aid of the gradual mobilisation of her remaining assets, could remain self-supporting in the rest of the world and also in the U.S. itself in respect of purchases by the sterling area on private account not made through the Purchasing Commission. We could, indeed, *undertake* to be self-supporting throughout 1941, and could hope to remain so indefinitely subject to the unforeseeable chances of war.

The possibility of this is largely due to the exchange control and payments agreements which the British Treasury has now established with the greater part of the neutral world outside U.S.A., and to the arrangements established within the sterling area,—an organisation which had no counterpart in the last war. But this system must be supplemented, particularly because there will be some substantial payments to meet in U.S.A. on behalf of the sterling area as a whole falling outside the programme of the Purchasing Commission, by a gradual use of our remaining gold and a gradual liquidation of our saleable securities in U.S.A.

If we are left with the remaining balance of these assets under our own control, it will not be possible to draw a sharp line where American assistance begins and ends. If we are stripped of them, the U.S. Administration will no longer be in a position to draw the line in any definable place and will, perhaps, be driven to attempt the impracticable task of establishing a general Treasury control over British expenditure abroad, certain to be ineffective and very hampering to the war effort in the attempt. Nor would there be any financial gain to offset this. The balance of our assets will be utilised just as much one way as the other; and there will be *more* pressure on us for due economy if we have pledged ourselves to be self-supporting within a defined sphere, than if we are allowed gradually and increasingly to depend on assistance of undefined scope, an arrangement demoralising to our side (and weakening to the British Treasury in its control over its own departments) and intensely irritating to the other.

(The suggestion that the proposed plan of assistance should take effect as from Jan. 1, 1941, does not necessarily involve its actual completion, including legislative sanction, before that date. It would be sufficient if it were given retrospective effect to that date, so that gold expended after Jan. 1 for the purposes of the Purchasing Commission would be subsequently refunded and thus made available for other outside commitments.)

The administrative advantages of this to both Treasuries are obvious. But the overwhelming argument for it is its *intelligibility* to public opinion. American assistance would be expressible in terms of materials instead of money. America would be doing exactly what both Presidential candidates have promised that she would do, namely supplying Great

Britain with all possible material assistance in the shape of munitions short of war. All extraneous questions and debateable matter would be automatically excluded.

Above all, it would, on this basis, be open to America, should she see fit, to cut out all financial relations, based on false commercial analogies, between the two Governments. A loan, and the terms of a loan, could be avoided altogether. America's aid might take the form of placing at our disposal without charge the approved American programme of the British Commission, expecting us to be self-supporting in other respects. How much better this would be, before the public opinion of both countries and of the world at large, than the humbug and dishonour of a 'phoney' loan or the subsequent embarrassments of a real one!

Perhaps it is not for us to ask for, or even to suggest, such a thing. But, truly and sincerely, the money involved is not of such importance to either party compared with the establishment of right relations, which will not lead to subsequent friction and estrangement, between the two countries. It would be well worth our while to pay the £100 million a year after the war, if, taking everything into account, it is this action which would make both nations feel that the right and proper thing had been done, exactly appropriate to the interests and responsibility of each and to the true character of the historical events in which we are participating.

(3) In conclusion, the question whether it is advisable for the U.S. Administration to ask us to part with our last ounce of gold raises a special issue worth mentioning.

The U.S.A. already hold the greater part of the gold in the world. The only value of this gold is as a means of settling international balances. If the convention—for it is no more—by which gold is used for this purpose comes to an end, the U.S. stock of gold becomes valueless. But the convention depends on not all the gold being in one hand. When in the game of 'Beggar my Neighbour' all the cards belong to one player, that is the signal for the game to come to an end. The pack becomes worthless paste-board; the fun is over. If, therefore, gold is to play some version of its accustomed part in the post-war world, more than one player must have some. Either they must be left with some; or alternatively there must be, in the literal sense of the word, a new deal—the U.S. Administration must deal out its stock all round, so that the game can start again.

I conclude that, in view of the stocks she already holds, it would be no advantage to the U.S. to acquire the last ounce of gold from the Bank of England,—and, indeed, that this would be an actual disadvantage to her. For either the gold must be given back after the war, or we must think out a way—which is not too difficult—for a post-war system in which gold plays no part. It is evident that we cannot have a gold system with no gold.

The minimum working gold reserve of the Bank of England might be estimated at about £150 million. We shall be hard put to it to retain this sum, even if, as proposed above, the commitments of the British Purchasing Commission are taken over from January 1 next.

27 October 1940   J.M.K.

At the meeting on 31 October, it was agreed that it was desirable to get American support from 1 January 1941, ideally for all the purchases of the British Purchasing Commission; that the Americans should be discouraged from forcing sales of securities, but if necessary such sales should occur, even after the war; that attempts should be made to obtain allied gold to meet commitments; and that sales of South American utilities should be considered.

After the meeting, Keynes circulated a supplementary memorandum, as the discussions continued into November.

SUPPLEMENTARY NOTE ON U.S.A.

I

Sir F. Phillips raised the question of whether, if we ask U.S. to look after our war-like expenditure as from January 1 next, we could make out a case for retaining in addition our unsold dollar securities. With a view to answering this question I have rearranged Prof. Robertson's figures as follows:–

If the U.S. Administration looks after our 'warlike' expenditure in U.S.A., our remaining liabilities which have to be met in dollars and gold are:

Debits	£ million	Credits	£ million
'Other' U.K. expenditure in U.S.A.	65	U.K. exports to U.S.A. visible and invisible	55
Adverse balance of sterling area with Canada	200	Rest of sterling area favourable balance with U.S.A.	45
Gold and dollar expenditure outside U.S.A.	70	Newly mined gold	120
	335		220

To meet this adverse balance we shall have

(*a*) Dollar securities not yet sold (£175 million)

(*b*) What we can borrow from Canada

(*c*) Direct U.S. investments and other assets outside U.S.

But

(1) Some of the newly mined gold may be needed to replenish the minimum gold reserve.

(2) We must budget to last at least three years.

(3) The above estimates assume that the Empire, outside Canada, will continue to sell us all their gold and lend us all their favourable balances *without* diminishing their favourable balance with U.S.

(4) They assume that we can maintain our exports even when our war effort is fully intensified.

(5) The figures are based on known commitments or on projecting the figures of the first year. If the war takes a new turn and involves greatly increased expenditure outside U.K. they may be considerably exceeded.

(6) No allowance is made for the reduction in our income due to sales of U.S. assets.

In my previous note I suggested that we should expect Canada to make her own arrangements with U.S.A. so as to relieve us from meeting our own adverse balance with her out of our U.S. dollar resources. If this were done up to the hilt, it would clearly give us a good deal in hand. For the above calculations do not rely upon this.

It would be possible, therefore, for us not to make this a condition of the new arrangement from the outset, but keep it rather as a safety valve and hope that Canada would at any rate succeed in borrowing enough in U.S. to reduce considerably the assumed adverse balance of £200 million a year. It is scarcely for us to make the arrangements between U.S. and Canada, and it would be an advantage that our own proposal need not be very precise on this matter.

Perhaps the main argument against stripping us of the dollar securities remains the importance of leaving us with some margin against contingencies. If we are spending in one place or another at the rate of £4,000 million a year, the value of the dollar securities, namely £175 million represents less than 5 per cent of one year's outgoings. It does not seem to me indecently greedy to aim at a reserve of this magnitude in addition to the minimum working gold reserve.

Moreover, if we allowed ourselves to be stripped of the *whole* of the £175 million, it would certainly be rash of us to promise that we could be self-supporting outside warlike expenditure in U.S.A. If it is a matter of selling a few and holding the rest, we have got into the realm of chicken feed and have left that of the grand principles on which we should ask U.S.A. to aid us.

1.11.40   J. M. K.

However, the atmosphere was transformed by President Roosevelt's announcement of lend lease at a press conference on 17 December 1940 and his fireside chat of twelve days later. For on the lend lease principle materials necessary for 'the defence of the United States' could go to Britain, if the president thought this the most efficient way of using them, subject to acknowledgement by some consideration subsequently negotiated.

At the end of 1940, however, Britain was not only attempting to become recipient of financial aid; she was also financing allies. With the Italian invasion of Greece on 28 October 1940, Britain had advanced the Greeks £5 million for their sterling area needs, adding that a part of this sum might find use, if necessary, as cover for the Greek note issue.[3] On 5 December, probably after a conversation with Keynes, Brendan Bracken suggested to the Prime Minister that Britain should aid Greece in the form of a gift to make it easier to obtain American assistance on generous terms. The Prime Minister consulted the Treasury the next day. Thus Keynes began a brief involvement in Greek finance.

On 6 December, Keynes wrote to Bracken.

To B. BRACKEN, *6 December 1940*

Dear Brendan,

It happened that I was consulted this morning about our financial assistance to Greece. It may be useful that you should see the enclosed copy of a note summarising my views.

You will see in a minute that there is a considerable obstacle to the proposal to make the assistance a free gift, that we are more or less committed to financing their internal as well as their external expenditure. If, therefore, we give them all this, we shall actually owe Greece large sums at the end of the war.

[3] The Greeks had asked for £20 million to cover any note issue expansion necessary for military purposes and to meet government purchases in the sterling area.

On the other hand, if we make a free gift of the whole of their external expenditure during the war, whether for military purposes or in respect of the adverse balance of trade on private account, we have a good argument, which might appeal even to the Greeks themselves, for limiting the assistance to this.

I had not realised last night that the Greeks had succeeded in establishing the principle, which they, and they alone, established in the last war, of getting their domestic expenditure paid for. It is one thing to make a present to Greece of their actual expenditure, another to make them a present, not only of this, but in addition perhaps of £50 million at the end of the war.   Yours ever,

[copy initialled] J. M. K.

To A. P. WATERFIELD,[4] *6 December 1940*

I understand our present commitments to Greece are as follows:–

(1) To meet all their expenditure in the sterling area, with an ambiguity as to whether this means Greek Government expenditure or includes the expenditure of all Greek nationals.

(2) To provide 'cover' in the shape of a balance at the Bank of England for an increase in the note issue to meet internal expenditure, with an ambiguity as to whether this covers all internal expenditure, including the deficit on the ordinary budget, or only war expenditure. We have not so far agreed to defray dollar expenditure, which the Greeks are at present meeting out of their own dollar reserves, these dollar reserves being, however, exiguous and likely to be used up before long.

We have made no commitments to meet domestic expenditure which is paid for otherwise than by an increase

[4] Alexander Percival Waterfield (1888–1965), Kt. 1944; entered H.M. Treasury, 1911; Principal Assistant Secretary, 1934–9; First Civil Service Commissioner, 1939–51, seconded to the Treasury.

in the note issue. Mr Hugh Jones[5] has, therefore, made an excellent suggestion, that requisitions should be paid for with non-negotiable bonds. The worst of the present position is that there is every incentive to the Greek Government to pay for everything with notes, since in that case we meet the payment, whereas otherwise they have to meet it themselves. Clearly Mr Hugh Jones's suggestion ought to be supported on our side, but it is not so clear that the Greeks have a sufficiently strong motive to agree.

During the last war the Greeks were the only allies who established a principle that they should receive financial assistance to meet their internal expenditure; and the result was that they ended the war with substantial sterling or gold balances. They are evidently aiming at the same situation now.

In view of our commitments, the only way of limiting what we are in for, which is estimated at £10 million a month is (a) to press for expenditure being made otherwise than by an expansion of the note issue, and (b) to interpret 'cover' for the note issue at less than 100 per cent.

(b) has been prejudiced because we have allowed them 100 per cent cover for the initial expansion of the note issue, but cover up to this figure is, of course, unusual and unnecessary.

The best proposal I can think of for the definitive settlement is the following:–

(1) To adhere to our commitments to meet Greek Government expenditure in the sterling area and to provide the Bank of Greece with a sterling credit at the Bank of England calculated on some formula according to the expansion of their note issue for military purposes.

(2) To provide that any balance of the Bank of Greece at the Bank of England at the end of the war should be used to discharge, so far as it is sufficient, our loans to Greece, and

[5] Llewellyn Arthur Hugh-Jones (1888–1970); British Delegate, International Finance Commission of Greece, 1936–46; Economic Adviser to Spears' Mission to Syria and Lebanon, 1941; Finance Adviser (Greece Mission) UNRRA, 1944–5.

that the *excess* of our loans to Greece over this total should be *cancelled*, being thus converted into a free gift and carrying no interest meanwhile.

This is a compromise with the proposal that our assistance to Greece should take the form of a gift and not of a loan. There is a great deal to be said for converting it into a gift. It will create a good precedent for America, a not unsatisfactory precedent for other potential allies, is likely to cost us nothing in the long run and will make it easier for us to claim that Bank of Greece balances at the end of the war should be used to discharge their obligations. It is a great obstacle to the proposal to make the loan into a free gift, that we should be financing Greece for internal expenditure. For it means that we should not only be making them a present of all their actual expenditure during the war, but would owe them a large sum at the end of the war, amounting perhaps to £50 million or more. If, however, we convert the actual amount of their expenditure out of our credits into a free gift, that will make it much easier for us to ask that the balance should be cancelled.

[copy initialled] J. M. K.

As the discussion continued, Britain offered to meet the cost of sterling area war supplies and to cover 40 per cent of internal expenditure, while the Greek demands grew more extravagant. On 22 January 1941, after a series of exchanges and Treasury discussions, Sir Richard Hopkins on advice from Keynes asked Keynes to prepare a brief for the Chancellor for possible Cabinet use. Keynes provided a draft on 31 January. This draft was accepted by Hopkins and Sir Horace Wilson on 5 February. However, the issue was not settled before the fall of Greece in April 1941. Up to that time Britain continued to pay £5 million per month into the number 3 account mentioned below.

To SIR RICHARD HOPKINS, *31 January 1941*

I have prepared this memorandum in consultation with Mr W. L. Fraser[6] as a first draft with a view to the Chancellor of the Exchequer's laying it before the War Cabinet and obtaining a decision how far we are to go. There are certain passages which may need bringing up to date when a further telegram has been received from Sir M. Palairet.[7] But that is not likely to affect the substance, so that it would save time if this document could be considered in its present shape.

No immediate action seems required except that I am unhappy about the *de facto* position of No. 3 account at the Bank of England. When this was established it was set up as an ordinary payments account and the Bank of England was not given any special instructions about it, since it was taken for granted that the Greeks understood it was only for note cover purposes or for transfer to No. 2. Mr Fraser has discovered in confidence that in fact the Greeks are drawing on it for general purposes; just as though it was No. 1 account, and ten days ago had already drawn £3 million, half of it for payments to various bankers in respect of coupons etc. and the other half credits for payment in the sterling area. I believe that a telegram has gone to Sir M. Palairet explaining to the Greeks that this cannot be allowed. But meanwhile should we not inform the Bank of England that no further payments should be made from this account on the instructions of the Bank of Greece except to No. 2 account? If the Bank feel embarrassed by such an instruction, it might be helpful to talk it over at the Exchange Control Conference, since they are equally interested with ourselves in preventing this abuse of the understanding. I attach Mr Fraser's original note about this.   [copy initialled] J. M. K.

---

[6] William Lionel Fraser (d. 1965), merchant banker, company director; served at the Treasury, 1939–45.

[7] Sir Michael Palairet (1882–1956), diplomat; Minister to Greece, 1939–42, Ambassador, 1942–3; Assistant Under-Secretary of State in Foreign Office, 1943–5.

THE GREEK FINANCIAL IMBROGLIO

As the mixed result of a strong sense of gratitude on our part, a lack of definition or possible ambiguity in the promises originally made, and, it must be added, an appetite on the part of the Greek financiers which grows by what it feeds on, demands are developing which are in excess of what is necessary to meet with the utmost generosity the real requirements of the situation.

On the other hand, the importance of satisfying the Greeks, and indeed of more than satisfying them, is so great and so obvious that this is not an occasion for financial strictness or too much care for the financial future.

For these reasons a direction from the War Cabinet how far the Treasury ought to go would be helpful. At present there is an exchange of detailed telegrams with the Greek Government, which do not improve the atmosphere or reach an agreed solution, and have reduced the mind of Sir M. Palairet to a state of high confusion. We are pressing for the despatch of a Greek financial delegation to London. It might be better to limit ourselves to that for the time being, to suspend further financial discussions until the Delegation has arrived, and meanwhile to arrive at a clear-cut decision in our own minds what to say to them when they get here.

The demands of Greece (or rather of the financiers of the Bank of Greece) have now grown, taken at their full face value, to the following:–

(1) We to finance the whole of their *external* expenditure on war supplies (including all purchases essential to the maintenance of the fighting forces and imported for their use) in the sterling area; the necessary sums to be paid into what is known as No. 2 account at the Bank of England.

(2) We to finance a large part of their *internal* expenditure inside Greece by paying an initial sum of £5 million and subsequent sums of £5 million per month into what is known

as No. 3 account at the Bank of England, these amounts to be at their free disposal for any purpose now or hereafter, and not, as intended by us, merely conventional cover for their note issue.

(3) Greece to retain, without being required to use any part of it to help the war, the whole of the current earnings from her exports to the sterling area, and from her shipping freights (estimated at £20 million gross per annum) accruing to their credit in what is known as No. 1 account at the Bank of England (the general account of the Bank of Greece before Greece entered the war).

(4) The Ministry of Shipping to pay for the hire of their ships at a rate not only much in excess of what we pay our own shipowners but so high in relation to what we are paying other allied shipping as to run the risk of upsetting our standards all round; this on top of insurance valuation on a high scale, which we have already agreed, irrespective of the age of the vessels for any losses out of the fine collection of old hulks which the Greek shipowners have collected at bargain prices. The Ministry of Shipping have recently asked the Treasury if the latter can use some financial weapon to make the Greeks more reasonable! We have already agreed to (1) and (3) in full, and (4) is a relatively small matter. We have also granted a credit of $5 million and have placed no restriction on its expenditure and have allowed purchases up to £600,000 in Turkey out of our own credit, although this involves us in some loss of gold. It may also be added that, whilst in principle the Greeks are to look to America for their dollar requirements, in practice they will be receiving from us substantial amounts of munitions of American origin or requiring replacement from America, because the allocation of supplies in the field is not made until they have actually arrived in the Mediterranean sphere of operations.

The difference of opinion, therefore, concerns the advances for internal expenditure under (2) above. The latest

Greek demands under this head are much in excess of their original expectations or of our promises and have gradually developed as a result of their discovering by experience that we are reluctant to say No or to take up a hard and fast line. If they were conceded, it would mean, not only that we should have met the whole of their external expenses during the war in the sterling area but that this country would in addition *owe* Greece at the end of the war a sum which would have reached (say) £120 million if the war lasts to the autumn of 1942. In terms of peace-time finance this would be a heavy burden, equal to the favourable balance of our trade with the whole of the rest of the world during the whole of the four or five years before the war; and it will be on the top of enormous obligations in other directions and of a great depletion of our earnings from former assets. In the view of the Treasury such an outcome is wholly inacceptable.

What we have actually agreed to is a lump sum of £5 million paid into No. 3 account, followed by monthly instalments, provisionally estimated at £4 million, provided this is required to maintain the cover of their note issue at 40 per cent (a total of £20 million having been advanced by us up to date).

The difference of opinion relates both to the amount of the credits to No. 3 account and the purposes for which they are to be available.

As regards amount, these credits were originally asked as cover for the note issue, which is being considerably expanded to meet internal war expenditure, and were to be based, according to us, on the principle of providing 40 per cent of the increase, which is the statutory proportion of the Bank of Greece. In the first instance the Treasury agreed to transfer sums calculated on approximate estimates; and there is no reason to suppose that the amounts transferred so far into No. 3 account (namely £20 million) fall short of 40 per cent of the Note expansion.* The fact that the Treasury agreed at an early stage to make lump sum transfers not primarily related to the note issue statistics has led the Greeks to hope that they might establish the principle of a large fixed monthly subsidy irrespective of the actual amounts of the note expansion or of internal expenditure.

As regards the availability of the sterling credits in No. 3 account, the Treasury have agreed that any surplus available in No. 3 account may be used to replenish the balances of No. 2 account. Since, however, they have also agreed, apart from this, to provide unlimited credits in No. 2 account to meet all war expenditure currently incurred in the sterling and associated areas, the only practical significance of the credits in No. 3 account is psychological and conventional for the purposes of the Bank of Greece's Bank Statement. The Treasury have taken it for granted—and have never even been asked to agree otherwise—that the credits in No. 3 account have no wider availability. But it has come to their knowledge that the Bank of Greece is in fact giving instructions to the Bank of England, based on the assumption that these credits are immediately available for unrestricted use on expenditure not connected with the war and are drawing on them substantially, without having so informed us, for miscellaneous purposes which ought to be met out of the general balances in No. 1 account. In view of this, it is not safe to leave room for any ambiguity.

Moreover, behind the question of the immediate availability of these credits lies the question of what is to happen to the large balance in No. 3 account which is likely to remain in hand as cover for the note issue after the war. If they were to be regarded as freely available without any question of reimbursement, this country would find itself liable, in effect,

---

* The total note issue as at 23 October was £21,700,000 and had risen by £5,300,000 to £27 million on 7 December.

to pay a peace-time indemnity to Greece on a scale which would be very large in relation to our probable capacity; though naturally it would be a great comfort to Greece to be able to reinstate their position after the war in a manner, which is, in effect, at our expense.

It will be easily appreciated, therefore, into what a dangerous position we are drifting. The Greek financiers are endeavouring to establish a *de facto* position quite different from what we promised or what we intended. Sir M. Palairet, not unnaturally, is reluctant to convey to the Greeks any messages we send him which he thinks might give the Greek financiers an opportunity to tell Monsieur Korizis[8] that we were falling behind our engagements. There is a real danger lest Monsieur Korizis might be persuaded that he has a genuine grievance, when all we are trying is to avoid falling into the deep pit which his financiers are digging for us.

The Treasury believes that the best way out is to be found in distinguishing sharply between the financial assistance genuinely required by Greece during the war which should be afforded her on the largest possible scale and on the most generous terms, and, on the other hand, what may be called, not unfairly, the *financial racket* aimed at establishing a position in which, after the war is over, *we* owe Greece large sums at her free future disposal.

The key to this solution is to be found in the fact that we have not at present undertaken to make free gifts to Greece. We have given her *credits,* the equivalent of which she owes to us and can be asked to repay. A dangerous situation can only arise after the war if Greece is allowed to treat her unspent credits at the Bank of England as freely available without offsetting them against the larger sum which she, in theory, will owe us. At present Greece is not entitled to make any such assumption. But unless we call a halt we shall inevitably drift into a situation in which she acts that way in practice.

[8] Alexandros Korizis, Premier of Greece, January to March 1941.

The Treasury proposal is, therefore, that all war supplies which we furnish to Greece, whether directly in kind or through orders which she places in the sterling area and we finance, shall be a *free gift*. But we on our side must not owe Greece anything, and the unspent balances at the Bank of England, which we shall have provided as a conventional cover against her internal note issue, must be offset in due course against the corresponding sums which she will owe to us. This does not mean that the credits will be cancelled immediately after the war, but they will not be available except as a conventional cover for the note issue and must be worked off by gradual instalments against the corresponding obligation from Greece to ourselves.

The Treasury ask, therefore, for instructions to negotiate as follows with the Greek Financial Delegation to be sent to London as soon as possible:–

(1) The whole of the external expenditure in the sterling and Allied currency areas incurred by Greece on war supplies, widely interpreted to cover all purchases for the maintenance of the fighting forces and imported for their use, shall be met by us as a free gift.

(2) A sterling credit equal to 40 per cent of the expansion of the internal note issue shall be established at the Bank of England in favour of the Bank of Greece which shall not be diverted from this purpose except by agreement with the Treasury, and remains a credit, not a free gift, the unspent portion of which will be offset by instalments at some later dates to be mutually agreed against the corresponding Greek obligations held by us.

Whilst the negotiations should begin on this basis, it might be reasonable to agree to a further clause embodying an additional concession if this was necessary to bring about a successful conclusion:–

(3) In the event of the commercial balances in No. 1 account (which are at the free disposal of the Bank of Greece for all purposes within the sterling area) becoming exhausted,

transfers up to a limited amount, to be agreed with the British Treasury on each occasion, may be made from No. 3 account to No. 1 account to replenish the latter at any time during the war or for two years afterwards.

A line must be drawn somewhere. To concede extravagant demands leads not to a contented alliance but merely to yet further demands, as experience is showing. The terms proposed above are the most generous and far-reaching which an Ally has ever received.

Chapter 2

WORKING OUT THE RULES
OF LEND LEASE

President Roosevelt's announcement of the principle of lend lease did not mean immediate finance for supplies to Britain. Rather it left open the details of the coverage of the principles as embodied in a Bill and the problem of interim finance before the Bill became law—the means of meeting the commitments which Britain had undertaken in 1940 and those she might make in the coming months. In addition, the Americans continued their pressure for the liquidation of Britain's overseas assets to meet current demands for funds.

After concerning himself initially with the details of the draft legislation before Congress and their interpretation, Keynes turned his attention increasingly to the problems of interim finance and the old commitments. On 31 January, he talked with Mr Harry Hopkins[1] over the interpretation of the Bill before providing the Chancellor with a draft *aide memoire* reflecting the conversation.

AIDE MEMOIRE

The outcome of the Lend and Lease Bill will be extremely satisfactory and will go nearly the whole way towards meeting British financial requirements, provided that the President can see his way to interpret it and use his discretion along the following lines:–

1. To treat British type munitions equally with common type munitions as defence articles within the meaning of the Bill.

2. To regard as within the ambit of the Bill machines and raw materials such as steel, oil, machine tools, drop forgings, alloy metals etc. which are used directly or indirectly for

---

[1] Harry L. Hopkins (1890–1946); U.S. Secretary of Commerce, 1938–40; head of Lend Lease programme, 1941; adviser and assistant to Roosevelt, 1941–5.

defence purposes but are also capable of being used for general as well as munition purposes. This would sometimes involve the principle of substitution, which was accepted by the U.S. Administration in a somewhat similar connection during the last war. According to this principle articles are defence articles if they are acquired to replace articles which have been used for defence. To give an example: the quantities of steel and oil purchased from U.S.A. will be considerably less than the total quantity of these commodities used for defence purposes. But it is impracticable to follow a particular consignment of, e.g., steel through all its processes. By the principle of substitution all such purchases from U.S.A. would be defence articles, provided they did not exceed the total quantity employed in defence.

3. To transfer to U.S. Government agents as soon as possible after the Bill becomes law all contracts for future delivery falling under the above two headings in respect of which the British Treasury have made advance payments or have incurred capital expense and to reimburse such payments to the British Treasury in cash, these transfers to cover British type munitions as well as common type.

It is estimated that such reimbursements might amount to $550 million in respect of the American type munitions and $170 million in respect of British type munitions. This would be approximately sufficient to restore the minimum working balance of $600 million required by the British Treasury and the Bank of England to meet contingencies in every quarter of the world (for it must be remembered that they have no other liquid resources whatever) and, in addition, to meet other commitments falling outside the Lend and Lease Bill for a period of about a year.

The anxieties of recent weeks have been due partly to the difficulty of finding sufficient liquid funds to meet payments during the interim period and partly by doubts as to whether British type munitions would be financed under the Bill (both future payments and the reimbursement of advance payments) as well as American type munitions. For, if British type munitions are not to be financed under the Bill, the British Treasury will be completely in the soup. Yet it is obvious that British type munitions are articles of defence equally with American type.

If the British Treasury are to be in a position to maintain their minimum working balance and to meet their gold and dollar commitments after the end of a year some further provision would be necessary. Perhaps the two following suggestions deserve consideration:–

(i) The above calculation is on the assumption that agricultural and forestry products purchased in U.S. partly for civilian use and partly for the forces, also agricultural tractors and machinery and fertilisers, will not fall within the ambit of the Bill. Perhaps, however, the Bill could be interpreted so as to cover some of these. Failing this, it is submitted that, if it is possible, even at this late date, to amend the Bill, the inclusion of these products might be actually advantageous to its prospects from the political angle.

(ii) Could the operation of the Bill be made retrospective so as to make it applicable (to take the easiest case) to any American type munition of which delivery has been accepted during the interim period or earlier? It is a particularly unfortunate result of the present arrangements that even American type munitions will have to be financed out of the free British resources in every case in which delivery has been accepted by them before the Bill becomes law.

If a further $300 million could be released by these means, the exhaustion of liquid resources might be postponed by nearly another year.

The above calculations are given under great reserve, since the position is highly fluid, and new demands are constantly coming forward. The figures on which they are based can be summarised as follows:–

(a) Munition contracts placed with the British Purchasing Commission and actually outstanding on 1 March next may not be much more than $1,000 million, but few fresh orders will have been placed for 2½ months and contracts under discussion at various stages of maturity (and of varying degrees of probability) would bring the total up to $8,500 million at August 31, 1942. These figures include both British and American type munitions.

(*b*) Purchases of machines and raw materials falling under (2) above which will come, it is suggested, within the ambit of the Bill will amount within the next year to about $600 million.

(*c*) The balance of trade, including both visible and invisible items, between the sterling area and U.S.A., apart from orders under (1) and (2) above, is likely to be slightly adverse by (say) $50 million in the course of a year if present estimates are realised. On the other hand, the need to save shipping by purchasing from the nearest market may make it necessary to increase such purchases beyond what is now contemplated.

(*d*) Expenditures which have to be met in gold and dollars in respect of commitments outside the United States are estimated at about $810 million per annum. Towards this newly mined gold within the Empire available to the British Treasury should furnish $560 million, leaving a deficit of $250 million. Adding this to the adverse balance of $50 million (which is perhaps an under-estimate) with the U.S. itself, we have a total deficit of not less than $300 million.

Thus reimbursements under the Lend and Lease Bill of $720 million will meet this deficit for a year and raise the working balance to about the minimum figure required. The release of a further $300 million by some further expedient would make the position reasonably safe.

Mr Hopkins assured the British authorities that when the Lend Lease Bill became law the President would provide all the assistance that was legally possible.

However, between the introduction of the Bill on 10 January and its passage on 11 March American pressure for the liquidation of remaining British overseas assets increased. On 11 March, in response to a request for comments on a Foreign Office memorandum for Lord Halifax, Keynes set out his (and the Treasury's) views. The first five paragraphs, very slightly revised, went to Lord Halifax in a message from Mr Churchill on 10 April.

From a letter to NIGEL RONALD,[2] *11 March 1941*

It is true that we have been resisting a hurried and indiscriminate handling of our direct investments in the immediate present. This is partly because in the present state of the American markets there are no serious buyers, so that hasty action, which would have to make use of untrustworthy middlemen and irresponsible bargain-hunters, would be liable to land both ourselves and the American Administration in some responsibility for grave scandals and gross individual injustices; and partly because some of the direct investments have an importance as part of our permanent industrial structure and mechanism for export wildly disproportionate to what they would be worth in the hands of another party dissociated from the parent business. (Indeed many of them would have a negative value separate from their parent and are not, properly speaking, foreign investments at all, but an intrinsic part of the organisation of the home firm.)

In the main, however, the controversy has been on a different matter. We are not resisting the ultimate liquidation during the war of the major direct investments, which have substantial value, provided a responsible purchaser can be found. The issue between the Treasury and Mr Morgenthau[3]

---

[2] Nigel Bruce Ronald (1894–1974), K.C.M.G. 1946; H.M. diplomatic service from 1920; Assistant Private Secretary to Secretary of State for Foreign Affairs, 1929–34; First Secretary, 1930; Counsellor, 1939; Assistant Under-Secretary, 1942; Ambassador to Portugal, 1947–54.

[3] Henry Morgenthau, Jr. (1891–1967); Under-Secretary and Acting Secretary, U.S. Treasury, 1933–4; Secretary of Treasury, 1935–45.

has been of a different description. He has been aiming, partly perhaps for political reasons, to placate opposition in Congress, and partly perhaps for other reasons connected with his future power to impose his will on us, at stripping us of our liquid resources to the greatest possible extent *before* the Lend Lease Bill comes into operation, so as to leave us with the minimum in hand to meet during the rest of the war the numerous obligations which will not be covered by the Lend Lease Bill.

It is our view that this situation will be of the utmost political and practical disadvantage to both countries. The liquid resources in question include, not only our American investments, but the whole of our gold down to the last £ sterling in the possession of the Bank of England to meet unexpected obligations in any part of the world. Apart from the fact that we shall have a fair amount of outgoings in the United States, and a very large amount in Canada, not covered by the Lend Lease Bill, we also have substantial obligations all over the place,—in Sweden, Persia, Venezuela, Bolivia and elsewhere, which we are under an obligation to meet in gold. Morgenthau has been aiming at a position in which the gold reserve of the Bank of England was virtually nil.

Now this would put us in a humiliating position, productive of perpetual friction in days to come, and treat us worse than we have ever ourselves thought it proper to treat the humblest and least responsible Balkan country. It means moreover that we should have to go on our knees with Mr Morgenthau before we could enter into commitments which were no concern of his. And, according to our understanding of the Bill, Mr Morgenthau would often find himself in a position in which he was legally unable to meet our request however much he might wish to do so. There is indeed every indication that the man is not merely tiresome but an ass. If we were to acquiesce in his policy, we should be laying up great store of trouble for everyone concerned.

I was through all this in the last war. The greatest cause of friction arose from the fact that when America came into the war our own private resources were virtually exhausted, with the result that we had to borrow from them for all sorts of necessary purposes outside U.S.A. This meant that their efforts at exercising Treasury control were bound to be unsuccessful. The fact that they had to finance us, not only for munitions, but for all kinds of expenditure throughout the world, was, during that war, a perpetual cause of friction, and a great aggravation of the problem of the war debt afterwards that it should have arisen in this way. I am sure that it is of the utmost importance for future relations that the Lend Lease Bill should only be used to finance clearly defensible transactions, namely, munitions proper and certain foods. For the various miscellaneous items which are less easily explained to the American public we should continue to depend on our own resources. But that would only be possible if we were left with adequate resources for the purpose.

Now, under the Lend Lease Bill it will, to the best of our belief, be lawful for the President to take over from us various contracts already placed and reimburse us the advance payments we have already made. This would give us enough resources to be independent for all the above purposes. But unless this transfer is made now (and it seems very doubtful whether Mr Morgenthau favours this), it does not appear to us that it will be legal hereafter for us to receive any actual cash whatever from U.S.A. This is the subject matter of our telegram 1303, which you sent off for us yesterday.

I come next to your post-war preoccupations. I do not believe that the American Administration have given any serious thought to this or that the President has more than the vaguest idea of what he will do. I expect we ought to allow the position to develop a bit further before even beginning to discuss it. The larger the amount, the safer the position will be. I should rather expect that the President intends to

47

make us a complete present of the whole thing financially speaking, but to ask in return certainly some political concessions or agreements and perhaps economic ones.

Meanwhile, the most pressing problem, if we are to avoid unnecessary friction, is, I am sure, the retention by us of enough assets to leave us capable of independent action. That is what the Treasury is trying to secure. It is an entire mistake to suppose that we are 'playing safe, guarding an imaginary post-war financial wicket'.

By 14 March, the situation was clearly developing in a manner not foreseen when Keynes had spoken with Mr Hopkins. A particularly pessimistic telegram, one of a series, from Sir Frederick Phillips led to this assessment by Keynes, portions of which appeared in a memorandum prepared for the Chancellor's subsequent briefing of the Prime Minister.

To SIR RICHARD HOPKINS, *14 March 1941*

We have been led to suppose hitherto that when the Lease Lend Bill had become law the President would give us all the financial assistance which was legally possible. It is not disputed, so far as we are aware, that it is legally possible for him to take over those of our existing commitments where we have not yet accepted delivery of the goods, accepting liability for the payments still to be made and reimbursing us in respect of our advance payments. On the assumption that the main part, if not the whole, of these commitments would be taken over, we have been pressed not to be over-reluctant in parting with our resources to meet the problems of the interim period, and we have been encouraged to enter into new commitments during the interim period, with Mr Morgenthau's express sanction of each such commitment entered into, on the expectation that these would be taken over in due course. Indeed, if this procedure was not to be followed, it is not obvious why we should have been required to obtain Mr Morgenthau's approval for each of them specifically.

Sir Frederick Phillips now explains that all this is a complete delusion, that there is no likelihood of the President's using his legal powers to act in the manner we had been expecting, and that if anything is done in this direction it will be on a small scale.

It is necessary, therefore, to take fresh stock of the position and to consider seriously a situation which hitherto, in our own minds, we have been regarding as outside practical possibilities.

If the President had acted according to our expectations up to the hilt, we should have been relieved of $m1,440 prospective payments, reimbursed $m780 against past payments, and the payment of these sums in full would have put us in a comfortable position. That is to say, we should have been able to accumulate a working balance of some $m600, repay the Belgian Government the $m300 in gold which we have borrowed from them and pay Canada some $m700 in gold or dollars, by which she could meet her adverse balance of trade with U.S.A. arising from our large expenditures in Canada. Indeed, this would have made us so decidedly comfortable that we could have been content with something less, since the calculation assumes only some $m200 sales of investments.

Sir Frederick Phillips now tells us that, instead of an expectation which might have been as great as $m2,220, the most we can hope to get is something between $m100 and $m350. Thus we look like being (say) $m2,000 worse off than we were hoping.

This means that, if we reduce our working balances and the gold at the Bank of England to nil, refund no part of the Belgian gold and make no payments to Canada, we should still be $m400 short, or approximately so. Against which, however, we should have such further sums as we can realise from the sale of market and direct investments in U.S.A.

Looked at from another point of view, the statistical position can be summarised as follows.

If we realise in the course of the next year (say) $m600 from

49

market and direct investments and were to make no payments whatever to Canada, we should about balance, with nothing left for contingencies. Broadly speaking, this seems to be the position as Sir Frederick Phillips views it. It appears that Mr Morgenthau made the following statement in his testimony before Congress.

'I believe that any amount of South African gold that the United Kingdom receive during this year they should use to pay for merchandise which they buy from us.'

Sir Frederick Phillips comments on this that Mr Morgenthau 'regards this as binding, so that, though we may get away with necessary gold payments to third countries, he does not propose to let us pay any gold to Canada'.

If this is accepted it is over our financial relations with Canada that the crisis will arise. It is estimated that we (and the rest of the sterling area on balance) will owe Canada about $m1,000 in the course of the next year. So far Canada has offered to lend us about $m300 towards this. We have not been regarding this as adequate and have had the intention of pressing Canada to raise her assistance at least to $m400 and perhaps to $m500. The last figure would seem to be somewhere about the maximum of her capacity if she is to meet her adverse balance with U.S.A. If we ask her to advance us the whole amount of $m1,000, then she will be able to avoid bankruptcy only by suffering the same stripping process that we are suffering of all her assets of whatever description capable of liquidation in U.S.A.

It should be added that the above calculation is made on very optimistic hypotheses as to the operation of the Lend Lease Bill in regard to future commitments. It assumes that practically the whole of our future purchases from U.S.A. can be financed under it, and reduces our miscellaneous payments and imports from America not suitable for finance under the Lend Lease Bill to no more than $m80. Since it is just possible that the President does not really intend to reduce us to such straits, it is suggested that it might be as well to call attention to the consequences of what is proposed in plain language and not submit to it in humble silence. It should be pointed out that there is an alternative prospect before us not so bad as the foregoing, but nevertheless infinitely tiresome and inefficient and productive of ever-growing friction. We had been supposing that when the Lend Lease Bill was through a definite settlement would be reached in regard to our existing commitments so that we should know where we stand. If we were to get the whole amount, this would be necessary, since as soon as we have taken delivery the time has passed when a future commitment can be taken over. But apparently so long as any of the future commitments have not yet matured some further relief is possible in this way, by such undelivered commitments being taken over. Thus, it will be open to Mr Morgenthau day by day to allow us just so much relief as is necessary to keep us on the mat but still breathing by taking over a small appropriate amount of the still undelivered future commitments. If he adopts this procedure he will retain power in his hands to bend us to his will on any matter of detail where he has a fancy to do so. There will be no branch of our expenditure in any part of the world which he cannot question before agreeing to give us that day's dollop. In fact we should continue to live for months to come in the same condition of anxiety and precariousness as has existed during the interim period. Here again one wonders whether it is quite certain that this is exactly what the President intends.

14.3.41   J.M.K.

These circumstances, plus Mr Morgenthau's demand of 10 March for a spectacular sale of a large British direct investment in the United States to ease the passage of the first Lend Lease Appropriation Bill through Congress, lay in the background as Keynes, and to a lesser extent other members of the Treasury, began regular conversations with Mr B. Cohen[4] of the American Embassy in London. Just prior to the first conversation, the British Government selected its firm for the 'show sale', Viscose Corporation of America of which 97 per cent belonged to Courtaulds.

The first conversation concerned Britain's dollar position, and Keynes supplied Mr Cohen with a broad outline afterwards.

To B. COHEN, *17 March 1941*

Dear Mr Cohen,

These are the figures which I mentioned to you this morning. We need to cover

	£ million
U.K. commitments in the U.S.A. on existing contracts	360
Payments by sterling area to Canada in gold or dollars, say	150
Reconstitution of working balance	150
U.K. payments in U.S.A. not covered by lease lend	?
Total, say, over	660+?

We have not yet had the information which would enable us to estimate the last figure.

Towards these needs we have

	£ million
U.K. exports to the U.S.A. visible and invisible	45
Favourable balance of the rest of the sterling area	25
New gold 120, less 30 gold outgoings elsewhere	90
Sale of marketable securities and direct investments	?
	160+?

[4] Benjamin Victor Cohen (b. 1894), lawyer; Adviser to U.S. Ambassador, London, 1941; Assistant to Director, Office of Economic Stabilisation, 1942–3; General Counsel, Office of War Mobilisation, 1943–5; Legal Adviser, Bretton Woods Conference, 1944; Senior Adviser, American Delegation, U.N. General Assembly; 1946.

Here again it is difficult to estimate the last figure in any particular period of time, but it would seem difficult to count on a figure higher than 150 within a year.

All this would mean a need for over £700 million, towards which not more than about £300 million is in sight. It looks therefore as if, when we can make a closer estimate, we might well find that we shall need to be relieved of commitments on existing orders in the U.S.A. to the amount of £360 million and to receive reimbursements in respect of advance payments and capital of £195 million, or at any rate a large proportion of this assistance, in order to be able to bridge the gap.

Yours sincerely,
[copy not initialled]

When Mr Cohen dined with Keynes on 18 March, the subject was sales of direct investments, a matter of considerable importance after Mr Harold Smith, the American Director of the Budget, announced to Congress on 15 March that no appropriations under Lend Lease would be used to take over Britain's previous commitments. After this meeting and a lunch with Mr Butterworth[5] of the American Embassy, Keynes circulated the following note.

To LORD CATTO, SIR RICHARD HOPKINS *and* SIR HORACE WILSON, *19 March 1941*

Mr Ben Cohen dined with me last night, and I had a long talk with him about direct investments. His constructive advice was that the best hope lay in getting the discussion on to a new plane by some fresh constructive proposal being put forward. He agreed that following what has become the line of least resistance will only lead to a mess.

Today Waley and I lunched with Butterworth of the American Embassy, who is returning to Washington on Saturday,

---

[5] William Walton Butterworth (b. 1903); U.S. Foreign Service, 1928; Second Secretary, U.S. Embassy, London, 1934–41; Department of Commerce, Washington, 1941–2; member Advisory Commission on Trade Policy in relation to Lend Lease, 1942.

where he will be attached to the R.F.C. and in close touch with Jesse Jones.[6] He was also strongly of the same opinion. I outlined to him the ideas in the attached paper. He said that, if I would let him take a note of this, he would very much welcome the opportunity of putting it up to Jesse Jones as soon as he got home.

Since the Director of the Budget has pledged Congress not to use the appropriations under the Lease Lend Bill to take over our back commitments, it seems that Morgenthau no longer has legal powers to assist us in any way. There seems no reason, therefore, why he should remain in the picture or why we should have any relations with him whatever from now onwards. Since he has no favours it is in his power to grant, there is no reason why we should ask for any. On the other hand, Jesse Jones comes into the picture, since he still has large funds which, if he and the President choose, can be made available. That is why I have adjusted the proposal below to the R.F.C. instead of to funds made available under the Lease Lend Bill. May I send this note to Mr Cohen and Mr Butterworth? I attach carbons of my letters to them, which have not yet been sent off.

19.3.41   J.M.K.

After the necessary clearances, Keynes sent the following letter and memorandum.

To B. COHEN, *19 March 1941*

Dear Cohen,

I am sure that the advice you gave me last night was good, that the only way of making satisfactory progress about the direct investments would be to produce some sort of a plan which looked like a new one and carried the discussion on to a new terrain. I have, therefore, reduced to writing the best version of this I could concoct at short notice. Please treat

[6] Jesse Holman Jones (1874–1956); U.S. Secretary of Commerce, 1940–5.

this as a purely personal suggestion of my own which has no official sanction or approval.

I met Butterworth at lunch today and heard from him that when he returns to Washington at the end of the week he will be attached to Jesse Jones at R.F.C. Since it would, so it seems to me, be vastly better for any new proposal to be put forward from your side rather than ours, I am taking the liberty of most unofficially sending him a copy of this same document.

I have drafted it in terms of the R.F.C. because, if I understand the Reuter telegram correctly, the statement made to Congress yesterday by the Director of the Budget completely tears up the possibility of the other solution. So far as we can make out, the Director of the Budget gave a pledge to Congress yesterday that *no part* of the appropriation now asked for would be used to take over our existing commitments and that the latter would be sufficiently cared for by the dollar assets which still remain to us. In other words, a pledge has been given that the legal powers which previously existed to take over our existing commitments will not be used. Morgenthau has burnt our boats and, as usual, without telling us beforehand, though he must be well aware of the consequences.

In making his statement the Director of the Budget gave a different figure for the amount of our existing commitments from our figure, namely, $m1,020 as against our figure of $m1,440. We have not at present any explanation of this discrepancy. Possibly it may mean that the difference is, one way or another, to be taken over. To that extent the problem would be mitigated. If we take as correct the figures of $m1,020 instead of our own estimate, if we forget the large payments we have to make to Canada, and if we do not replenish our working balance, it might not be impossible for us to meet the bill out of our resources. I imagine that it is in this way that Morgenthau has worked his arithmetic.

It was a very great pleasure to me yesterday to see you again. The suggestion that we should try to have some regular system by which you would keep in touch with us here is extremely approved. Would you be free to look in at my room, here, somewhere between a quarter to one and one o'clock on Tuesday? You could then have a talk with Lord Catto and anyone else who was available, and Lord Catto would be very glad if you could lunch with him a little later in the morning.

Yours sincerely,

J. M. KEYNES

P.S. You may like to have a note of how the sale of American Viscose has worked out as we see it here. The business, which is shown in the accounts at, I think, $128 million, well written down, without any allowance for goodwill, has been sold for $36 million *plus* 90 per cent of the extra which the banking syndicate make by re-selling the shares. This appears to place us entirely in the hands of the banks. They are fortunately responsible people. Nevertheless, if they come to the conclusion that the market is unsuitable for an issue during the next six months, they will then be entitled to take final possession of the shares and obtain for $36 million assets which brought in some $11 million profit last year. They can re-sell it at favourable prices to their friends. Even if they get the very best price on re-sale, their commission is enormous. They have already had some $1,800,000 as commission. If the business is eventually re-sold for $120 million, they will net an additional $8,400,000 as commission. And all this without taking any vestige of risk, since the assets are obviously in excess of the amount they have paid down.

DIRECT INVESTMENTS

1. The R.F.C. or other appropriate body to advance $900 million against the lien of all the direct investments.

2. This would not mean that these investments would be vested or become owned by the U.S. Administration. They would remain the property of their present owners and continue to be managed by them. It would mean that the sale proceeds of any which were found suitable to be sold should be turned over in reduction of the advance, and in the case of those that were retained the whole of the income would be turned over to the R.F.C. (or other body).

3. The present owners would have the same inducement as at present to earn as large an income as possible, since the dollars representing their profits turned over to the R.F.C. would be purchased from the owners by the British Treasury against sterling. Indeed the plan would have the advantage that the earnings would probably be materially greater in their present ownership than if these businesses were divorced from the parents and ceased to have the important advantages of the connection.

4. Above all, the plan would have the advantage that it would not interfere with the future export organisation of Great Britain. Many of the direct investments are not foreign investments in the usual sense, but are part of the organisation of the parent body for the purposes of foreign trade and the use of British processes and brands abroad. All this would be maintained intact to the mutual advantage. On the other hand, the income thus earned in U.S.A. would be turned over to the U.S. Administration. So that the financial, as distinct from the economic, advantages of the arrangements would be secured by the U.S. probably in ampler measure than under any alternative arrangement.

5. The plan would have the further advantage that it would not be necessary to organise sales or transfers of property or to fix any market value for any of the assets in question, except in particular cases where it was agreed that an outright sale was suitable and advisable. If the direct investments are worth more than the approximate globular figure, the U.S.

Administration would get the advantage of this in the shape of the income. If they are worth less, they would be no worse off than through an outright sale without the friction and difficulty of establishing the lower genuine value.

6. The plan is advanced as a method of helping the financial situation without disturbing the economic relationship to future mutual disadvantage.

7. In the first instance this would be a temporary arrangement for the period of the war. The ultimate settlement would be cleared up along with other associated problems at the end of the war.

In the weeks that followed, discussions continued with Mr Cohen and others in the Embassy on these matters. The following letter and memoranda by Keynes summarise the drift of opinion.

To S. D. WALEY, *22 March 1941*

Mr Ben Cohen rang me up on the telephone on Friday to say that he was very greatly attracted by the plan I sent him for dealing with direct investments. On the other hand, he was most doubtful about the wisdom of attempting to bring in R.F.C. and Mr Jesse Jones. He thought it would raise political difficulties and internal rivalries in the Administration. I told him that this had not been an original part of the plan but had been brought in because Mr Morgenthau seemed to have deprived himself of any funds with which he could assist us short of bringing in a completely new Appropriation Bill, which one could scarcely expect in the near future.

Mr Cohen replied that he would like to see the exact text before he could feel sure that this really was the case. He was evidently taken greatly by surprise, just as we were. I promised to let him have the full statement as soon as we received it from Phillips.

Meanwhile he has discussed the position with Butterworth,

who is aware of Cohen's feeling about this and has agreed to refer to the plan, when he gets back to Washington, with great discretion and perhaps leave out any reference to R.F.C. in the first instance.

I have now seen Phillips's telegrams 1230 and 1233. As you were meeting Cohen at lunch to-day, you will very possibly have told him all that he ought to know of the substance of these telegrams. The upshot seems to be that the statement made to the Committee on Appropriations contains no loop-hole, but Morgenthau, in his career of double-crossing every-one and providing false assurances on both sides, believes nevertheless that he is still in a position to give us such assistance as he has promised not to give us to the extent that he is inclined to from time to time. I should be interested to know how much you thought it discreet to tell Cohen and what his reaction was.

[copy initialled] J. M. K.

To B. COHEN, *22 March 1941*

Dear Cohen,

We told Phillips of the figures which I gave you and he has sent us the following comments.

£360 million represents total outstanding liabilities, not only those due in the year from March 1st.

The figure of £150 million for payments by the sterling area to Canada in gold or dollars was simply a repetition of the figure which Mr Morgenthau gave in the table which he presented to Congress in January. It seems clear that in existing circumstances and unless fresh decisions are taken, it will be hardly possible for us to pay any gold or U.S. dollars to Canada.

While Phillips has always represented that we shall need a reserve of £150 million free of encumberances after the war, in memoranda recently given by him to the U.S. Treasury covering the six months immediately ahead, he has pressed for £60 million to be accumulated mainly in that period.

The net dollar expenditure not covered by the lease lend system cannot yet be estimated. Phillips apparently thinks it may be somewhere between £25 and £175 millions.

As regards the sales of marketable securities and direct investments, Phillips suggests a figure of £225 million in the year rather than £150 million. We shall, of course, do everything we can, and if we reach the figure suggested by Phillips rather than the more cautious estimate which we suggested, so much the better.

Yours sincerely,
[copy not initialled]

To LORD CATTO *and* SIR HORACE WILSON, *2 April 1941*

I had a long talk with the American Ambassador yesterday evening. He took the initiative in broaching the topic of direct investments. Evidently he has been well briefed in our complaints by Mr Ben Cohen, and made a speech of indignation on our behalf scarcely less eloquent than Lord Catto could have made himself. He liked the proposal which had been put to Mr Cohen,—which circumstance fits in very well with sending him the proposed memorandum which Sir H. J. Wilson has asked Mr Bewley[7] to prepare. As I mentioned before, this will give Mr Winant[8] the opportunity of endorsing it when he forwards it, which I should say he can be relied on to do. He evidently attached much importance in this connection to Mr Harry Hopkins having been made Administrator of the Lend Lease Bill. He told me that the President had promised him that he was doing this before he left and that he had been disappointed at so much delay in the

[7] Thomas Kenneth Bewley (1890–1943); Treasury, 1913; Financial Adviser, British Embassy, Washington, 1933–9; Principal Assistant Secretary, Treasury, 1940–3.
[8] John Gilbert Winant (1889–1947); Governor of New Hampshire, 1925–7, 1931–5; Assistant Director, International Labour Office, 1935, 1937–9; U.S. Ambassador, London, 1941–6; U.S. representative on European Advisory Committee, 1943.

appointment taking effect. But Mr Hopkins is now effectively in charge.

I may add one or two other points of interest he touched on. He said he had just completed yesterday making a long report to the President on his first impressions of the situation here, and I inferred that he had probably taken this opportunity to make some reference to the direct investment business. He also said he wanted to strengthen his staff here considerably for dealing with British Government Departments and mentioned in particular the name of Mr Winfield Riefler,[9] whom I know very well indeed and who would be particularly suitable.

I fancy the point he had considerably stressed in his report to the President was the difference of psychology here and in America arising directly out of the fact that we are taking a *personal* part, as distinct from the two countries being agreed in their fundamental anti-Nazi sentiments. He thought it most important for American psychology that they should be actually participating in a non-business way. He suggested that half the trouble over the Lend Lease Bill and direct investments comes from the fact that the whole of the American participation is still presenting itself to the average American too much in the light of a business transaction, so that they treat it in the tough spirit which they consider appropriate to such transactions. Even small things which made them feel that they were doing something of a non-business complexion would, he thought, be of great psychological importance. For this reason he liked very much a mild idea I had mentioned to Mr Cohen, who seems to have passed it on to him, that Americans should go without cheese one day a week in order to supply our workers with their midday

---

[9] Winfield William Riefler (1897–1971); Economic Adviser to Executive Council of Federal Reserve Board, 1933–4; Chairman, Central Statistics Board, 1933–5; Economic Adviser, National Emergency Council, 1934–5; Professor, School of Economics and Politics, Institute for Advanced Studies, 1935–48; Special Assistant to U.S. Ambassador, in charge of Economic Warfare, London, 1942–4.

meal. On the grander scale he seemed to think that there was a strong argument for America's undertaking convoying, not merely on the grounds of material benefit to us, but that action of that kind would make everyone in America feel much better psychologically. His point all through this was that the Lend Lease Bill had been a great inspiration of the President for getting away from the purely business aspect of things, but that it had only partially succeeded because the general psychology had not yet had time or opportunity to get sufficiently weaned from the business side of things.

Since writing the above, I have had a message from the Ambassador's Secretary asking me to go to see him this afternoon.

2.4.41   [copy initialled] J.M.K.

To S. D. WALEY *and* SIR RICHARD HOPKINS, *7 April 1941*

Phillip's telegram 1465 on the scheme for direct investments I proposed to Mr Ben Cohen:

(1) What Mr Cohen told me confirms Phillips's view as to the inadvisability of bringing in Mr Jesse Jones. I understand that Waley is sending to Sir F. Phillips by bag today a copy of my record of a conversation with Mr Cohen to this effect and explaining that nothing is being done to raise the plan with Mr Jones so far as we are concerned.

(2) Sir F. Phillips is surely right that it would be dangerous to acquire a lump sum so long as the stripping policy is in full operation and the lend lease arrangements unsettled. The worst of it is that the latter are likely to remain to an important degree permanently unsettled. That is to say, they will be at all times in a position to be benevolent or hard-hearted to us in its detailed operation according to how they are feeling; so that they will always be in a position to put pressure on us to sell a direct investment on bad terms if they are in the

mood. It follows that nothing can do us any permanent good except a change of heart. Since the plan I suggested in regard to direct investments could only come about with the blessing and approval of the American Administration, I have been assuming that it was part and parcel of a change of heart. And it was for that reason, and that reason only, that the risk Sir F. Phillips envisaged was not prominent in my mind. If they were to fall in with my plan, it would be with the express and designed purpose, not of increasing pressure on us in another direction, but for relieving us from pressure and over-anxiety.

(3) I am not clear what Sir F. Phillips's own policy really is in the situation which has now developed. Is it in fact proposed to sell by hook or by crook every direct investment which can conceivably find even a bad market in the course of the next six months or so? If so, this is capitulation to what most of us, and no doubt he himself, think excessively undesirable. Surely we cannot contemplate that without a struggle.

If, on the other hand, he contemplates only going on with selected direct investments at the rate of disposal which circumstances render practicable, not in fact likely to be very rapid, we shall be seriously short of funds. How short depends on Mr Morgenthau's decision, which has not yet been communicated to us, as to the extent to which he proposes to bridge the gap between old commitments which we estimate at $m1,300 or a little more and $m1,000 which he has mentioned to Congress.

In order to avoid this dilemma, I should like to persevere with my plan, which, I think, improves on acquaintance, provided it can be fitted into the legislative framework over there. I will develop this in connection with the memorandum on direct investments which is being prepared by Mr Bewley.

(4) Since Mr Waley has taken steps to relieve Sir F. Phillips's mind about bringing in Mr Jesse Jones, perhaps this

telegram does not need any reply at the present moment, though, of course, it would do so if the suggestion it is criticising was to come to life again. If any further telegram is to be sent meanwhile, its object should be, I suggest, to elicit from Sir F. Phillips exactly what his policy is,—i.e. whether it is complete submission to Mr Morgenthau without a further struggle and cost what it may or whether he has any other plan or hope in view.

[copy not initialled]

During these discussions, Keynes also saw Samuel Courtauld, who raised a point concerning the prospective sale of American Viscose.

To s. COURTAULD, *10 April 1941*

My dear Sam,

When we met the other evening I think you mentioned that Hanbury-Williams had offered Morgenthau to raise something like $100 million on the security of Viscose rather than sell outright. I mentioned this to Horace Wilson yesterday when we were talking about such matters, and as he had not heard about that particular offer before, he asked me to make sure that I had not misunderstood what you said and to get an exact account.

Could you let me have this? Obviously it is a point very essential to have on record, since if the eventual price obtained in America is less than $100 million we should have an even bigger grievance than otherwise.

Yours ever,

[copy initialled] J. M. K.

From s. COURTAULD, *18 April 1941*

Dear Maynard,

I have been travelling about, and only got your letter of the 10th at Coventry yesterday.

My conversation with Hanbury-Williams by telephone was not completely definite. The full particulars of the various expedients which he tried to get accepted are on the way by letter, and should arrive in a day or two. He said by telephone, first, that the American investment bankers had always maintained that they would not be able to float the new 'American Viscose Corporation' Company for more than $100 million, and that he had told them, and continued to tell them, that this was an absurdly low figure. He then said that he had offered (not to these bankers of course) to go out and raise some such sum, himself, and meantime to deposit the whole of the scrip of the A.V.C. with the American Treasury as security. He said he was not allowed to take any step in this direction, and that this and various other expedients which he wished to try were immediately and definitely turned down. He was told that nothing would be considered but an outright sale of the undertaking. I do not know who turned him down, but Peacock knew all about it.

I cannot understand how it is that the Treasury seems to know practically nothing of the details of Peacock's negotiations, and did not even know of the terms of the actual A.V.C. deal until I told them, as the result of an earlier conversation with Hanbury-Williams. Peacock knows exactly what Hanbury-Williams' alternative proposals were.

I should be glad if you would ring me up on Monday afternoon and tell me if you have anything more to say about the P.S. of your letter.[10] I asked the Governor of the Bank this morning whether there is any possibility that Courtaulds might yet be dealt with on similar lines to B.A.T. He said he did not think so.

Yours
SAM. C.

To S. COURTAULD, *19 April 1941*

My dear Sam,

Thanks for your further information about Hanbury-Williams's negotiations. If you get any more information by post, I should be glad to have it, for, as you say, we at the Treasury are not kept particularly fully informed about details from the other side.

As you guess, my postscript had reference to the procedure

---

[10] This did not appear on the carbon copy. [Ed.]

adopted in the case of the B.A.T. subsidiary.[11] We have no solid reason for hoping that this procedure will now be adopted generally. But there is at least one other important case where it seems to be under consideration. Obviously it is very much the best way out of the situation. My feeling was, and is, that if the syndicate find difficulty, as they probably will, in floating the new Viscose Corporation at a reasonable figure within the six months period, the Americans might perhaps be persuaded to substitute the loan procedure for the flotation. Indeed, it would, I should have thought, be very difficult for them to resist this if a good case could be made out for a loan which reached or exceeded the probable amount which could be realised from the flotation. No doubt the reply given you by the Governor of the Bank is the safe and cautious thing to say. But I should have thought that it was well worth working with other hopes in view.

Yours ever,

[copy initialled] J.M.K.

Also, at this time, Keynes prepared an *aide memoire* on direct investments for Mr Winant.

To SIR HORACE WILSON AND OTHERS, *16 April 1941*

AIDE MEMOIRE ON BRITISH DIRECT INVESTMENTS IN U.S.A.

1. There are two issues which must be kept distinct:–

(1) The machinery and method by which the dollar equivalent of the British direct investments in U.S.A. can be made available to meet war commitments;

(2) Whether it is in the interest of the two countries that *all* the direct investments should be thus liquidated.

---

[11] In April 1941 the Reconstruction Finance Corporation loaned the Brown Williamson Tobacco Corporation, a subsidiary of British American Tobacco Company, $40 million, of which $25 million went into Britain's exchange reserves. B.A.T. retained all the common shares in Brown Williamson, a significant departure.

Misunderstanding has arisen because proposals of which the only object was to secure orderly and efficient marketing under (1) have been mistaken for dilatory action designed to prejudice the issue under (2). We have been given to understand that we can only escape this suspicion by hasty, and therefore inefficient, marketing,—action which, in our judgment, is capable of leading to recrimination and criticism hereafter. But we have not received any considered statement of the views and wishes of the U.S. Administration on the problem as a whole. We feel that, for reasons given below, the time has come when we ought to ask the Administration to give us clear guidance and to accept responsibility for what is done at their instance.

2. We ask the U.S. Administration to agree with us that realisation of our direct investments to the best advantage has political, and not merely financial, significance.

It is obvious that forced sales at low prices will produce a disappointing yield of dollars and thus defeat the whole object of realising these assets.

But there is a further argument against hasty sales which is important to us and is not without importance to the U.S. Administration. We shall have to compensate the British owners of the direct investments at a *fair* price, arrived at by arbitration if necessary, out of moneys voted by Parliament. The British Treasury will take precaution to see that the price is fair and not excessive; but if arbitration discloses that the price obtained in America is much below a fair price and that the terms were such as no business man in his senses would have accepted except under duress, this will be, sooner or later, a matter of publicity and of adverse comment in business circles and in Parliament. (It is already with difficulty that the matter is being kept in the background.) When this time comes the Chancellor of the Exchequer may have to explain that his action was intended to meet the wishes of the U.S. Administration; and he is, therefore, anxious to make certain that the implications of the present situation are fully understood on both sides.

That such transactions would soon become a matter of public knowledge is inevitable. Will they be approved by American public opinion? Will it seem suitable that, to the financial disadvantage of both Treasuries, a method of sale has been approved—indeed urged—by the U.S. authorities which sacrificed the British assets to speculators and interested parties at prices below their intrinsic value, or that excessive commissions had been paid to financial groups out of relation to any services rendered?

3. If the U.S. Administration share our views that for these reasons sales should not be effected hastily, we believe it to be beyond doubt that a considerable time must elapse before the direct investments can be turned into cash on a substantial scale—for the following reasons:-

(1) Shares in these undertakings are not (for the most part) quoted on any Stock Exchange and there is no public record of earnings and dividends. Thus they have not been subjected to valuation by the collective judgment of markets over a period. Accordingly a purchaser cannot be expected to offer a satisfactory price until he has had a prolonged opportunity of study. Under the Sherman Laws, firms in the same line of business are, in general, precluded from purchasing, so that a business must be sold to outsiders, competent neither to understand its value nor to manage the concern when they have acquired it; unless time is given for the existing management in U.S.A. to prove their case and find responsible backers. These considerations operate both ways. For there will be cases, some of them important, where it will be necessary to protect the American private investor from having a business floated on him which cannot hope to survive in the new, less favourable, conditions.

(2) It is exceedingly difficult to assess the value of an American subsidiary divorced from its British parent. Many of the direct investments (the great majority in terms of number

though not of value) are not separate businesses and depend almost entirely on the existing connection. These will indeed have no selling value worth consideration. But there is also an important group which have appreciable value apart from the connection with the British parent firm, but where this value is most difficult of assessment, so that the intending purchaser must examine closely the probable effects of separation and the prospects of the truncated business carrying on with success.

(3) American stock markets at the present time are inactive at a depressed level as a result of the many uncertainties and risks of war-time. The finest businesses in America could not be sold to new purchasers to-day at a figure approaching their real value. Is there a single outstanding enterprise in U.S.A., with however fine a record, which the proprietors could turn into cash in the next three months at a figure approaching its real value by selling to new outside purchasers, particularly if the prospective purchasers were well aware that the business *must* be marketed within that period?

4. These are arguments against the hasty disposal of assets which ought to be the subject of sales in due course. Whilst some of the direct investments represent important sums individually, the great majority of them in number, as distinct from value, will not realise significant amounts in the best of circumstances. Many of them are part and parcel of the export organisation of the United Kingdom, including the use of British processes and new ideas in the American market, and have little significance apart from this. If the present owners are dispossessed of this element of their organisation, there will be much heart-burning and bitterness in this country, especially as the loss to the vendors will be out of all proportion to the price which the outside purchaser can be expected to pay on any justifiable estimate of the value of what the property will be worth to *him*; and questions will arise whether the British vendor is to be prohibited from opening up any alternative organisation in future to replace

what he is losing. Would this fairly represent the deliberate policy of the U.S. Administration? Ought we not to receive clear guidance from them? For it would be a misfortune that we should proceed along mistaken lines out of pure misunderstanding.

Is it the purpose of the U.S. Administration to strip us of all assets within their jurisdiction? The maintenance of future contacts between British and American industry has much more than merely financial value; and we hope that the U.S. Administration would favour our retaining these contacts in some cases at least. It scarcely needs to be pointed out that the liquidation of British export organisations in U.S.A. will gravely affect British capacity to purchase American goods after the war; and will affect it much more than can be measured merely by the divisible profits of the British subsidiary companies operating in U.S.A.

5. Both the amount to be realised from the direct investments and the rate at which they can be liquidated are relevant to our ability to meet the old commitments which we contracted before the Lend Lease Act became law, and the new commitments which we may have to contract from now onwards owing to inevitable delays in bringing the Lend Lease machinery into operation or to difficulties in bringing certain expenditures within its terms, especially those relating to other parts of the sterling area. We cannot see our way more than a short period ahead. We have no clear understanding what is to happen. If we knew the worst, we could take measures to adapt ourselves to it; if we knew the best, we should be greatly heartened. But we know nothing for certain. Meanwhile our financial policy throughout the world is overshadowed by anxiety and uncertainty how these issues will be finally resolved. Each month that passes increases the difficulty of an eventual satisfactory solution, since after an old commitment has matured there is no way under the existing law by which the U.S. Administration can help.

6. The questions of the financing of the old commitments

and of the disposal of the direct investments have reactions on the future administration of the Lend Lease Act.

If we are left to meet the old commitments unaided and the receipts from the liquidation of the direct investments are inadequate over the relevant period, we shall only be able to pay our way with the help of a very wide and liberal interpretation of the Lend Lease Act by which our future purchases in U.S.A., almost without exception, are brought under the terms of the Lend Lease Bill whenever it is by any means possible to do so under the law.

Is this advisable? It may involve great administrative difficulties and delays if every individual purchase has to be placed through the Lend Lease machinery. It is also likely to involve long and difficult debates just where the line should be drawn, and the final decision will not always be easily defensible before public opinion, which may regard fine legal points as a means of subterfuge.

How much better it would be, both administratively and politically, if the operations under the Lend Lease Act could be kept on broad and easily defensible lines leaving minor, marginal and doubtful items to be paid for out of our own British resources!

But for this to be possible these resources must not be kept as near zero as possible. The bulk of the old commitments are munitions of war in the strictest sense, which could be taken over under the Lend Lease Act in the full spirit of that Act and of the President's intention in promoting it. If this course were taken, the British Treasury would be left with enough resources of its own to give it that proper measure of independence to which it is entitled, and a margin out of which it could be expected to meet all those expenditures which in the urgency and unexpectedness of war it will be very desirable to incur without the delays of explanation, debate and complicated procedure.

[copy not initialled]

Chapter 3

WASHINGTON, 1941: FINANCING PRE-LEND LEASE COMMITMENTS

By mid-April Keynes was preparing for his first wartime visit to the United States. On this visit he was to improve communications between Whitehall and British officials in Washington by providing them with background information not easily communicated by cable, as well as conduct negotiations on several lend lease problems surrounding the old commitments and the level of Britain's reserves.[1] He was also to discuss problems surrounding stocks of surplus commodities and war aims.[2]

Keynes arrived in New York from Lisbon on 8 May. He then discussed the A.V.C. sale with Sir Edward Peacock, Mr Carlyle Gifford[3] and representatives of the bankers involved before going on to Washington on 9 May.[4] After discussions with Sir Frederick Phillips and other British

---

[1] Keynes had no instructions, nor did he intend, to take part in the negotiations for the sale of American Viscose Corporation. However, he was kept informed of developments and communicated London's view of certain problems connected with the sale, in particular the political difficulties that might arise if the total dollar proceeds of the sale negotiated with American bankers were less than the amount awarded Courtaulds by the British arbitrators appointed to decide on compensation. (The arbitration procedure was adopted because with A.V.C. as an integral part of Courtaulds' operations, no market valuation existed as a basis for compensation as in the case of vested securities.) For the complete story of the sale of A.V.C. see D. G. Coleman, *Courtaulds: An Economic and Social History*, (Oxford, 1969), vol. II, ch. xv.

[2] On these matters, see Volumes XXV and XXVII.

[3] Thomas Johnstone Carlyle Gifford, Scottish accountant and company director, sent to America in 1941 by the Bank of England to advise on the sale of requisitioned American securities.

[4] As a result of Keynes's discussions in New York, it was agreed that the British should approach Mr Morgenthau about the possibility of using a loan from the Reconstruction Finance Corporation to repurchase A.V.C. from the bankers' syndicate, thus retaining British control. However, on his arrival in Washington, Keynes wrote to Sir Edward Peacock on 12 May that the sale of A.V.C. had 'a symbolic, almost a mystic, importance' to the Americans and that it would be 'most unwise to treat it purely on the business basis'. He was therefore inclined to let the arrangements for a public sale through the bankers go forward. In the circumstances, the Treasury should not be unhappy with the price, then expected to be about $75 million.

Despite further information, in the form of an offer from the Reconstruction Finance Corporation of a loan of $65 million to A.V.C. which led to meetings attempting to postpone the public offer and discussions with Mr Morgenthau, the sale went ahead on U.S. Treasury insistence. The public issue on 26 May yielded

officials concerning his proposals for Mr Morgenthau, Keynes visited the Secretary on 13 May. On 14 May he again visited the Treasury with Sir Frederick Phillips, at Mr Morgenthau's request, before putting his proposals to Mr Morgenthau in writing on 16 May.

To H. MORGENTHAU, *16 May 1941*

Dear Mr Morgenthau,

I now enclose the memorandum which you asked Phillips and myself to prepare for you. There is only one thing I should like to add to what is written in the text.

I believe that, if something of this sort could come to pass, there would be intangible advantages beyond those considerations of administrative convenience etc. which are mentioned in the enclosed. We have great anxieties and preoccupations, much to concern us and much to decide, in all parts of the world. It is natural, therefore, that sometimes we should worry a bit. The *uncertainties* of the exact financial arrangements over here in the past months—inevitable though they were in the light of the political and other difficulties—have weighed on the Chancellor of the Exchequer and his advisers, although at no time has he had any doubt that in the end, if we could have faith, all would be well. If from now on we could have a clean-cut settlement on the lines suggested, which would give us an immediately assured position against contingencies and remove all debateable points of any significance, it is difficult to exaggerate what a comfort this would be to everyone in the Treasury at home.

It is easy to argue, indeed I am sure it would be true, that many of our worries have been quite unnecessary and that we have wasted time and thought on what was certain to come right in the end. But in London it is difficult to be sensitive to the background in Washington—it makes all the difference in the world to come here in person—and I stress, therefore,

the Treasury $54·4 million. However, Keynes's involvement soured his initial relations with Mr Morgenthau, who believed that the main purpose of Keynes's visit was to kill the sale of A.V.C.

73

that the advantage of a clean-cut arrangement of the kind which the Chancellor of the Exchequer has instructed me to propose to you would be much more than is apparent on the basis of mere statistics and accounting and strict logic, and out of proportion to the sums involved, which are only a fraction of the vast assistance you are giving us.

I venture to say all this, since you will have a fellow-feeling for the Chancellor of the Exchequer in the burden he is carrying.

Yours sincerely,

J. M. KEYNES

MEMORANDUM

1. Experience of lease lend already shows that there are certain British requirements which are difficult to bring under lease lend procedure because of either (*a*) mere administrative complexity or (*b*) legal or political difficulties under the Act. This memorandum makes suggestions for a re-arrangement by which it is considered that those difficulties could be largely overcome without increasing total lease lend appropriations. It is suggested that the difficult categories should be dealt with by ordinary purchase outside lease lend altogether. This will naturally increase the current charges for which the British Government will have to find dollars, and correspondingly reduce the charges on the lease lend appropriations of the U.S. Government. If a sum corresponding to these savings could be applied at the outset towards taking over existing British commitments, no net increase in total appropriations would be called for, but the British Government would be placed in a position to remove the 'difficult' categories from lend lease altogether.

2. As shown in Appendix A hereto, the categories which are likely to be administratively difficult (difficulty (*a*) above) appear to call for some $200 million per annum. For easing legal or political difficulties under the Act (difficulty (*b*) above) a figure of $125 million per annum is provisionally suggested,

but it would be for Mr Hopkins to say what reserve he might think it prudent to set aside. Assuming, however, $125 million for difficulty (*b*), the total requirement to make this scheme effective would be $325 million per annum, so far as the U.K. is concerned.

3. The question of the provision to be made for supplies (whether strictly warlike or other) to the sterling-using Dominions is still uncertain. But:

(*a*) if nothing—i.e. not even strictly warlike supplies—is lease lent to the Dominions, a further provision would have to be made under this head.

(*b*) if, however, strictly warlike supplies are lease lent to the Dominions, no addition would be needed to cover the purchase of non-warlike supplies, since Sir F. Phillips' estimates already submitted to Mr Morgenthau assumed as a statistical basis that the U.K. would have to find the main part of the dollar finance for such supplies.

4. Thus, assuming no addition on account of the Dominions, the total amount which would be removed from the scope of lease lend under these proposals would be $325 million a year, which would, of course, result in a corresponding reduction in the charges on lease lend appropriations. As explained in 1, the proposal is that a sum corresponding to those savings should be applied at the outset in taking over existing British commitments. But, since this method of providing relief against existing commitments has to be applied at this stage or not at all, it would seem advisable to provide for two years' requirements at the present time, making $650 million for the two years.

5. Since this $650 million relief from existing commitments would subsequently be re-absorbed by cash payments on new commitments outside lease lend, it would be additional to the relief of $300 to $400 million already agreed by Mr Morgenthau in his interview with Sir Frederick Phillips on March 19th. (It will be recalled that this referred to contracts which the Army and R.F.C. would take over.) Thus the total relief

from old contracts would be $950–1,050 million (less some $70 million which represents progress already made towards the $300–400 million referred to above). As payments due under the existing contracts outstanding on 1 May were approximately $1,300 million and advance payments outstanding at that date $700 million, making a total of $2,000 million, there is ample scope *now* to cover the $950–1,050 million mentioned above. In six months' time, however, this would become difficult or impossible as the existing commitments are running off rapidly.

6. The advantages claimed for this re-arrangement are the following:–

(1) The Lease Lend Act would be restricted to materials directly related to warlike purposes and to agricultural products; with the elimination of marginal cases, no further questions of the eligibility of any materials under the Act would arise, and the U.S. Government could claim that the Act had been administered much more strictly than its wording required.

(2) The administrative burden on both governments would be greatly reduced with a gain to efficiency and to promptness of action.

(3) If the British Treasury had a reasonable reserve against contingencies, both they and the American Administrator of the Lease Lend Act would be subject to much less embarrassment whenever items came forward which the latter felt to be for any reason open to criticism, since the British Treasury would have no difficulty in accepting those criticisms immediately. It would also mean that the British Treasury could take the responsibility of itself financing any entirely unforeseen requirements which might develop, which it might be difficult for legislative reasons to bring within the ambit of the lease lend procedure except after an inevitable delay.

(4) If the British Treasury were relieved from a position where their resources are likely to fall to a dangerously low

level in the near future, they could face with far greater assurance the various unforeseen risks and contingencies which may face them in any part of the world during the particularly anxious period of the ensuing twelve months.

(5) All this would be achieved without inflating the total appropriations which would be required under the Lease Lend Act as compared with the alternative course now in operation, of working that Act as hard as possible and bringing under it virtually all British purchases in U.S.A.

Appendix A

The break-up of the total of $200 million referred to above is as follows:

	£ million
Certain machinery components etc.*	40
Certain chemical manufactures, drugs	30
Sundry materials,† machinery and consumption goods	18
Vehicle parts	8
Civil road vehicles, including fire pumps, cranes, etc.	24
Abrasives	4
Rutile, bentonite, diatomaceous earth, tin residues and certain minor non-ferrous metals	6
Timber other than aero-sitka and aero plywood	10
Bagasse, other paper, cotton and linen rags	7
Borax, razorite, sundry chemicals, fibestos and synthetic resins, carbon black, pine tar, rosin, turpentine and asphalt	6
Agricultural machinery	12
Agricultural seeds	4
Oil plant equipment	30
	199

Note. The inclusion of a description in this table does not necessarily mean that the whole of that description will be 'difficult'. The values attributed above are intended to refer only to the 'difficult' part of such categories.

* The heading 'machinery components' comprises, *inter alia*, miscellaneous wireless apparatus, accumulators and parts, electrical heating and cooking apparatus, electric lighting apparatus, air and gas compressors, boot and shoe making machinery, hydraulic, pneumatic and separating machinery, prime movers, pumps, textile and knitting machines, bearings (a very large item), and scientific instruments.

† The heading 'sundry materials' comprises such diverse requirements as brass screws and fittings, implements and hand tools, needles for sewing machines, hosiery machines, refractory bricks, electrical testing apparatus, moulding and presses.

It should be stressed that all these articles are essential, having been subject to the strictest criticism, and that many of the larger items, particularly machinery components, are in fact used for defence purposes. Some of these essentials, however, are for use or consumption on private account, and in all the above cases it is difficult to isolate and route them for purchase through the lend lease procedure.

Many of the above products are highly specialised, are bought to particular specifications and in comparatively small quantities from particular U.S. suppliers. A large part of the machinery demand is not for machines as such, but for bearings, parts etc. Many of the requirements mentioned are obtained by English firms from U.S. suppliers with whom they have maintained close trade connections for many years, and it would be a great waste of effort to interpose official machinery on both sides of the Atlantic between the regular purchaser and the regular supplier. It is relevant in this connection to point out that the import licences for the U.S.A. outstanding on 15 March last (to select a recent date at random) were over 10,000. Apart from the administrative difficulty of handling the question of purchase, the reception, storage, distribution, etc. of the goods after arrival in the United Kingdom would require the establishment of a special Government organisation. At present such arrangements are carried out through the ordinary channels of trade. Given the very large number of transactions, documents etc., which would have to be handled, the administrative difficulties would be out of all proportion to the sums involved.

The same day as Keynes wrote to Mr Morgenthau, Mr E. Playfair,[5] then with the British Supply Council in Washington, wrote to S. D. Waley in London setting out Keynes's position.

[5] Edward Wilder Playfair (b. 1909), K.C.B. 1957; Inland Revenue, 1931–4; Treasury, 1934–56; Control Office for Germany and Austria, 1946–7; Permanent Under-Secretary of State for War, 1956–9; Permanent Secretary, Ministry of Defence, 1960–1; since retirement, company director.

... Maynard has safely arrived, and is forging thunderbolts. We all agree that his idea of an allowance is an excellent one, and I think Morgie and Hopkins and everyone else thinks so too. The only trouble is that it mightn't come off because it means more appropriations too soon. However, we can but try and are doing so. We have slightly pared down the scale of his operations, but it seems to require about $100 million, which is a mint of money.

On the whole, I think we have found much less divergence between our ideas after all this time than might have been expected. I think the main difference—very important as regards approach although it makes little difference to our main objective—is that Maynard thinks we are a great and independent nation, which on the financial side is patently not true; some months' experience here have shown us that the Americans don't see it in that light. I think he is inclined to ask as a right what they are only prepared to give as a favour. It seems to me necessary to keep moral indignation out of these discussions if we are to get anywhere. I find experience in credit negotiations with Spain, Roumania, etc. very useful. I recognise in ourselves the sentiments which we found so unreasonable in the Spaniards, and in the Americans the sentiments which the Spaniards found so unreasonable in us. In fact it has astounded me how true human nature runs to type.

During his negotiations, Keynes kept London informed of developments by cable and through letters to Sir Horace Wilson and the Chancellor. As the letters covered a much wider range of subjects than the cables, they serve as a good guide to his activities.

To SIR HORACE WILSON, *19 May 1941*

Dear Wilson,

By the time this reaches you, fully three weeks will have elapsed since I left London. I wish I could have written sooner. But all I could have said would have been half-baked. Indeed, it is half-baked still, but the issues, personal and otherwise, are now beginning to disentangle themselves.

Another great discouragement has been the difficulties in the way of communication. This is a major obstacle which it is important to overcome. You cannot believe how isolated people are and how discouraging it is to write a letter with little chance of getting a reply under six weeks,—which has been the position up to date. Now I am told a bomber service three times a week has been, or is about to be, organised, and I am hoping to take advantage of that in sending this budget of news.

I enclose separate notes on different aspects. I shall also be sending, either in this bag or in a later bag this week, a letter to the Chancellor of the Exchequer about the American attitude to the war,[6] a letter to Waley about China,[7] a letter to Catto about direct investments,[8] and a letter to Ronald of the Foreign Office about the statement on economic aims which Mr Eden wants to make, of which I will let you have a copy.[9]

Please excuse the verbose and rambling character of the enclosed. I am overwhelmed with engagements and forced to talk my head off for fully twelve hours a day. The rambling verbosity of the enclosed is just a small indication of the general state of mind that I have been reduced to and lack of genuine leisure and time for reflection.

Yours sincerely,

J. M. KEYNES

THE COURSE OF MY NEGOTIATIONS

I

Everyone in the British Mission is now satisfied that the proposals I have brought out would be a great step forward if they could be put into operation and would facilitate every-

---

[6] Below, p. 103.
[7] Not printed. [Ed.]
[8] Not printed. [Ed.]
[9] See *JMK*, vol. xxv. Robert Anthony Eden (1897–1977), 1st Earl of Avon, 1961; M.P. (C.) Warwick and Leamington, 1923–57; Parliamentary Private Secretary to Secretary of State for Foreign Affairs, 1926–9; Parliamentary Under-Secretary, Foreign Office, 1931–3; Lord Privy Seal, 1934–5; Minister without Portfolio for League of Nations Affairs, 1935; Secretary of State for Foreign Affairs, 1935–8, for Dominion Affairs, 1939–40, for War, 1940, for Foreign Affairs, 1940–5, also Leader of the House of Commons, 1942–5; Prime Minister, 1955–7.

one's task. Phillips and I are working together closely and agreeing all matters. Purvis[10] is enthusiastic for the scheme, and so is Monnet. Thus the whole team here is working unitedly.

On the American side, after an early hesitancy as to just what I was at, I am not conscious of any real ground of opposition on principle, and Purvis reports the same. The difficulty is on the technical side, how to do what we want without raising difficulties with Congress. This difficulty is very great and can easily be used as a good pretext for doing nothing. The danger is that I shall get bogged down without anything tangible to oppose, and no way in which to make progress without reforming the whole financial system! Thus progress is slow. I am warned that this is inevitable and that it would be a mistake to try to hasten matters. This week the Treasury have been wholly preoccupied with a new tax programme about which they have been having a serious controversy with other Departments. One has to contend here with an extraordinary confusion of authority, and, in addition to that, difficult personal cross currents, which run not only between Departments but within Departments. Thus it is necessary to open up in several different quarters and make sure that each of them separately appreciates what one is driving at and is satisfied that all is on the right lines.

Let me take the three principals in order.

I spent last week concentrating on Mr Morgenthau and his officials. I expect this was prudent. I am sending a separate note on Mr Morgenthau's general attitude to us.[11] He clearly wants to be helpful and, whilst—as he has said to me with a smile—he has committed himself as yet to nothing, I am sure that his bias at the moment is to agree, unless some compelling reason arises to the contrary. His officials can be divided into

[10] Arthur Blaikie Purvis (1890–1941); Canadian company director; Director-General, British Purchasing Commission, 1939–40; Chairman, Anglo-French Purchasing Board, 1939–41; killed in aircraft crash, August 1941.

[11] Printed below, pp. 87–91.

two groups. There are first of all what one could call the regular civil servants, particularly Bell[12] and Cochran.[13] Phillips and I have had useful separate conversations with them. They understand the point and would like to help us. Phillips is on the best of terms with them and believes that they are our good friends, approaching questions like this as clear-headed, competent officials. Apart from these, there are the advisers of the Treasury, economic and legal, who represent the New Dealers as such, led by Harry White.[14] This group is more energetic than the other, and Morgenthau is often reluctant to act unless he has them behind him. They are politically more important and have closer affiliations with the other Departments and with the White House. It is these who at times have been more difficult for Phillips to deal with. Owing to the accident of Harry White having been away on short leave, I am not yet in touch with them, but it is expected that Morgenthau will ask me to continue the discussions with a group to which they will be called in.

I got Walter Stewart[15] to come down here from Princeton. He has no position in the Treasury, but turns up in Washington every other week to advise Morgenthau, who told me that he attaches much importance to what Walter Stewart tells him. Stewart is keen on our plan and has talked to the Treasury officials and to Morgenthau most helpfully. He takes the view, I hope rightly, that I shall be received friendly-wise by Harry White and his associates, since the New Deal group here regard me as one of them.

[12] Daniel Wagena Bell (1891–1971); U.S. Treasury Department, 1911–45; Assistant to Secretary of Treasury on financial and accounting matters, 1935–40; Under-Secretary, U.S. Treasury, 1940–5; subsequently a banker.

[13] W. Merle Cochran, State Department Official seconded as Special Adviser to the Secretary of the Treasury on monetary matters, 1935–41.

[14] Harry Dexter White (d. 1948), economist; Assistant Director of Research, U.S. Treasury, 1934; Director of Monetary Research, U.S. Treasury, 1940; Special Assistant to Secretary of Treasury, 1942; Assistant to Secretary, 1943–5; Assistant Secretary, 1945–6; U.S. Executive Director, International Monetary Fund, 1946–7.

[15] Walter W. Stewart (1885–1958), American economist; Economic Adviser, Bank of England, 1928–30; Bank for International Settlements, 1931; member, U.S. President's Council of Economic Advisers, 1953–5.

I might interpolate at this point that Walter Stewart told me confidentially that Morgenthau was a little surprised that I had not brought a letter of credentials from the Chancellor of the Exchequer and had begun by being suspicious of what I was here for, probably wondering whether it was not direct investments. However, Stewart thought that his suspicions were now at rest and there was no need to do anything.

I come next to Harry Hopkins. I am in touch with him but have deliberately not hurried an interview, since it seemed important to clear the position with Morgenthau first of all. Morgenthau has spoken to Hopkins; there is every reason to think he would be sympathetic, and I am to see him shortly. But what I expect him to say is: 'God bless you, but don't expect *me* to solve the technical difficulties in the way.'

Finally, there is the President, who, as you know, has been ill. He has sent me a personal message that he wants to see me and will summon me for a talk as soon as his doctors allow him to return to full work. When this happens, it will certainly help my position in every other quarter. I spent Sunday with Lauchlin Currie,[16] who is economic adviser to the President and sits in the White House. I expounded my ideas to Currie, who thought that they would appeal to the President. He advised me to put them to him in the plainest possible terms when I see him.

The up-shot is that the difficulty is technical and not in principle. But if the Americans really want to do what we ask, surely they should be able to find a way round. My personal impression is that this will be difficult without recasting their present approach to lend lease appropriations. They have tied themselves up in an unworkable system, which needs recasting, apart from this particular issue. I will prepare a short note on this when I understand it better.

[16] Lauchlin Currie (b. 1902), economist; with Federal Reserve Board, 1934–9; Administrative Assistant for economic affairs, Executive Office of the President, 1939–45; Deputy Administrator, Foreign Economic Administration, 1943–5.

The division of authority here can be illustrated by the following examples.

All orders under lend lease have been taken entirely from Morgenthau's purview and he knows nothing whatever about them, but the old commitments remain his responsibility. Then when I want to substitute aid to meet *old* commitments instead of aid to meet *new* commitments there is no one Department which can give me an answer. Formerly the Director of the Budget was part of the Treasury, but under the recent reorganisation he was entirely divorced from them and is now seated as an independent authority in the White House, with no particular responsibility to Morgenthau. Morgenthau intensely—and I should have thought quite naturally —dislikes this arrangement, which did not exist during his earlier years of office. He has no control over what the Director of the Budget may tell Congress and is often in disagreement with him. Last week Morgenthau stated publicly that Congress ought to save a billion dollars out of the more extravagant peace-time expenditures to make room for war finance,—an obvious and, one would have supposed, sound observation. But the extraordinary thing is that economising on expenditure has nothing to do with the Secretary of the Treasury in this country, who for practical purposes seems now to be confined to the task of raising taxes plus a multitude of miscellaneous activities which run in the most perplexing way across those of other Departments. The Director of the Budget took great exception to Morgenthau's call for economy on the ground that the appropriations in question had been passed through his office with the authority of the President and approved by Congress, so that Morgenthau had no business to suggest to Congress that they should reconsider the matter. But this is not all. Morgenthau formally has the responsibility for proposing taxation, and recently made recommendations to Congress. Two other Departments, with, I think, some encouragement from the President, then got together, namely Marriner Eccles,[17] Chairman of the Federal Reserve Board, and Leon Henderson,[18] the Price Controller, criticised Morgenthau's proposals publicly and made alternative recommendations to congress. These were in fact superior to Morgenthau's and have had a better reception. Since there were indications that the President preferred them, Morgenthau has now had to put forward compromise proposals, and in the last few days that has occupied his whole attention and ruffled his temper. It is as though the President of the Board of Trade and the Governor of the Bank of England publicly criticised the Chancellor's Budget proposals, got hold of the Prime Minister and then compelled him to modify them, none of this being behind the scenes but carried on in the press.

The result is that no one is safe and no one can really decide anything except the President. My particular problem cannot be solved unless I can simultaneously square Morgenthau about the old commitments, Harry Hopkins about the new commitments and the Director of the Budget about the relation of these to the appropriations.

20 May 1941   J. M. KEYNES

P.S. Since dictating the above I have spent the morning with Mr Harry Hopkins. This carries the story so much further that I must not hold up this letter to complete it, though there may be time to add a further document in the same bag.

The upshot is that he is determined to do what we want

[17] Marriner Stoddard Eccles (1890–1977); Governor, Federal Reserve Board, 1934–6; member, Board of Governors, Federal Reserve System, 1936–51; Chairman, Board of Governors, 1936–48; member, Board of Economic Stabilisation, 1942–6; National Advisory Council on International and Financial Problems, 1945–8; Advisory Board, Export–Import Bank, 1945–8; U.S. Delegate to Bretton Woods Conference, 1944.

[18] Leon Henderson (b. 1895); economist; Economic Adviser and Director of Research and Planning, National Recovery Administration, 1934–5; member, National Industry Recovery Board, 1934–5; Commissioner of Securities and Exchange Commission, 1939–41; Administrator, Price Administration and Civilian Supply, 1941–2.

if it can possibly be managed and that Morgenthau is of the same opinion. He is, however, much against doing it by taking up old commitments and is trying to think out another way. I am to see him again shortly. But we also discussed the question of what is called here 'consideration'. That is to say the ultimate terms of settlement of the Lend Lease Bill and the sort of return we are to be expected to make in respect of it. I shall be informing Lord Halifax of the upshot of this later to-day. It is difficult to reduce to precise form a long and, in some respects, vague exposition. He has, however, been discussing the matter with the President and believes that at least the first and most important step ought to be settled in the next fortnight. The matter is to be handled by the State Department, as being political rather than financial, and not by the Treasury. Mr Sumner Welles[19] already has a draft prepared, with which Hopkins partly agrees and partly does not. The President has not declared his mind, but is ruminating it with a view to early action.

P.P.S. (21.5.41) I have now, at the request of the Ambassador, sent a cable on 'consideration', so need add nothing to that. On the other issue the position is fast clarifying itself. I had a short conversation with Harry White last night and he tells me that the Treasury will be ready for a further general consultation shortly. The information from all quarters is that everyone is now agreed that it would be a good thing to do what I am asking. Hopkins was categorical about this and added that Morgenthau was of the same opinion. Indeed psychologically the atmosphere could not be better. There is nothing but friendliness and good will.

On the other hand they are all equally definite that the end cannot be achieved by re-opening the question of the old commitments, and I am strongly advised to abandon this.

[19] Sumner Welles (1892–1961); Assistant Secretary of State, 1933–7; Under-Secretary of State, 1937–43; Special Representative of U.S. President to report on conditions in Europe, 1940.

They say some other method must be found. If they can find it, well and good. But I have no conviction that any of them has a workable plan, and the hints which have been thrown out so far about assistance from Jesse Jones etc. do not seem to me to be plausible. In my own mind I am still convinced that the re-opening of the old commitments is the decent and sensible way of handling the matter and that, if they would make a clean breast to Congress and explain all the circumstances, they could easily re-open them. At the back of my mind, therefore, I remain obstinate, though meanwhile I do not press the point and wait to hear the other concrete suggestions which it is up to them to make.

Hopkins was particularly friendly and open. He made it clear that I had access to him at all times and that I could also see the President at any crucial or critical moment if I had to invoke his help. But he added, with which I agreed, that it would be much better if we could get this particular issue settled without bothering the President, so that when I see him we should be free to talk on more general matters. He seemed to me to hint that the President would like to discuss 'consideration'. But I shall, of course, say nothing on that except after the fullest consultation with the Ambassador, whom I am now seeing frequently.

All the above will probably be out of date and without interest by the time it arrives. But it may possibly have secondary interest in giving a picture of the odd way in which life here is conducted.

MR MORGENTHAU

He is certainly a difficult chap to deal with. I have seldom struck anything stickier than my first interview. One seemed to be able to get no human reaction whatever, which is, I suppose, his method of protection until he is quite sure what you are after. It is also most difficult to get him to see one's real point, and misunderstandings peep out of every corner. Everybody agrees that he is jealous and suspicious and subject to moods of depression and irritation.

On the other hand, I am satisfied that any suggestion of his being fundamentally unfriendly is untrue. He really wants to do his best for us. My wife, who sat next him at dinner one evening, summed him up in a phrase, which those who know him better think apt. 'He is a good man', she said, 'and will do you no harm *on purpose.*'

In particular, there have been two passages in the recent past where we owe him a big debt of gratitude.

The first was in connection with the actual terms of the Lease Lend Bill. After this very general idea had sprung from the brain of Jove, it had to be clothed in detail by the lawyers. Two drafts were prepared, one in the State Department and one in the Treasury. The State Department draft was on the basis of pledging as security almost everything we possess in the world outside the British Empire, including all our remaining foreign investments. The draft prepared in the Treasury, on the other hand, went to the other extreme, kept the $ sign out of the Bill in all contexts and provided for no specific security whatever on our part, not even our remaining assets in U.S.A. This was the draft sponsored by Morgenthau. There was an acute controversy behind the scenes between the two drafts. Morgenthau, I am told, took his life in his hands. He told the President, and this is said to be the first time he has gone so far, that if the State Department draft was adopted, he would refuse to defend it before the Congressional Committees. In the end Morgenthau had a complete victory, and the Bill as adopted follows the lines of his draft. I have also had this story from other sources. I am sure that the substance of it is true and that we do owe him real gratitude in this connection. If the draft bill had got on the other lines, a most difficult position would have been created for us.

In conversation with me Morgenthau was insistent that he is misrepresented when it is said that his aim was to strip us of all our assets. He points out that his evidence before Congress, when he talked about our assets being put on the auction block, related solely to the sum necessary to meet the outstanding old commitments. He emphasised that he has always aimed at drawing a firm line at this point and of protecting any remaining assets we might have in excess of that sum. He holds that for political reasons he had to go as far as that and had strongly resisted efforts to push him further.

On the other hand, this is inconsistent with the statement in the Report of the Committee on Appropriations to Congress (page 4), where the following passage occurs:

> The Committee is also advised that the British assets in this country, in so far as they are not needed for payment on their orders here, will be given as security on defence articles which the United States may furnish to them.

The reconciliation is to be found, I suppose, in the difference of opinion between Morgenthau and the Director of the Budget (who, as I have explained elsewhere, is not, as we supposed, one of his servants). This Report of the Committee on Appropriations is so important and so tiresome that I append a copy. It will not be the first time that the Administration have gone back on what they have told Congress if a good deal of what is said in this document is subsequently forgotten.

The second occasion was in connection with the placing of orders during the period between 1 January and the Lease Lend Act coming into force. It is generally agreed that this was done by Morgenthau on his own responsibility and that he took a risk in doing so, since he could not be sure that Congress would not introduce something into the Lease Lend Bill, then under discussion, which would conflict with the commitments he was making. If these new orders had not been placed, the war effort would have been seriously impeded, and yet no-one, apart from Morgenthau, seemed prepared to take the necessary responsibility. Nor is that the end of this episode. He gave Phillips to understand at the time, as you will all remember, that he would ultimately find the finance for these additional commitments. He has reiterated that promise and, indeed, has now mentioned a figure, namely, $300 to $400 million, which is in excess of the new orders placed during that period, this excess being in order to implement encouragements he had given us to believe that *something* would be done to replenish our balances.

He has recently reiterated to Phillips and to myself and also to Walter Stewart and to Harry Hopkins that it is an absolute undertaking on his part to find some way of providing for us that sum of $300 to $400 million. Yet how he is to do so under the existing arrangements is still obscure. He has scrounged about $70 million from miscellaneous sources and might raise that figure somewhat further, but it is not clear how he is to reach the full total. I rather think that this commitment of his may be helpful in connection with my own proposals. His difficulty arises out of the absurd way in which they have allowed themselves to be tied up by the appropriations and the statements made in connection with them. If he could find a way of taking over the old commitments for his own purposes, that same method would enable him to overcome his many difficulties. The obstacles in both cases are the same. The fact that he has committed himself to find a way of overcoming them in the one context is a favourable feature for solving the other also.

In this connection it is worth repeating a remark of Harry Hopkins, made a few days ago, as reported to me. He said: 'The Secretary of the Treasury has told the British that he will find them this sum of $300 to $400 million. He was fully entitled to make that commitment. We must find a way in which it can be fulfilled. But how to do it God knows.' In conversation with me Hopkins further emphasised this and added that the commitment was made with the knowledge of the President.

All this does not mean that Morgenthau is not almost intolerably tiresome to deal with, for his colleagues and his own officials also and not only for us. On the other hand, a certain firmness in his character and a persistency and freedom from wrong motives does seem, in the course of years, to have built up a position for him which is exceedingly strong. Everyone goes through a phase of falling out of favour, his own officials just as much as ourselves. Sometimes Cochran and Bell, his capable permanent officials, carry weight with him; sometimes they do not. The same is true of Walter Stewart. Phillips, at first in favour, spent a period of several weeks in which Morgenthau refused to see him altogether, but now is again in excellent relations. He began by distrusting Gifford, but now speaks of him most highly. Peacock has had a period of extreme disfavour. The ultimatum about Viscose began with a demand on London for Peacock's recall, which was not passed on. He is still not too favourable to Peacock, which is extremely unjust in my opinion, since no one could possibly have behaved with more wisdom and dignity and *bona fides* than Peacock has shown. My own relation to him is, in my own judgment, still rather indefinite. Certainly I am not in disfavour (my wife and I have been asked to his major dinner party this week to meet the Crown Princess of Norway), but I feel that quite innocently and inadvertently one could easily do something which would put the position back. He will do one no harm *on purpose*. But how easily he might without intending it!

May 1941

The cable Keynes referred to on 'consideration' ran as follows.

Following for Treasury from Keynes.

[*Begins*] Following a conversation with Mr Hopkins on my own particular proposals, he told me that he had spent the previous evening with the President discussing consideration under lend lease. The President's ideas are not yet crystallised but he wishes to make statement about consideration under the act when he makes his first periodical report to Congress on 13th June. This would mean that an agreement must be reached with us in course of the next fortnight. The President has entrusted the negotiation to the State Department and not to the Treasury, on the grounds that it raises political rather than financial issues which is all to the good. Under-Secretary of State has already prepared a draft which Hopkins described to me as 'liberal'. It is clearly understood on their side that this is an issue which must be handled with the Ambassador direct and not on departmental dictation.

2. Hopkins went on to outline his own thoughts which are not necessarily the same as Under-Secretary of State's draft though they may be in line with them. Hopkins divided lend lease commitments into two categories, strictly warlike, and the rest including food, tobacco and miscellaneous. Of the 7 billions, probably 5 would clearly qualify in the first category, and if ships and warlike raw materials were included perhaps 6, leaving only 1 or 2 billions for second category. He thought warlike category might be dealt with on basis of our returning any unused and surviving material at the end of the war, and that the United States would be ready to forget about material or ships expended in warfare or lost, without expecting any further consideration beyond satisfaction that they had been used for the common purpose.

3. For non-warlike category, on the other hand, President might want to give Congress a list of kinds of consideration to which we were ready to agree in principle without speci-

fying at this stage exactly what should be called for. He mentioned islands, bases, tin, and rubber. I pointed out that any form of economic consideration had the disadvantage of impairing our post-war capacity for American goods, and that it might be better to keep the consideration strictly and without any exception within the political field. He agreed with this and had evidently mentioned tin and rubber not because the items [*grp. undec.*] them but to make the list more plausible. Distinction between warlike and non-warlike is potentially dangerous though it is what I have always expected. But if in effect no consideration is asked for warlike, and only political consideration for non-warlike, American view that an early settlement is in both our interests may be correct.

4. Whilst apparently Administration believes the Congress will expect the President to make a statement about consideration on the occasion of his first report, there is no legal reason why he should do so and it is not clear to us that there is any compelling political reason. If proposals when made are not of a kind we can easily agree to at short notice, Phillips and Purvis think we could circumspectly ask for more time. In particular consultation with Dominions may prove to be necessary. [*Ends*]

Please see my immediately following telegram.[20]

As noted above (p. 83) Mr Morgenthau initially believed that Keynes's purpose in coming to America was to sabotage the sale of A.V.C. Sir Frederick Phillips attempted to disabuse him of this belief, but Mr Morgenthau was initially unhappy dealing with Keynes when he could deal with Phillips over the same matters. This is particularly clear in some of Morgenthau's comments to his subordinates, as recorded in the Morgenthau Diaries. The solution of the problem took up some of Keynes's next report to Sir Horace Wilson.

[20] Not printed. [Ed.]

To SIR HORACE WILSON, *25 May 1941*

Dear Wilson,

I enclose a second note on the course of my negotiations. It speaks for itself, and I need add nothing to it. If all goes well, I should think that I ought to have accomplished, for better or worse, all that is possible within a fortnight and be free to leave this city somewhere about June 6th, though one can foresee nothing with any confidence. I am, therefore, making preliminary enquiries about the possibility of getting a clipper somewhere about that date. Meanwhile, however, the question of what is known here as 'consideration' has arisen. You will have had my telegrams, first of all on the 21st reporting my conversation with Mr Harry Hopkins, and secondly to-day giving early news of what is likely to come from the State Department. This was based on a conversation with Mr Dean Acheson,[21] who had been in charge of drafting the document. I imagine that an official paper will reach the Ambassador from the State Department sometime this week at latest. I do not know whether you will think it advisable for me to stay here in that connection or whether I can be of as much service at the London end in that context as here. The solution will turn, I think, as much on good drafting as on anything else. They are anxious, I believe, to do what is most helpful to us, provided we can find a formula which looks reasonably plausible to Congress. Broadly speaking, the outline in the telegram I sent to-day, if it proves correct, would be, I think, extraordinarily satisfactory. Perhaps you might be ready to give me instructions about this, should I feel I ought to telegraph for them at a later date.

The other matter where I have not yet finished is in connection with the surpluses. I have arranged to visit the State Department on Tuesday to have a round table talk with Dean

---

[21] Dean Goodenham Acheson (1893–1973); Assistant Secretary of State, U.S.A., 1941; Under-Secretary of State, 1945–7; Secretary of State, 1949–53.

Acheson and his leading assistants in charge of surpluses, explaining our point of view and endeavouring to discover theirs. It is quite likely, I think, that this will extend over more than one meeting.

In spite of all the difficulties, one cannot exaggerate the strength of sympathy and good intention in almost every quarter here. In my recent experience there is not a single exception. Though you may find it difficult to believe, Mr Morgenthau himself is passionately with us, believes that he has at every stage fought our battle and is sensitive to criticism which he thinks misunderstands the excellence of his intentions and the magnitude of his success in fulfilling them,—and, in spite of everything, there is great truth in this. He has in his own queer way genuinely aimed at helping us to the full extent that the political situation allowed and, as I explained previously, has protected us from serious dangers. Everyone connected with the Administration is miserable at the apparent inaction here and concerned to discover the right moment and the right ground on which they can come to our full aid. I spent last night dining with Felix Frankfurter,[22] the other guests being Bob Brand and Dean Acheson. The whole evening was occupied by a debate between Acheson and Frankfurter,* the former holding passionately that the President should, in his capacity as Commander in Chief, forthwith declare war or its equivalent by ordering the fleet to its battle stations. Frankfurter held that this would be a grave political mistake and expose the President to a rebuff from Congress. Nor would it be safe for him to ask Congress to declare war as such. The right course was for the President to consult Congress and to obtain its consent for some specific action which did not amount to declaring war as such but necessarily carrying that implication with it at a later stage. If the President had obtained this initial cover from Congress,

[22] Felix Frankfurter (1882–1965); Supreme Court Justice, U.S.A., 1939–62.
* Who is very close to the President and sees him every week.

95

then the rest could follow without their taking umbrage or having any ground of complaint under the constitution. I understand that this view is held strongly by Mr Hull.[23] I should expect it to prevail, and probably it is right. But that Mr Acheson had such impatience and felt so strongly to the contrary was an interesting sign of how some people in the Administration are feeling at the continued delay. It is also consoling to notice that the only division amongst the President's advisers is how and when.

All this may be resolved before this letter arrives. No-one here seriously doubts the ultimate outcome. From the point of view of the Administration, the worse the news is the more they will want to help, but from the public point of view bad news does nothing but harm, since the whole of the opposition to action comes, not from sympathy with the other side, but from the feeling of defeatism about ours.

I had intended to send the Chancellor a separate letter dealing with my general feeling about the atmosphere here in greater detail. But I am endlessly preoccupied with seeing people and have not yet managed to put my thoughts on paper. Doubtless, you will be passing this on to him.

Yours sincerely,

J. M. KEYNES

P.S. If the outline of the draft about 'consideration' which I have telegraphed proves correct, it seems to all of us here extraordinarily satisfactory. Mr Hull is as anxious to get the Administration committed to a reduction of the Hawley-Smoot tariff as to get us committed to abandoning the Ottawa Agreement. People in the Embassy on the commercial and Board of Trade side feel that a solution of this sort would be the culmination of all their work. It may very well be that the actual text of the draft will raise serious questions. But

[23] Cordell Hull (1871–1965); Secretary of State, U.S.A., 1933–44.

if by any means it were possible to agree out of hand so that the President could actually say the thing was fixed by June 10th, this would be a very wise thing to do. Could not consultation with the Dominions take the form of communicating to them the text of the State Department when it is received without comment, saying that H.M.G. proposed to accept it (subject to certain specific amendments, if such were necessary) within a week unless objection is raised immediately, which it is much hoped will not be the case. To get into a prolonged wrangle about details of the Ottawa Agreement would be disastrous. The only difficulty I see about this is that the text itself may not directly refer to Ottawa. If so, it would be necessary to us in transmitting to the Dominions to point out the possible implications of the actual wording in this connection.

THE COURSE OF MY NEGOTIATIONS

II

On the surface there has not been much progresss during the past week, but I am told that officials have been at work seeing what can be done. The lack of further developments has been due partly to the preoccupation of the Treasury with the Viscose transaction, with consultations behind the scenes between them and the State Department on 'consideration' and certain difficulties of their own about the tax programme etc. The other obstacle has been due to my having to go through the usual personal upset with Mr Morgenthau.

After my meeting with him on May 14th, which seemed to end very favourably, I did not see him again and had no word from him for a little more than a week. Meanwhile I heard from many quarters that he had been making trouble about what I was here for. First of all, on Sunday he rang up the Ambassador from the White House to complain that I had no credentials. The next day he told Phillips that he had from a sure source that my real purpose in coming to Washington was to upset the Viscose transaction. Phillips assured him that this was without foundation and a complete falsehood. Nevertheless on Thursday morning, after showing great temper towards Jesse Jones and the Viscose business, he again repeated to Phillips and Peacock, who were there with him about Viscose, the same story that that was all I was here for.

It, therefore, seemed to me plain that I could not hope to make further progress unless I could reach an eclaircissement. I sent him a private note on Thursday asking him if he could see me privately for a short time on a purely personal matter. Accordingly an appointment was fixed on Friday afternoon. I told him that these reports had reached me and that unless I cleared away these grounds of suspicion I did not see how I could usefully continue in conversation. He repeated the story, without disclosing the source, and told me that that, combined with the fact that I had no credentials and apparently the Ambassador had no knowledge of my visit, etc. etc., had led to these difficulties. I then opened out frankly on what seemed to be the only possible source of them, namely, my conversations with Mr Ben Cohen, and this turned out to be the right clue. To make a long story short, the interview ended in my having, I think genuinely, cleared his mind of misapprehension and in the restoration of relations much more cordial than they had ever been before. Indeed, he beamed on me, pressed my hand and told me that I need have no further concern and that he would do the utmost possible to clear up all the difficulties. We had started on the wrong leg, he said, and must now start all over again, and all was forgiven and forgotten; though exactly what it was that was forgiven and forgotten I shall never know for certain!

Nevertheless, I have formed a clear idea of where the root of the matter lay, which all those who know him tell me is completely convincing. The roots of his suspicion were, as usual, complicated. I do not think Viscose really had much to do with it except as a slogan and pretext. I feel sure the real point is that he has seen reports from Mr Winant and Mr Ben Cohen in London relating conversations with me sometime back (some of which, as will be remembered, related to Viscose), that he considers these communications from London as an attempt to upset his policy and to get at the President behind his back, that he is therefore cross with Mr Winant and very angry with Mr Ben Cohen, that he was regarding me primarily as an emissary of Mr Ben Cohen to work behind his back with the extreme New Dealers with a view to substituting Mr Cohen's policy instead of his own. The fact that the announcement of my visit to Washington came from Mr Winant and was, as he thought, not backed by the Chancellor of the Exchequer confirmed his opinion that I came primarily as an agent of Winant and only secondarily as representing the Chancellor of the Exchequer. Thus the comical thing is that what I regarded as my strong card, namely that I had been strongly recommended by Mr Winant to the President and Mr Morgenthau in a special telegram, was precisely my undoing! One can never remember, I find, in this place to make enough allowance for the extreme jealousy between colleagues. (As another example, the final stage of the Viscose deal and his rejection of the obviously right solution was not due to any dissatisfaction with us or desire to do us down but solely to do down Jesse Jones, about whom he spoke with open profanity in his last meeting with our people.) The interview ended by his telling me that he appreciated our difficulties, that he was passionately sympathetic to our case (which I believe to be true) and that he would now go to the limit of finding a way to do what the Chancellor wants, appealing to the President, if necessary, for help against the other Departments.

Phillips and I are to see the officials of the Treasury to-morrow to hear the details. My wife and I have since dined with him, the atmosphere being one of the utmost cordiality, and everything is now on the best of footings!

My interview with Mr Harry Hopkins, it will be remembered, ended in his also expressing a strong desire to do what we wanted, but confused as to how to attain the end, and his making suggestions that the best way out was to be found in the use of some of Mr Jesse Jones's funds. The more I have thought about that the less promising that method seems. I still think that some handling of old commitments is the only feasible method.

That, I am glad to say, is the line of approach they are still considering in the Treasury, unless I have misunderstood the position. When Mr Morgenthau promised Phillips the sum of $300 million in respect of the old commitments, he was acting on the authority of a letter of the President of some date in March instructing, so I gather, Mr Jesse Jones and more particularly the War Department to buy from us any old commitments that Mr Morgenthau might designate. This was how he intended to make his promise good. For unfathomable reasons, a subsequent instruction went, without Mr Morgenthau's knowledge, from the White House to the War Department to the contrary effect. He is now going to try to work something out on the assumption that the first letter still holds good. If the War Department appeal to the second letter, then it may be necessary to mobilise all forces in an appeal to the President to return to the earlier position. I am sure that such an appeal would be successful.

The principal snag in my opinion, and Phillips agrees, is that it may be difficult to find suitable commitments to transfer to the War Department sufficient in value to cover, not only the $300 million necessary to meet the commitment to Phillips, but also a further amount of $650 million to meet my proposals. We shall know more about this in a short time.

Meanwhile the usual obstacles to really rapid progress have arisen. Mr Morgenthau went off on Saturday for one of his periodic vacations and will not be seen again in Washington for ten days. Mr Hopkins has retired to his bed, and is not easily available for conversation. Mr Morgenthau, however, urged on me that this would not cause any real delay, since Phillips and I might make good progress during his absence with his officials. I hope this may prove correct.

You will see that Washington is a very odd place, with difficulties unsuspected to our more innocent minds!

26.5.41   J. M. KEYNES

Keynes's cable on the consideration for lend lease, referred to above, ran as follows.

Following for Treasury from Keynes.

State Department, in collaboration with Treasury, spent last week preparing proposals on consideration—under lease lend—for immediate submission to Mr Hull and President. I am led to believe that general outline of proposals is along the following lines, the details of which must however be treated with reserve and are only transmitted to allow a little more time for thought.

1. Any warlike articles surviving the war to be returned.

2. Warlike articles used up during the war to be written off.

3. Precise line of division between warlike and non-warlike articles to be left somewhat hazy at the present stage.

4. An account to be kept, whether in terms of disposable articles or dollar value not clear, in which all material aid from us to America is set off against list of non-warlike articles supplied by them to us.

5. Against any balance outstanding at the end of the war, no economic consideration will be asked in the sense of delivery of goods, but only politico-economic consideration taking the form of declarations of common purpose during the war and common economic policy after the war, particularly the latter.

6. Preliminary version of such declaration will then follow

statement of common purpose in the struggle against the Axis followed by a mutual undertaking of assistance on our part on lines of lease lend, should rôles of two countries be reversed at any time hereafter.

7. Next would follow declaration of common post-war economic policy on lines of Mr Hull's recent declaration and well-known opinions covering non-discrimination, in the presence of free trade bias, unrestricted access to raw material and equal economic treatment of all countries, tacitly including ex-enemy countries. Terms might possibly conflict with Ottawa agreement and the like but State Department officials are aware of our probable unavoidable dependence on exchange control and import licensing after the war, and will endeavour to agree to declaration in a form which would not involve us in any lack of candour.

8. Final sum of statement as to surpluses and their use after the war and some agreement as to nature of our collaboration concerning their disposal with United States.

9. Above outline which contains no reference to bases may be incomplete, but probably embodies main ideas under consideration on strictly economic side.

10. President desires to inform Congress in his report on June 10th that proposals have been made by him to us and are under consideration. But it is appreciated that it may well be impossible for us to agree to exact terms of so fundamental a declaration before that date especially if it involves consultation with Dominions.

11. Phillips' telegram yesterday giving outline of what we might tell State Department about our post-war exchange policy might be considered in connection with above.

On 2 June, Keynes sent some more general impressions of Washington to the Chancellor.

To SIR KINGSLEY WOOD, *2 June 1941*

Dear Chancellor of the Exchequer,

I have been meaning for some time to send you a few reflections on the general state of opinion and action here. But it is singularly difficult to concentrate one's ideas in a letter when one has been forced to talk and listen such an inordinate number of hours every day.

In some important respects the position is much better than I had expected. At any rate in the circles in which I move, which include the leading columnists (who are very important here in forming and interpreting public opinion) and academic people as well as a vast concourse of civil servants and advisers and people connected with the Administration and with politics, sincere and even passionate sympathy with our cause is practically universal. In Washington, whatever may be true elsewhere in the country, isolationism is an entirely negligible and ineffective minority. But the state of national doubt and hesitation is obviously most painful to those who want to see something done. Walter Lippmann asked me whether I had seen a single happy American. The President's speech was some consolation to most people,[24] but they would have been happier if he had gone further and spoken more concretely. The general sympathy and magnanimity of mind towards us is touching. But, all the same, it leaves one extremely homesick, missing the complete feeling of unity of purpose and of decisions finally made which we have in England.

I also find more drive and determination behind the defence programme than I had given them credit for. The leaders and the great body of assistants in the War Departments and in the various mushroom offices (OPM, Opax etc.

---

[24] On 27 May, President Roosevelt had declared a state of national emergency in a broadcast and said he would take measures to strengthen the American defence position.

etc.) connected with defence show an energy and determination to get on with the job as great as you could find
anywhere. I have not the least doubt that the long-term
programme will be all that it pretends to be. Most people here
claim that what seems to me an excessive concentration on
the long-term programme as against the immediate future is
not interfering with the latter, but is in fact helping it. As this
is the almost universal opinion, I suppose it must be right;
yet I am not quite convinced.

For example, they are still hesitating over what I find to
be the most clearly obvious decision and one with which, I
believe, every well-informed person concurs, namely, that
they should forthwith cut down the output of the automobile
industry for private purposes. This is at present 80 per cent
of normal. It ought to come down immediately to 50 per cent,
and more than that after a little notice. This would give an
immediate increase of the right kind of labour and management and materials. Or take agricultural tractor manufacturers. These must be ideally suited to make tanks. They have
longer experience of making tracks than any other firms in
the world. Yet none of them is at present engaged in making
tanks. Being full of their normal business, they have not
sought such contracts, and no-one has forced them. I find it
hard to believe that such concerns as the Caterpillar Company
could not make tanks more efficiently and more quickly than
complete newcomers to the business. So I remain a little
unconvinced whether the immense concentration on 1943
and later years could not, in some cases at least, be replaced
by more urgent thought for the immediate future. Until the
output of consumers' durable goods is compulsorily curtailed,
the highly experienced firms producing them will be well
content to continue as they are and will not seek defence
orders.

It is universally admitted that two grave mistakes have been
made by the business advisers to the Government,—namely
in respect of supplies of steel and aluminium. Last autumn

both were declared by the highest business authorities to be in ample prospective supply. The economic advisers who maintained the contrary from the start and said that big business was biassed by the fear of excess capacity after the war have gained much credit from being so quickly proved right. For it is now admitted that the quantities available are very deficient and that it would take a long time to make good the gap. The President told me that according to a report just made to him an increase of steel capacity by 20 million tons would itself absorb 8 million tons. Thus the only way in which the gap can be made good in time is by curtailing civilian consumption of these articles. That will have to be done. But it is not being done fast enough. (Here again postponement in cutting down the automobile industry is a good example, since that is a huge consumer of steel as well as of other raw materials.)

Generally speaking the plants manufacturing for defence are completely new and are not adaptations of existing plants. One is told that this is more efficient in the long run, but meanwhile business is much more occupied in building plants than in building machines. Perhaps manufacturers have preferred this because it enables them to continue with business as usual alongside the defence programme which is merely superimposed. All this will, I am sure, result in a fabulous output in due time. Nor does it mean, I think, that the near-term programme will disappoint estimates. It may even be a bit better than the estimates. It is only that I am not perfectly convinced that the near-term programme could not be still greater than it is going to be, if full attention was concentrated on it. The precise date at which we shall be ready to deliver the knock-out blow is relatively so unimportant compared with having the maximum equipment over the next nine months. This is understood in general. But it is in the ultimate fabulous programme that they are most practically interested.

The other main criticism which must strike one's attention

here relates to the organs of government. To the outsider it looks almost incredibly inefficient. One wonders how decisions are ever reached at all. There is no clear hierarchy of authority. The different departments of the Government criticise one another in public and produce rival programmes. There is perpetual internecine warfare between prominent personalities. Individuals rise and fall in general esteem with bewildering rapidity. New groupings of administrative power and influence spring up every day. Members of the so-called Cabinet make public speeches containing urgent proposals which are not agreed as part of the Government policy. In the higher ranges of government no work ever seems to be done on paper; no decisions are recorded on paper; no-one seems to read a document and no-one ever answers a communication in writing. Nothing is ever settled in principle. There is just endless debate and sitting around. But this, I suppose, is their characteristic method. Suddenly some drastic, clear-cut decision is reached, by what process one cannot understand, and all the talk seems to have gone for nothing, being the fifth wheel to the coach, the ultimate decision appearing to be largely independent of the immense parlez-vous, responsible and irresponsible, which has preceded it.

Nothing is secret, nothing is confidential. The President laughed when I said that his method of deceiving the enemy was apparently to publish so much vital information that they would not have time to read it. (There really is something in this, having regard to the difficulties of rapid communication!) There is practically no information you cannot get by just asking for it. When I emerge from Mr Morgenthau's room, I am immediately surrounded by pressmen who sit all day in his anteroom to note the name of every private visitor and ask him to tell them what he has been talking about with the Secretary and what was said. The same thing occurs immediately outside the President's study. Almost before you are through the door of his room you are assaulted by the reporters for a full account of all that has passed inside.

In the higher offices of State there is not a single individual who is both young and vigorous. Hopkins is an invalid. Three are very old indeed. By common consent they cannot easily switch their minds to a new subject suddenly introduced or understand what they are told about it. Their professional advisers work, therefore, under a severe handicap on personal grounds, as they are only too ready to explain to one. On the other hand the younger Civil Servants and advisers strike me as exceptionally capable and vigorous (with the very gritty Jewish type perhaps a little too prominent). The people the President surrounds himself with are most attractive and sympathetic. There is a splendid choice of talent out of which the survivors of two years hence will have been selected.

So you will see it is a very mixed picture.

The favourable elements, in my opinion, far exceed the unfavourable. The unbounded energy and good intentions must prevail in the end. But it would be a mistake not to expect time-lags here even more serious than with us.

The President's broadcast probably said everything that it was possible for him to say at this juncture in a statement of that kind. It means more, not less, than the words. Its main purpose, I should say, was to get a step forward by a formula which would involve no disruption of the national unity. The isolationists are fighting a rearguard action. Every day there are reports of prominent individuals and newspapers who have deserted their ranks. Each declaration by the President, which is not unduly controversial, causes some further section to feel that they must fall in with the national decision. Many half-sympathisers with the isolationists have come over to the President with his last speech because they feel that the decision has now been made and the time for criticism and argument for something different has gone by. Whilst to us

107

it may seem disappointingly slow, the President is unquestionably securing far greater ultimate national unanimity by
this process of gradually detaching supporters from the other
side without using words which will sting them into indignation or persisting opposition.

On the day after the great broadcast the President asked
the Ambassador and myself to lunch with him, and we spent
nearly 2½ hours in his company, mainly listening to him talk
at large over a wide range of topics.

The President sat at his big flat-topped study desk without
ever moving or getting up. We sat at each side of it, small
napkins for our plates, with nowhere for our knees (in both
our cases awkward objects!). The negro servants brought in
a serving waggon containing the lunch which they put by the
President and then finally withdrew. From this he gradually
took out the courses of an excellent lunch and handed them
to us with much courtesy and dexterity. I thought he was in
grand form. I had heard many reports how I should find him
much older and very tired compared with my memories of
what is now seven years ago. He was also said to have been
pulled down by his recent prolonged attack of acute diar-
rhoea. One is told that sometimes life and force goes out of
his face and that he looks like a tired old *woman* with all the
virility departed. But this was certainly untrue that morning.
Perhaps his speech and its success had raised his spirits. I
thought him calm and gay and in full possession of his own
personality and of his will and purpose and clarity of mind.
He still had that supreme equanimity which I have seen in
him before, and I again felt an extraordinary charm in his
expression and countenance, especially when it lights up with
an upward glancing quizzical expression when he has used
some teasing or half serious expression. I do not see how
anyone can doubt in his presence that he is the outstanding
American to-day, head and shoulders above everyone else.

I am told that he wastes much time in details which are of

no importance, in general talk on things which do not matter (which is probably his method of relaxing), in press conferences which are useful from one point of view but are exhausting and dangerous from others. But he still seemed to me to have the quality of thinking in simple terms on broad lines, of choosing his men and trusting them, and, in fact, seeing and handling things in the big way that he should. Those near him tell me he is well aware of the need to conserve his strength and knows well how to do it as the result of his long semi-invalidism of body.

We had gone ostensibly to discuss with him the draft I had prepared for Mr Eden on the post-war economic settlement.[25] The President had read it carefully. You may have seen the comments he made on the paper itself which the Ambassador telegraphed that day. But the following points are perhaps worth adding.

The President was emphatic that he would have no discussion at the present time of any post-war details. On this he spoke very much in the same terms as our own Prime Minister. He was all in favour, he said, of such matters being talked about behind the scenes provided it could be done without publicity. But there should be no public statements of any kind whatever, and even as regards private discussions he would be a bit timid for fear that complete privacy for them could not be safeguarded,—which in this country, of course, it could not. He then went on to mention some of his own post-war ideas. There were two points on which he was emphatic.

This time there must be unilateral disarmament. Europe must be entirely deprived of all weapons of offence. But England and America must retain fully adequate equipment ('no sinking of ships this time', he said) to act as the policemen of Europe. (When I mentioned Russia—'Now you are making things difficult', he smiled.) The second point was that

[25] For further details on this see *JMK*, vol. xxv.

on this occasion America would not pull out. He refused to consider the possibility that America would not take her full share of responsibility for the post-war situation in Europe, political as well as economic. The Europeans, on his view of the matter, are to be told just where they get off. Whatever federal or other arrangement may be set up between groups of European states, he clearly contemplated that a British–American police force should take all the necessary responsibility for maintaining order for some time to come.

In this and other contexts he put great emphasis on pan-Americanism. He seems to attach importance to carrying the South American states with him and associating them in any project, so far as possible.

He recalled a conversation he had had with Clemenceau in 1917, when that old man told him his purpose that a French child should be born and live for seventy years without fighting a German, something which for many centuries past had never yet happened, and that to break up Germany into small constituent parts was the way to secure this. The President wondered whether a federal Germany of small constituent parts entirely deprived of armaments, which Clemenceau failed to get last time, might not be the remedy now.

Whilst we sat, telegrams from the public commenting on his speech were arriving in thousands. Miss Le Hand brought them into the room in large bundles from time to time. The President said he had been expecting at least 25 per cent criticism. Actually they were running steadily at only 5 per cent in opposition. He said that this could be regarded as insignificant and was the most favourable response he had ever received to any public utterance. Since a critic is more likely to send in a telegram than an adherent, less than 5 per cent certainly seems negligible.

On the Ambassador asking him whether he proposed to repeal the Neutrality Act, he replied (what was subsequently made public) that he did not intend to do so. The consequent debate in Congress, he said, would give the isolationists the perfect platform they were wanting; they could prolong the discussion for months and extract the maximum nuisance value. He was convinced that he could do all he wanted without repealing the Act. He hinted that his immediate intention was to modify the danger zones so as to extend the areas into which American ships could sail. It is also open to him under his emergency powers to requisition merchant ships and turn them in effect into government vessels, whereupon the Neutrality Act will no longer apply to them. It was clearly in his mind to extend the frontier of American responsibility in the first instance almost to the other side of the Atlantic covering all the islands. He emphasised the greater ease with which he could carry public opinion at the present stage to any Atlantic island as compared, for example, with the African mainland. Here followed a long conversation about Iceland, the Azores and the Cape Verde Islands, the substance of which the Ambassador telegraphed after the interview. I thought that Iceland in particular was prominent in his mind and that he intended to make Iceland an American island for the time being and to develop transit arrangements both by air and by sea from there to the British Isles.

Through all this part of the conversation I had the impression that there were no adequate staff conversations between the Americans and ourselves of the kind I had assumed to be going on. I had no sense whatever of any close or continuous contact between the experts of the two countries on such matters. The President seemed very much in the air, and treated as a matter of pretty vague, inexpert conversation subjects on which I had supposed the general staffs would have reached the minutest conclusions long before now. I believe that representatives of our general staff are due here before long. But so far as the President himself is concerned, it certainly seemed that he had not those sources of continuous contact with our own strategists which one would have assumed to be essential.

He then passed on to what seemed to be a favourite project of his, the suggested 1,500-ton boats to be produced by the thousand, having shallow draught and various other notable advantages. Salter tells me that all the experts disbelieve in the whole thing. But the President evidently means to give the experimental stage his full protection; and the idea did sound to the layman extremely attractive and practical,— indeed, just the sort of thing that one would expect all the experts to declare to be quite out of the question!

Like most Americans, the President seemed to take a much more gloomy view about our holding Africa than is usual amongst ourselves and, also like the rest of them, attached much less importance than we do to our keeping Suez. He thought that every territorial expansion by the Germans from now onwards might weaken them on balance. The more thinly they are spread about the world, the better in the long run for us. Of course, he agreed that we should resist to the utmost, but he would not view a failure in that quarter with any excessive long-run concern. I am astonished by the extent to which nearly all responsible people over here seem to have written off Africa altogether. It has, at any rate, this advantage, that when bad news does come it does not for them create any particularly new situation. The President's confidence as to the ultimate result is quite unbounded, and nothing that can happen in the meantime will, I should think, make the slightest difference to his state of mind.

This letter is much too long, but there is one other facet of American opinion I ought to mention. It is widely believed here that there are important groups in London and even in the Government who are still appeasers and would welcome peace talks and a negotiated peace. These ideas exist every-where. I find it most difficult to gain credence for the statement that all such notions are completely wide of the mark and do not bear the slightest relation to any significant fact. If anything could be done to give the coup de grace to such ideas, which are most harmful, it would be a good thing. Americans really talk as though defeatism in England was at least as widespread as isolationism over here.

Yesterday, week-ending at Princeton, I paid a call on Einstein. The old sage was in bed with his vast olive corrugated countenance crowned with the white shock of Struwelpeter hair, and a big toe protruding from under the counterpane. He was full of gusto and enthusiasm and urged above everything with all the emphasis he could command that if, when we are ready, we bomb Germany continuously and without remorse they most certainly will not stand it.

I have already stayed here longer than I intended. But things move very slowly owing to the dissipation of authority, the reluctance to settle anything in principle and the fact that all important matters are conducted orally. But I am still hoping that another fortnight will see me through—for better or worse.

Yours sincerely,

J. M. KEYNES

Keynes also continued his reports to Sir Horace Wilson.

To SIR HORACE WILSON, *8 June 1941*

Dear Wilson,

It is not unlikely that the enclosed will be largely superseded by telegrams before it reaches you. On the other hand, it may be in time to give you a better background of what I may be telegraphing.

You will see from this that, if my forecast is right, my hopes of getting away by the end of this week will be disappointed. I do not mean to stay a day longer than is necessary. At the same time, although these particular negotiations are going slowly, I am not wasting my time. The Jesse Jones loan,[26] the question of 'consideration' and the surplus problem, as well as occasional dabbling in other matters, keep me busy; though what keeps me busiest perhaps is the establishment of a growing number of contacts in this vast official world. Everything is done, so to speak, backstairs, and unless one spends three-quarters of the day seeing people on one pretext or another, one knows nothing and can effect little.

I have no means of knowing if any of my various communications have reached you and, if so, at what date. I shall be grateful for a telegram, *en clair*, telling me by what date you have received this one. My important previous communications are two previous sections describing the course of my negotiations, I and II, sent to you, and a very long letter on the general situation to the Chancellor of the Exchequer.

Yours sincerely,

J. M. KEYNES

THE COURSE OF MY NEGOTIATIONS
III

The whole of the last fortnight has been occupied by the U.S. officials trying to work something out for us within the limitations which have been set them. There can be no doubt as to their good-will or that they have been told to do their

---

[26] The Jesse Jones loan was the culmination of the ideas Keynes had discussed with Mr Cohen in March. The idea had been revived after the Brown Williamson loan in connection with the American assets of British insurance companies. It became more probable as legislation moved through Congress increasing the resources of the Reconstruction Finance Corporation and allowing it to lend to foreign governments using U.S. securities as collateral, and as the problems of the A.V.C.-type of solution to Britain's need for funds became even clearer. Keynes and Phillips proposed borrowing against direct investments and securities enough to provide the money required from sales of investments in 1941. After lengthy negotiations following Treasury approval in principle on 6 June, the U.K. borrowed $8 million on the shares of U.S. subsidiaries of U.K. insurance companies, dollar securities and the earnings of 41 insurance companies not incorporated in the U.S. The loan was signed on 21 July.

best. But the limitations set are such as, in my opinion, to make anything like a complete solution almost impossible.

Their instructions are to discover what can be done without applying again to Congress and without conflicting with those various statements made to Committees of Congress by officials, of which we are only too well aware and which they only too keenly regret.

During the whole of the week before last the Treasury officials were engaged trying to see what could be done in taking over old commitments on the basis of those which came after certain critical dates. There was nothing that we could do except to supply them with all the statistics they needed, each application for new statistics inevitably involving a short delay. The Treasury officials came to the conclusion that, so far as Morgenthau was concerned, he had said nothing which would prevent him from taking over all the commitments subsequent to January 1, as well as various other oddments which add up to a certain amount. This would have been a great help. They had to wait for Morgenthau's return from a ten day absence for him to approve this and they then had to convince the lease lend department under Harry Hopkins that something on these lines would be acceptable.

Unfortunately, the lease lend department have ruled that, whilst Morgenthau is not bound by what the Director of the Budget said to Congress, they are. This meant that the critical date became March 11 instead of January 1, with a big curtailment of what could be taken over.

Since then they have been exploring for expedients, which have not yet been communicated to us officially, and indeed have been kept unusually secret; though in fact I do know what they are. Their revised proposals have not yet been approved in higher quarters, and we are told that we shall have to wait at least until tomorrow, June 9th, and probably a little longer, before having them communicated to us.

My own opinion is that none of the expedients under

consideration can be made, with the utmost ingenuity and good-will, to yield much more than $420 million. Off this has to come the $300 million already promised to Phillips, leaving a balance of only some $120 million towards my request for $650 million. I am afraid we have to accept the position that, if the commitment of the Director of the Budget is held to, this is all that can be done, so far as the old commitments are concerned, without going to Congress. I have, therefore been pondering all the alternatives, some of which I have already suggested to you by telegram. The position can be summarised as follows:–

(1) The view is widely held amongst the more responsible officials that the present ban against asking something fresh from Congress is only temporary, and will not hold at a later date, particularly if America's participation develops as we all expect it to. Indeed Cox[27], who is Harry Hopkins' principal assistant and a very good man indeed, has told me that he thinks Congress might be approached on new lines as early as September 1. Cox's own personal idea—I do not think it has any higher authority at present—is that, increasingly, strictly military supplies should be ordered in the first instance out of American war appropriations for subsequent transfer to us and that lend lease appropriations in our name should be limited hereafter to miscellaneous raw materials, agricultural products, agricultural machinery and the like,—roughly speaking, the items corresponding to the bracket of $1,350 million in the existing $7,000 million appropriation. But it is thought they might go to Congress about September 1, or soon after, asking for a further lump sum appropriation under this heading, and that lump sum appropriation might include an item which would be in effect cash, though limited, of course (which would do us no harm at all), to expenditure

---

[27] Oscar Sydney Cox (1905–66), lawyer, Assistant to General Counsel, U.S. Treasury Department, 1938–41; General Counsel, Lend Lease Administration, 1941–3; General Counsel, Foreign Economic Administration, 1943–5.

in U.S.A. other than old commitments. If this were done, it would release all our currently accruing gold etc. to replenish our reserves. I feel that there would be no harm in having what was substantially a cash item under lease lend, since it is now clear that that would be treated, as far as 'consideration' is concerned, on all fours with agricultural products.

(2) I do not think that any exaggerated confidence should be felt in the above, though it certainly represents the line along which all the responsible people here are thinking. The question for us is whether in view of it we should be content with getting a sufficient sum to cover our miscellaneous expenditure for one year rather than for two. I expect to be asking you before long by telegram whether the Chancellor is prepared to be content with this. My own inclination is to say 'yes'. My reason for this is the general trend of events taken in conjunction with the fact that those concerned here are now entirely conscious of our needs and wholly sympathetic with them. Cox, for example, entirely accepts the advisability of our having important free uncommitted balances and regards all the statistical exercises, on which he and the others are now wasting their time, as nothing more than a pretext for giving us those balances. He recognises the building up of balances and our financial independence as the ultimate aim. The same can be said in slightly varying degrees of all the other people I am in contact with. The disposition is now not merely accepted in the Treasury, the lend lease department and the State Department as our attitude, but it is sympathetically adopted as something which is proper for them to aim at. Thus, in the light of what I now know, I should be content if we could get provision for something less than two years, leaving the remoter future to look after itself, thus being satisfied with an appreciably smaller total than $650 million.

(3) Included in the annual total of $325 million there is an

item of $200 million for articles which I was previously
instructed it would be difficult to borrow through lease lend.
As a result of recent telegrams it is clear that this total can
be appreciably reduced. As a result of telegrams from London
and consultations here, I am satisfied that we could quite
safely reduce that figure from $m200 to $m140.

(4) I feel some confidence that I can obtain approval to the
general principle of lease-lending to the Dominions, apart
from Canada, those classes of raw materials which are being
lease lent to us. I have been told that in the case of steel
particularly they may be highly critical of Dominion demands,
but this will be from the priority point of view. If they are
satisfied on priority grounds, then I believe they will agree
to lend lease the articles. Now from the financial point of view
this is perfectly satisfactory. So long as all the steel etc. which
goes is lent-leased, we need make no financial provision to
pay for it out of free dollars. The loophole here is that the
priority machinery is at present far from watertight. So that
Australia, e.g., having failed to get tin plates through the
priority machinery, can then succeed in placing a private
order and getting stuff away which we shall have to finance
out of free dollars. Probably, however, before long this will
have tightened up. I have sent you a telegram asking you how
much relief would follow if the above principle is granted.
I have not yet received this figure, but I should expect that
it would be not less than $m50 per annum. If so, the effect
of this and the reduction under (3) above would reduce the
two years' total of $m650 to $m430.

(5) The next most plausible source of funds is by selling
assets otherwise unrealisable to Jesse Jones for payment out
of R.F.C. funds. I have already asked for instructions about
the advisability of this by telegram. The argument against
it is that, of course, we appear to be parting with assets which
would have a post-war value. The arguments in favour are:–

   (i) that we should be obtaining immediate liquidity;

(ii) that we should be disembarrassing ourselves of post-war surpluses which may otherwise be troublesome;

(iii) that we are extremely likely to have to throw in any surpluses we possess at the end of the war along with other people's surpluses for purposes of European relief and re-construction; and

(iv) if the transaction is being carried through as a means of supplying us with as many dollars as possible, we should probably get a liberal price, representing a very full value of the property transferred.

On balance, therefore, I am rather decidedly in favour of turning an appropriate portion of our surpluses into free dollars, (say) $m100, which might be chiefly lead and wool. Undoubtedly jute would also qualify, but that at present belongs to India and not to us. And there would also be other articles.

Something on these lines might fit in extremely well with the bold proposals set forth in Pursa 373 of June 5th, which I have just seen, outlining Harriman's proposals, of which I was already aware, but extending them into a new field. Under this scheme the U.S. could buy from us a pool of raw materials stored in other countries and not for immediate shipment. If the Harriman proposals come into operation, I should say that, if we have not turned these commodities into actual cash, they would naturally be set off against lend lease and would certainly not remain on our hands as a post-war asset. Under the Harriman plan they might reach a much greater value than $100 million. But a prospect of anything like the Harriman plan would be a reason for our not being reluctant to turn such commodity assets into liquid cash.

(6) It is possible that there may be other assets which we could dispose of to Jesse Jones for much more than a normal price. For example, Cox has suggested that we might, instead of attempting to sell the Borax Company in the market or borrow against it, dispose of it to the United States Govern-

ment on the ground that it had command of the sources of supply of an important war material. I believe that Peacock has come to the view that the utmost we could borrow against Borax Company would be some quite trifling sum, $m2 or $m3. If this was lumped together with other transactions, as for example under (5) above, it might be put in for some far greater figure than this, such as $m50, the idea being to put on it the greatest nominal value which could possibly be substantiated.

(7) There remains the possibility, which I mentioned in my telegram, of our selling some sterling to the U.S. Treasury (for dollars) to be used by them for military expenditure hereafter in the sterling area. The argument in favour of this is that otherwise we should probably have to supply them with such sterling, not for dollar cash, but as an off-set under lend lease.

(8) The above can be summed up as follows: the annual requirement of $m325 might be reduced to $m215. Towards this we may hope to receive $m120 in respect of old commitments etc. (namely, $m420 in all, of which $m300 has to be deducted to meet the promise to Phillips); $m100 to $m150 from selling assets to Jesse Jones; and perhaps a further sum for the purchase of sterling. The above brings enough in sight to give us the necessary provision for fully one year and perhaps more. It is quite true that this would not augment our immediate cash balances nearly so much as a settlement for two years. On the other hand, the whole of the $m420 from old commitments etc. is likely to be so arranged as to benefit us in 1941, when we need the money most. If we are also able to borrow $m400 from Jesse Jones, we should, it seems to me, have quite a decent balance at all the critical dates.

If the above outline of a possible settlement meets with approval, it would be helpful for me to have some indication to that effect by telegram; though I may be requiring instructions before this document has reached London.

I may as well add to the above such fresh news as is available about the proposals for 'consideration'. My telegram on May 31st gave you, I think, an accurate account of the draft prepared in the State Department. During the last week much time has been occupied in wrangling over this draft between the State Department and the Treasury. (Indeed the time so occupied has been one cause of the slow progress over the negotiations outlined above.) The changes, which were provisionally made by the Treasury, were very far from improvements, and there is reason to think that tin, rubber and also jute raised their heads again. I have recently heard some gossip as to the progress of affairs from no less than four different sources, and it is not quite easy to be sure which represents the latest phase. But I was told yesterday that, if the draft is proceeded with, it is unlikely that the Treasury changes will be accepted by higher authority and much more likely that it will go forward substantially in the form prepared by the State Department. Whether this is true remains to be seen. The main thing which now remains to be done is for the President to decide whether he feels that it is politically advisable for him to make us an offer on these lines at once or whether it would be more prudent to delay. June 10 is now so near that he can at best either tell Congress that he has discussed, or is about to discuss, the question with us, and there can be no question of any prior settlement. It may be easier for the President to make his statement about 'consideration' as part of a wide statement as to what he is going to do next in response to Ambassador Winant's visit. This would take it out of the financial sphere, which is much to be desired. I am keeping in touch with all this in a number of different directions and doing what is possible to steer opinion along the right lines.

A word, too, about the Jesse Jones loan. Peacock expects to be asking Morgenthau in the course of the next few days for his benevolent approval of our opening direct negotiations with Jesse Jones. Meanwhile there has been the queer episode of the loan to Coats[28] of which you will probably have heard by telegram before this reaches you. The Coats proposition is complicated by a Court decree, which is in suspense but not revoked, which might render them liable for dissolution under anti-trust legislation. Clearly this impairs their security. Peacock had been saying that he doubted whether he could borrow much more than $m6 or $m7. Clarence Dillon[29] then busied himself to get a better offer and arranged for a loan of $16 million which Peacock thought magnificent. Morgenthau approved this, and at first it was thought that Jesse Jones did too. Indeed Peacock expected that Jesse Jones would fight shy of Coats because he would not want to get involved in the Court decree in question. The latest gossip is that, on the contrary, Jesse Jones is interested himself, does not want any outside bankers to get the loan and is declaring that $m16 is entirely insufficient and that the property is good for a loan of $m30.

There is, I think, very strong reason to hope and to believe that, if we can get a substantial Jesse Jones loan with the earnings of the more obvious direct and market investments ear-marked to its repayment, we shall hear no more of the disposal of the equities of any of them. Those which are not included as security for the Jesse Jones loan will be forgotten altogether and those which are included will be liable in respect of their current income only. So the horrible Viscose business may after all bear fruits.

8.6.41   J. M. KEYNES

Meanwhile Keynes continued his lend lease negotiations.

---

[28] J. and P. Coats had almost concluded a loan for $16 million from a group of banks and insurance companies, using their American subsidiaries as security. Eventually the loan was brought into the Jesse Jones arrangement and the sum raised to $25 million.
[29] Of the merchant bankers Dillon Reed & Co.

To D. W. BELL, *9 June 1941*

Dear Mr Bell,

Since the Memorandum dated May 16th, 1941, was submitted to Mr Secretary Morgenthau, we have been in telegraphic communication with London as to whether some items included in Appendix A to the Memorandum could not after all be handled administratively at the British end under lend lease arrangements without too much difficulty. These communications have also been supplemented by discussions with our officials here in the light of their actual current experience. The result is that we can now replace the previous list by a revised list attached below, which adds up to $m140 instead of $m199. The main part of the difference is due to four items:

(1) It is now agreed that agricultural machinery can be conveniently handled by us under lend lease, provided this category is acceptable at your end, which I gather it is.

(2) In practice, the item previously included for civil road vehicles, including fire-pumps, cranes etc. is going forward under lend lease.

(3) It has been possible to divide up the paper and timber items into two categories and take out some of the larger items which seem to present no excessive difficulty under the lend lease procedure.

(4) The item for oil plant equipment can be reduced, since it is now proposed to requisition under lend lease for tin plate and drum sheets.

The items still remaining contain no margin for orders not thought of at the time when the list was compiled, and there is a sign that they are likely to increase moderately on account of unforeseen additions during the year. It would be advisable, therefore, to give a little margin and to think of the total as amounting now to (say) $m150 as compared with the strict total of $m140.

Yours sincerely,

J. M. KEYNES

P.S. The above is, of course, on the assumption that the items now declared administratively practicable at our end are eligible for requisition under lease lend at your end.

Appendix A

	($million)	
	Original	Revised
Machinery components	40	37
Chemical manufactures, drugs	30	30
Sundry materials, machinery and consumption goods	18	18
Vehicle parts	8	8
Civil road vehicles, including fire pumps, cranes, etc.	24	0
Abrasives	3	2
Rutile, bentonite, diatomaceous earth, tin residues, bismuth and miscellaneous non-ferrous metals	6	9
Miscellaneous paper, bagasse, cotton and linen rags	8	3
Timber (other than aero spruce and aero plywood)	10	3
Borax, razorite, sundry chemicals, fibestos and synthetic resins, carbon black, pine tar, rosin, turpentine and asphalt	6	6
Agricultural machinery	12	0
Seeds	4	4
Oil plant equipment	30	20
	199	140

Chapter 4

WASHINGTON 1941: THE CONSIDERATION FOR LEND LEASE

Keynes began more serious discussions on the Consideration on 9 June. The opening meetings were still preliminary and vague, but the trend of Keynes's thinking at the time came out clearly in his letter to the Ambassador on 12 June.[1]

To LORD HALIFAX, *12 June 1941*

Dear Lord Halifax,

My conference yesterday at the State Department about 'consideration' was scarcely more definite than before. They have no further instructions either from the President or Mr Hull. Nevertheless, we conversed for about an hour and a half, and I suppose that some sort of vague progress was made. At the end Mr Acheson agreed that they on their side must seek strenuously for more definite instructions with a view to our meeting again on, perhaps, Saturday.

A good part of the time was occupied with talk arising out of two suggestions which I made, as I was careful to explain, personally and without authority. I hope I was not indiscreet in this. On the one hand, it is doubtful policy for us to take the initiative. On the other hand, if we draft the phrases, we can give them the turn we prefer.

The two papers in question are attached. I had discussed both of these beforehand with Purvis and Phillips, and in the opinion of both of them they were quite harmless and even desirable. In any case, they commit no one, and it is under-

[1] Lord Halifax had cabled Keynes's ideas to London on 10 June. Keynes received permission from London to continue his informal discussions on 15 June, but later in June he received instructions to be very discreet and to 'avoid making far-reaching suggestions'.

stood that I put them forward merely with a view to making the conversation a little more precise.

On the paper marked I the phrase which I introduced—'in respect of the aid which is accorded no cash account shall be set up' is an example of the advantage of using one's own draft. I attached importance to this phrase whatever the items in the ensuing catalogue might be and made, I think, some impression along these lines. When I was asked what (3) might comprise, I said that I could think of nothing important except ships, but the main purpose of this clause, which we should certainly prefer left out, was to emphasise and make clear the distinction between the produce of Great Britain and other parts of the Empire, which we did not own and would have to purchase for good money. As a possible additional item they threw out the old proposal about our holdings of South American Railways and Utilities. I said that if they really attached importance to this, which I much doubt, they could put forward such a proposal and I would ascertain the British view on it.

The second paper marked II I had the impression they distinctly liked. You will see that I made no attempt to define the terms of reference.

Since they had shown some inclination to leave altogether too wide open until the end of the war the question of what 'consideration' should be given under Category C, i.e. non-warlike articles, I emphasised the grave disadvantage of this from our point of view. I pointed out, and they agree, that the nominal sum due under Category C in terms of dollars might be very great indeed. If a way was left open by which in effect a subsequent administration or a subsequent President could demand the cash equivalent of this, we at home would feel gravely threatened and disturbed on the financial side. This was agreed especially by Mr Dean Acheson, who made an excellent statement admitting the desirability of settling now, so far as possible, the kinds of items comprising 'consideration', so as to make this list exclusive of other less desirable possibilities.

My feeling was that we might quite easily, perhaps even rapidly, come to a satisfactory conclusion if only they, on their side, had firmer instructions and a free hand in matters of detail. I wonder if it would help for you to see the President. I think it might. Should I sound Acheson as to whether, from their point of view, this would be a helpful thing? It is vitally important that the President should give the right kind of instructions, and no one on our side has yet had a chance of a word with him about this from our point of view.*

Unless you feel otherwise, it seems to me that there is no need to make a further report to London at the moment. The conversation raised no new points on which there is any need to ask instructions.

I enclose a copy of the President's report under the Lend Lease Act. The passage out of which the present negotiations arise appears in the last paragraph of page 13, where the President reports that 'work has started on the agreements to fix the terms and conditions under Clause 3(b) upon which the Foreign governments receive the aid.'

Yours sincerely,

[copy initialled] J.M.K.

I

Category A. Warlike articles and raw materials in a condition to be returned.

Category B. Ditto consumed or destroyed.

Category C. Non-warlike articles and raw materials for the use of the civilian population.

A separate list will be kept of the deliveries belonging to Category C. In respect of the aid thus accorded no cash account shall be set up but the President shall be entitled at

* Is not this *very* important? I could see Acheson immediately to discover his view.

any time before the end of the emergency period to ask in return for any of the following:-

(1) Any deliveries under the reciprocal lend lease arrangement provided for under Clause   above.

(2) Information and inventions of any description valuable for the purposes of the defence of the U.S.

(3) Any goods produced or manufactured within Great Britain required for the purposes of a strategic reserve.

(4) Co-operation in any measures which may be agreed for post-war relief and reconstruction requiring the use of surplus stocks of goods and materials in the ownership of the British Government.

II

Furthermore, whereas it is a primary purpose of the President of the United States in accepting this agreement to avoid encumbrances which might interfere with the free and healthy flow of normal economic intercourse between nations after the war, the British Government, deeply appreciative of the magnanimity of its terms, agree for their part to make such contribution as lies in their power to this same end and in particular, to join with the Government of the U.S. in setting up forthwith an Anglo-American commission charged with the purposes and subject to the terms of reference set forth below, and in carrying out the agreed recommendations of this body.

Meanwhile, Keynes's negotiations with the U.S. Treasury continued and reports of these and the 'consideration' discussions became intermingled.

THE COURSE OF MY NEGOTIATIONS

IV

We are not yet at the end of the discussion as to the amount of old commitments which can be taken over, since there seems endless opportunity for the discussion (and generally for the rejection) of countless sophistries. It is all rather an absurd way in which to spend one's time in conditions of war. I can only say that the officials of the U.S. Treasury have been doing their best and wasting their own time even more than ours. At the moment the position is the same as that which I reported in my telegram, namely that the utmost expectation is $420 million, which would leave over a balance of $120 million for me after satisfying Phillips's request for $300 million. The worst is about $175 million which falls seriously short of Phillips's requirements.

Until this discussion had reached its last lap, I felt that it was inadvisable, even though it led to a fearful waste of time, not to bring forward my own constructive proposals for meeting my own specific requests. For there was the gravest danger that, if I did so, any ideas I might have would be stolen to satisfy Mr Morgenthau's promise to Phillips, they being at their wits' end how to find this money within the limits of the law and the commitments made.

But at last it seemed safe to crystallise the position and make my proposals more explicit. Yesterday, therefore, I sent the letter of which I attach a copy to Mr Harry Hopkins. I discussed it previously with Mr Oscar Cox, his principal adviser, who approved the letter, and I think I have a reasonable chance of getting his backing for it when Mr Hopkins consults him. Indeed, I have satisfied myself that the proposals here made, which I hope the Chancellor will approve, follow the line of least resistance and most promise in all quarters. Both the proposals are workable, I think, and should yield fairly substantial amounts.

18.6.41   J. M. K.

To HARRY HOPKINS, *17 June 1941*

Dear Mr Hopkins,

In the five weeks which have passed since I gave Mr Morgenthau a memorandum outlining what the Chancellor of the Exchequer had sent me to say, no positive progress has been made. But the possibilities of the situation have been very carefully explored by Sir F. Phillips and myself with the officials of the Treasury Department and with Mr Cox, who have been most kind and sympathetic and helpful but have been up against difficulties which were none of their making.

I am given to understand that, as a result of this examination, Mr Morgenthau will be advised shortly of the utmost which is possible by way of relieving us of existing commitments. But it is clear, I think, that the amount, if any, available after satisfying Mr Morgenthau's promise to Sir F. Phillips to find relief of from $300 million to $400 million, will not go far towards satisfying the needs which I outlined in my memorandum.

The time has come, therefore, when I need guidance from you how it would be useful for me to try to make progress, in so far as this is possible through the lend lease machinery. Leaving details and minor sources on one side, and assuming that we are already putting in requisitions in respect of all U.S. exports to U.K. which can be handled administratively on our side and are acceptable on yours, there appear to me to be only two methods which are of substantial importance:–

(1) The financial estimates made in London assume that munition exports to the British Commonwealth outside Britain (excluding Canada) will be lent-leased but that we shall have to pay cash for other exports to those destinations. If you were prepared to apply to requisitions under lend lease on behalf of other parts of the Empire outside North America the same general criteria that you apply to requisitions from Britain, this would afford us a material relief.

I do not mean by this that you should not apply to Dominion applications stricter tests under the priority arrangements where commonsense and the necessities of the situation suggest that stricter tests are appropriate; but that types of cases which would be eligible for lend lease if they were for the U.K. should also be eligible when they are for other parts of the Empire in all cases where the stuff is available for them to take.

This would, I suggest, be a sensible sort of arrangement to make, since it would amount to substituting lend lease supplies which present no administrative or other difficulties in place of U.K. requirements which do present such difficulties.

It is unlikely that the relief obtainable in this way would do the whole trick, but it would go a long way. It is a difficulty in the way of my obtaining reliable estimates at short notice that London might think it inadvisable to encourage the Dominions to draw up requirements along these lines unless there was some reasonable hope of their getting satisfaction. Our total disbursements in respect of exports from the U.S. to the British Empire outside Great Britain and Canada are estimated at $450 million a year, but only a proportion of this, say a third to a half, is likely to prove workable through the lend lease machinery, at any rate in the first instance.

What I contemplate in making this suggestion is not independent lend leasing direct to the Dominions, but lend leasing to Great Britain with authority to transfer to the Dominions. This procedure has the advantage that it does not complicate the 'consideration' agreement or the organisation which is now conveniently centralised under Mr Purvis. Otherwise the President would have to make five distinct consideration agreements and you would have to deal with five independent requisitioning authorities. Moreover if the requisitions on Dominion behalf are not centralised and criticised by us before they reach you, considerable waste of time may ensue. There are also other difficulties which I need not labour.

(2) The only other important way in which you can help us would be by obtaining fresh authority from Congress when next the President asks for an appropriation.

We estimate that we are spending currently in the United States at least $700 million a year, which, for one reason or another, is not being paid for through the lend lease machinery, of which $250 million is for Great Britain and $450 million for the rest of the Empire exclusive of Canada (as mentioned under (1) above). As you know, we have a common purse with the Dominions, apart from Canada, for dollar expenditure, and we must provide the dollars needed for their essential purposes as well as for our own. It is these heavy disbursements, *additional* to our pre-lend lease commitments for munitions, which are the source of our financial difficulties. If we could be relieved of a substantial part of these, we should be—relatively speaking—in an extremely satisfactory position.

To be more precise, would it be possible for the President to take authority, when next he approaches Congress for a lend lease appropriation, to ask for a sum of (say) $500 million a year (or $250 million if the Dominions are being dealt with under (1) above) which he was free to make available for expenditure in the U.S. otherwise than through the strict lend lease procedure of requisitions etc.?

This would enable him, in effect, to make a cash transfer to us provided we undertook to expend it in the U.S. for current needs other than on pre-lend lease munition commitments which we should continue to meet out of our own resources as we have agreed to do. He could point out to Congress that a few months' experience has shown that the lend lease procedure is convenient and appropriate over 95 per cent of the field, but that there remains a margin where it is administratively inconvenient or impracticable, so that he needs a little elbow room to deal with this marginal field.

Otherwise, it is a case of spoiling the ship for the sake of a coat of paint. We have this magnificent conception of lend lease; 'consideration' is being discussed on lines more magnanimous than any hitherto recorded transactions between great nations; and yet, on account of our resources having been so completely exhausted before lend lease came into operation, we suffer anxiety and possible embarrassment through being unable to accumulate the minimum reserves which are necessary to carry the vast financial responsibilities of London. At the present moment the total gold reserves of the Bank of England are less than $50 million, and the cash reserves of the British Treasury less than $100 million—which would be laughable if it were not so embarrassing. To build these up, except very slowly, out of our accruing resources is impossible while we are facing the double task of paying off old commitments and financing current expenditure of the sterling using parts of the Empire in the U.S. outside lend lease. Yet it needs only a trifling addition to the assistance we are already receiving to give us the necessary comfort of mind and freedom from daily cares—a gain to our Administration in all the circumstances of the present hour altogether out of proportion to the sums involved.

I am sending Mr Morgenthau a copy of this letter so that he will be aware of what I am suggesting.

Yours sincerely,

J. M. KEYNES

To SIR KINGSLEY WOOD, *21 June 1941*

Dear Chancellor,

(1) I find that Sir Edward Peacock can take a letter to you if I write it quickly. I will send a duplicate by bomber bag.

(2) My negotiations with the Treasury have now taken a favourable turn and, unless there is a new kind of hitch (which is always possible), we ought to get virtually all we have asked for. The latest sophistry in relation to old commitments,

which looks like going through, should mean that they would take over on one ticket or another from $400 million to $500 million. For the rest the idea is to lend lease all possible supplies to Dominions etc. which lend themselves to that treatment. I should be hopeful that this might reach $250 million a year. The two sources between them should reach my full request, if not more.

In addition to that, as you will be hearing from Peacock, we expect $425 million from Jesse Jones. It also seems likely that Jesse Jones will buy the wool, the title of which we have already transferred to U.S., as a strategic reserve, thus bringing us in about $70 million cash. There are also other minor possibilities on these lines.

So far, therefore, as the above is concerned, I might at an early date consider my job finished and hurry home.

(3) But there remains the vital question of 'consideration'. The position here is that I am to see the President personally in the course of the next few days. I am advised by Hopkins and by those in the State Department who have been dealing with this question that the possibility of progress will entirely depend upon the success of this conversation. The President regards this subject as very much his own, and no one but himself is going to have much to do with decisions about it. For this reason he has discarded the State Department draft, though I have no doubt that, when we get down to business, something very much on these lines will resurrect itself. He has not given any sufficiently clear instructions to provide the basis for an alternative draft. But it is felt that he will talk to me at large on the whole subject and that a point may be reached from which we can proceed. Methods in this country are so odd that it is probably I who will have to pass on to the State Department the President's instructions on the matter![2]

---

[2] Keynes was so instructed when he saw the President on 7 July, much to Dean Acheson's amusement.

Meanwhile I am warned that the matters prominently in his mind may include the following:–

(*a*) Far and away the most important snag is the President's doubt whether it is politically possible for him to put over just at this juncture the right kind of agreement, indeed the only possible kind of agreement. I gather that his reaction to the State Department draft was that it would be politically difficult for him to get it across and that he would much rather have an entirely provisional settlement now, leaving over all substantial matters to a later date. The State Department and Hopkins are entirely on our side in this matter. They point out that a later date might mean two years after the war, that this Administration and this President may be no longer there and that it would be an enormous relief to us to get a really satisfactory settlement finally determined at this date. I sympathise with the President's standpoint without sharing it, for certainly the 'consideration' we are in a position to offer does not look very plausible. But they say that the President is in a mood to be much too delicate about public and congressional opinion and that his nervousness about the reception of the document is very likely unnecessary. At any rate I shall do my best.

(*b*) On points of detail, the President has not decided whether it is advisable to make the distinction between warlike and non-warlike goods. I gather it might not be difficult to persuade him that the division is inadvisable. My instructions from you and the Prime Minister are that you do not like the division, so I will try to persuade him that he should give instructions for all the deliveries to be treated on the same basis.

(*c*) I am told that he is taking a great deal of interest in the question of an international police force after the war. The question has been raised behind the scenes whether part of the 'consideration' might be that we should take a major responsibility for equipping and arming this international police force. That sounds to me, at first sight, rather a good idea, but it needs thinking about. It would be helpful for me to know how it strikes the Prime Minister and you. This would have to be vaguely drafted at this stage, as something which the President could ask for if he wished.

(d) I have had hints that the President might want to include in the 'consideration' we give the South American railways and other public utilities which we own. It would not be his purpose to acquire for the United States an economic, income-earning asset, but rather to hand these back to the South American Republics as a gesture and a present. The President is strongly of the opinion that foreign ownership of public utilities is an anachronism. He is very strong on pan-Americanism and anxious to bring the South American Republics in to the utmost possible extent. When he visited Brazil he expressed to President Vargas, as he drove through the city, admiration of some of the public utilities there. 'Yes,' said the President, 'but how would you like it if the subways of New York were owned by Portugal and the Japanese?' And that remains prominently in the President's mind. I have myself heard him talk on these lines and think it very likely that he will attach great importance to something of this kind from us. Here again it would be of great help to me to know how it strikes you at home. I have, of course, given no encouragement to the idea. Nevertheless, it does seem to me that there might be a great deal in it. Here is a vulnerable and depreciating asset, having a book value (I am guessing from memory) of perhaps as much as £500 million and bringing us in (again I am guessing) an income of not more than £5 million, if that. This would look something splendid. Would it not be worth while making the offer to get the whole thing through?

(4) My strong feeling is that, if the President agrees to a substantial settlement now, we shall without doubt get a good settlement. In order to fix my ideas I have prepared a skeleton

draft, which I enclose. This has been merely for my own purposes and has not been communicated. But, if there is anything in it to which you take exception, may I have a cable? Though I shall be careful to commit no one, it is extremely likely that, as the only way of getting on, I shall have to be a little constructive, at the expense of being indiscreet, behind the scenes.

If to a draft on the general lines of this paper could be added financial responsibility on our part towards an international police force after the war and the offer of the railways and public utilities of South America, I believe we could succeed. And it is not impossible that we could get away without these further concessions. On the whole, I like these concessions for their own sake as making the thing look much more magnanimous and better and responsible from our point of view than a document which would be so empty as the enclosed draft.

I call particular attention in the enclosed to the overriding clause I (3). I think there is a good hope of getting in a clause of this kind. If, as I propose, it is an overriding clause, we can be a good deal freer in the subsequent details, since, in any case of doubt, they would be governed by that.

Yours sincerely,

J. M. KEYNES

P.S. The Ambassador is away, but I am taking his instructions on all this as soon as he is back.

Keynes's skeleton draft for the suggested announcement ran as follows.

I

(1) A declaration of common purpose.

(2) A declaration by the President that the carrying out of

this common purpose is the main object of the aid accorded under the Lend Lease Act and that the benefits thereby obtained are, in his judgment, the signal advantage secured by the United States under Section 3(*b*) of the Act.

(3) In respect of the balance of aid accorded under the Lend Lease Act not thus compensated no cash account shall be set up and no delivery of goods or assets shall be asked which would interfere with the normal economic relations between the United States of America and the British Commonwealth after the war or with the capacity of the British Commonwealth to purchase American goods and services.

(4) But the British Government, deeply appreciative of the magnanimity of these terms, agree for their part to furnish in return the further considerations and co-operation set forth in the subsequent clauses below.

II

The British Government agree to return at the end of the war all goods received under the Lend Lease Act which have not been destroyed or consumed in any case in which the President calls for their return.

III

The British Government agree to accord a reciprocal lend lease arrangement if asked for by the United States at any time hereafter.

IV

The President shall be entitled, at any time before he declares that a final settlement has been reached, to ask for all or any of the following payment or repayment in kind or property or for direct or indirect benefits under the following heads:–

(1) *The Defence of the United States*

(*a*) A further provision for bases and other similar facilities required for the purposes of the defence of the United States.

(*b*) Information, operational methods, inventions and

secret processes of any description valuable for the purposes of the defence of the United States.

(c) Any other delivery of goods or property or services deemed by the President to have value for the purposes of the defence of the United States.

(2) *Post-war Relief and Reconstruction*

(a) A common policy after the termination of hostilities for the economic reconstruction of Europe and of all other areas afflicted or disorganised by the ravages of war.

(b) Cooperation in any measures which may be agreed for post-war relief requiring the use of surplus stocks of goods and materials in the ownership of the British Government.

(c) An agreement to facilitate the disposal by the Government of the United States in such manner as they shall see fit of any property and other assets now 'frozen' within the jurisdiction of that Government.

(3) *Post-war Trade and Economic Policy*

Whereas it is a primary purpose of the President of the United States in accepting this agreement to avoid encumbrances which might interfere with the free and healthy flow of normal economic intercourse between nations after the war, the British Government agree to make such contribution as lies in their power to this same end and in particular to join with the Government of the United States in establishing a post-war economic order which shall promote the freedom of trade, of travel and of intercourse between the nationals of all countries and more particularly between the citizens of the United States and of the British Commonwealth of Nations

(a) by maintaining the freedom of the seas throughout the world for the shipping of all nations;

(b) by opening all sources of raw materials within their control to every purchaser on equal terms;

(c) by participation in schemes for the regulation of output and prices of internationally traded raw materials;

(d) by the abatement, as circumstances allow, of all special privileges and discriminations in trade navigation and commerce and the reduction of trade barriers;

(e) by the maintenance through an appropriate exchange and currency organisation and in other ways of a due equilibrium in the balance of payments between national systems;

(f) by the provision of liberal and convenient facilities of every description for the movement of traders, tourists and students and for the exchange of all information and knowledge and the fruits of research and discovery.

V

And furthermore it is agreed that at an appropriate time an Anglo-American Commission shall be set up charged with the preparation of plans for Anglo-American co-operation both in the economic reconstruction of the post-war world and for the better ordering of economic intercourse between nations after the transitional period has been ended.

To SIR KINGSLEY WOOD, *22 June 1941*

Dear Chancellor,

I attach a duplicate copy of a letter I have sent you by the hand of Sir Edward Peacock which may or may not have reached you before this one. As I now have a little more time to complete what I have to say, I add this supplement.

The 'consideration' negotiations can be tackled in either of two ways. We can take up the position of objecting to any item which from our point of view represents real money and endeavour to confine our concessions to intangibles and policy. If we take this line strongly, it is possible that we shall be successful. People here are conscious by now of our prospective economic difficulties after the war and are unwilling to add to them. If your instructions are along these lines, I should say that the chief risk would be that the President would postpone the real settlement to a time which might be politically easier for him, not that he would press for the items we were objecting to.

The alternative course would be to approach the matter on somewhat grander lines and be ready to accept clauses which might really cost us something. Anything in the least comparable with, or of the same order of magnitude as, what we are getting is, of course, utterly out of the question. It is no use our making any offer to the United States where the gain to them is merely an economic profit equal to the economic loss to ourselves. It will be easy to persuade them that this sort of concession on our part would do no-one any good in the long run. We should, I suggest, firmly reject any items which were merely the equivalent of so many dollars and had no other significance. But where it is a case of conceding something which has a non-economic significance to the President and to the future ordering of the world, then we might consider whether it would not be proper for us to concede it even though it did cost us an economic price.

Two good examples are those I mention in the enclosed letter, namely, the expenses of an international police force hereafter and the railways and public utilities which we own in South America. It may turn out that the President does not attach much significance to either of these matters. But, if he does, should we resist?

It seems to me that there might be real advantages and also great propriety if any means can be found (which will not be easy) to make the agreement something which satisfies the President in his heart and will be regarded as a little bit of a triumph for him, however out of proportion to what he is doing for us. The post-war world will bring such vast changes that we may gain little if we hang on too resolutely to our nineteenth century economic anachronisms. If the Americans are of a mind to continue their assistance after the armistice, we shall, from the strictly economic standpoint, gain much more than we are likely to be called upon to sacrifice as 'consideration'. Possibilities of Anglo-American co-operation after the war open up wide, fruitful fields. The main thing we can offer is our sacrifice and our endurance in the war. They know that, and it is, of course, the background and the entire reason for their generosity. But it will all go forward much better if we do not hang back too much in *details*.

It would, therefore, be helpful to know in which mood you and the Prime Minister wish the negotiations to be carried on. I suggest that the distinction might be that which I have made above, namely, that we should argue against any items which are, in the last analysis, just so many dollars' worth or, at the best, little more than that, but that we should be ready to throw in items, though they have economic value to us, which have a super-economic significance to them, if the President, for whatever reason, deems them important. They will not mount up to much, but they would at least be a symbol of our recognition of the vastness of the magnanimity on their side.

I fancy that the attitude of the officials we are dealing with must have changed out of knowledge within the last six months. Six months ago in the Treasury we felt that they were trying to strip us of everything and reduce us to the lowest possible state. Whether this was really their intention or merely a concession to what they thought politics required, I am not sure. But there were several episodes which were not easy to explain except on some such hypothesis. To-day I find it hard to detect anything of this sort in major matters. They are still sensitive to real or imagined political difficulties and want to expose the least possible surface to Congress. But, subject to this, they are going out of their way to find means of relieving us of dollar obligations and of allowing us to build up a free reserve of $600 million, which is now the generally accepted objective.

We may not have received more than five billion dollars of lease lend money in the next twelve months, but the rate thereafter should approach or exceed ten billion dollars a year. If we make the utmost concessions which would be called for on the above criterion, I should be surprised if the real economic value of the 'consideration' we returned would reach one billion dollars.

You will see from these two letters how difficult it will be to carry these negotiations to their best success by the exchange of telegrams on specific points unless the background and the mood of the negotiations have been agreed and established.

Yours sincerely,

J. M. KEYNES

At this stage in Keynes's 'consideration' discussions, another element of his many activities in Washington came to impinge on what followed.

During the early stages of his visit, Keynes had become involved on the fringes of Anglo-American commercial policy discussions. These had their origins in British attempts late in 1940 to maximise dollar export earnings by forcing exports to the United States. Discussions arising from these attempts led to suggestions that Britain was trying to alter the Anglo-American Trade Agreement so as to make the American market more accessible to British exporters. Discussions with the Americans naturally brought proposals for British concessions, a request for a reduction in the Imperial Preference from the end of 1942 for tobacco, dried and fresh fruit. These requests, plus the 1938 Agreement's prohibition of peacetime quantitative restrictions on all the more important U.S. exports raised the problems of Britain's post-war financial position and post-war trade policy. Accordingly, when the Board of Trade on 6 May asked for Treasury permission to continue negotiations on a more formal plane, the Treasury drew attention to the difficulties Britain's post-war exchange problems might raise. The Board reported however, that the American State Department already appeared to appreciate the possibility of an exchange resources reservation to any agreement, and the United States Government accordingly proposed to begin negotiations with the British and any Empire Governments that would be involved in any changes in Imperial Preference.

At this stage, Sir Frederick Phillips, after consulting Keynes, reported to London that it was far from clear that the State Department realised that Britain might have to continue both import licensing and payments agreements after the war. He also suggested that heavy indebtedness might also provide grounds for discrimination between sources of supply.[3] On Bank of England advice, this caveat about indebtedness as the only cause for discrimination disappeared from the instructions to Phillips and J. A. Stirling[4] of the Board of Trade, but the possibility of such discrimination remained, as later telegrams made clear.

In the course of June, Keynes continued to take an interest in the problem and Stirling thought it would be useful if Keynes met Mr H. Hawkins,[5] to set out the problem of Britain's post-war position. Keynes met Hawkins on 25 June and stated the probability of post-war discrimination so forcefully that he effectively deadlocked the negotiations. This led to a major row between Keynes and Stirling, which had its reverberations in both London and Washington.

Keynes's attitude at the time is best reflected in a draft telegram which never got to London because Stirling and Phillips, who did not remember looking closely at the draft, managed to block it while Keynes was away from Washington over the weekend. However, Keynes's views as to the shape of the post-war world were transmitted to London by Lord Halifax on 4 July. On 16 July the Chancellor, the President of the Board of Trade and the Foreign Secretary cabled Washington to the effect that post-war restrictions would have to be applied in a discriminating way and that they would continue for some time. This telegram effectively ended the exploratory talks.

Draft Telegram to Treasury

The following for Treasury from Keynes.

You will have seen Stirling's three telegrams to the Board of Trade. The position can be summed up as follows:

1. Under the existing trade agreement we are obliged to abandon the system of import licences on the termination of 'hostilities or war'. Government monopoly purchasing bodies

---

[3] As far as can be ascertained Keynes strengthened Phillips' drafting at this point.

[4] John Ashwell Stirling (1891–1965); Department of Overseas Trade, 1917–27; Export Credits Guarantee Department, 1927–35; Commercial Relations and Export Department, Board of Trade, 1935; Assistant Secretary, Board of Trade, 1935–51.

[5] Harry C. Hawkins, Chief, Division of Commercial Treaties and Agreements, U.S. Department of State until 1944; Director, Office of Economic Affairs, 1944; Counsellor to the Embassy on Economic Affairs, London, 1944–5.

such as Ministry of Food [will also be] prohibited by the agreement [as soon as the war is over] from preferring a particular country for purchasing because we have means of payment there.

A new trade agreement is under discussion in which it is proposed by the State Department that similar terms should remain in force subject only to exceptions, the need for which is 'clearly demonstrated to the satisfaction of both parties', the party assenting to receive compensation. Thus we are asked to agree that our future arrangements for the control of imports and exchange throughout the world shall be subject to the approval of the State Department here.

2. The above is not merely a matter of words and form. The State Department representative expressed himself as deeply shocked at our substantial aim. He rejects the idea that our choice of where we buy should be influenced by whether we possess means of payment in that place. He maintains that goods should be sold for money and that a system by which in effect goods are traded for goods is uncivilised, a view more easily sustained by those who have all the money than by others. He does not yet appreciate our vital need to establish a new equilibrium after the war considerably different from the old by greatly expanding our exports.

3. The words of the present trade agreement relate to import licences and do not clearly prohibit exchange controls, though the non-existence of the latter is presumed in the preamble. It is not so clear that the same would apply to the proposed new agreement, but it is possible that the same distinction might be observed there also. This is because the State Department think in nineteenth century terms and are not so anxious to protect themselves against methods which did not exist at earlier dates. The difficulty of having any clear idea of the arrangements which will govern the post-war world, particularly during the transitional period, is a great obstacle. For example any commitments we enter into should

take account of the system of exchange and import controls prevailing in South America and in Europe. Yet it is thought reasonable to ask us to enter into positive commitments at a time when we are in the dark about this. Indeed it is because we ourselves can have no clear idea of what our future arrangements can be that any clear-cut commitments will be unsafe. We cannot tell the State Department what our post-war arrangements are going to be because we do not know. Yet that we should enter now into an agreement which presumes the abolition of all controls whatever immediately after the war is a lunatic proposition.

4. I suggest therefore that the only reasonable course is to negotiate a new agreement with provisos such as those proposed by Stirling in the second paragraph of his first telegram with the addition that the matter should be re-discussed between the parties within, say, two years after the termination of hostilities, so that the agreement is avowedly limited to the transitional period, with an understanding that it will be reconsidered when the arrangements of the post-war world are better known to both of us. Transitional arrangements of this kind surely cannot be avoided whether we stick to the old agreement or aim at a new one.

5. I share Stirling's hopes that the negotiation of a new agreement may be possible since it offers important advantages to both parties which it may be easier to obtain in present circumstances than hereafter. But time will be wasted unless you decide at once either to capitulate on the lines of paragraph 3 of Stirling's first telegram, which is surely unthinkable, or make it clear that provisions are essential like those in Stirling's second paragraph supplemented if necessary by a further clause that these are only accepted as governing a limited, transitional period and can be re-opened thereafter. It is so obvious that we shall require special provisions during the transitional period whatever our ultimate arrangements may be, that I cannot believe the State Department officials, who are reasonable and friendly, would

refuse it in the long run if only they could be brought to understand what it is all about. There is much to be hoped from a full and frank discussion in which, so far from glossing over our need for future liberty of action to evolve a sound system, we emphasise it. From what Mr Morgenthau has said to me I think U.S. Treasury is likely to sympathise with the view that it is impossible to legislate now for the post-war world.

6. Phillips agrees with above. He suggests that we might tell Mr Hull that we court enquiry into the facts of our post-war position so far as they can now be forecast and that if he would like any recognised U.S. economic authority to look into it we should be happy to co-operate. I like this suggestion which could not be efficiently carried out except in London. Full enquiry might persuade State Department that precipitate action would profoundly prejudice our post-war hopes of economic health and that it is vital for us to retain full liberty of action at least during transitional period. Perhaps Chancellor of Exchequer will communicate this to President of Board of Trade.

However, Keynes's lend lease negotiations seemed to be proceeding smoothly.

To H. MORGENTHAU, *2 July 1941*

Dear Mr Secretary,

I should like to confirm what I said to you at luncheon the other day, namely that the arrangements which are now being worked out at the Treasury should, it seems to me, satisfy the best hopes of the Chancellor of the Exchequer as I explained these to you in earlier correspondence.

Everything depends, of course, on what you called the McCoy[6] (I hope I have got that right!) going through;—that is to say, certain tanks and aeroplane engines contracted for

---

[6] Keynes had picked up the phrase from Mr Morgenthau on 1 July (*Morgenthau Diaries*, volume 416, p. 178). The phrase caused some confusion in London.

by us being taken over by your War Department and certain shipping contracts replaced by deferred contracts for a later date. (Though I understood from Mr Cox that the shipping proposition would have to be postponed for the time being until the Maritime Commission had further appropriations.)

If we get the relief provisionally forecast under these headings as well as the various miscellaneous sources of relief which have been already arranged, this, in conjunction with the good work you are doing for us at the committee, should more than fulfil our best hopes and should leave us endowed with adequate reserve balances during the fairly long interim period before they will begin to be replenished out of our own currently accruing resources.

I am hesitating to telegraph definitely to the Chancellor of the Exchequer so long as the big items under discussion by Mr Cox are a little bit in the air. But, as soon as these seem reasonably definite, I shall hasten to advise him how very generously his wishes have been met. We have already sent him some general indications of the ways in which you are helping Phillips and myself to a satisfactory conclusion.

I feel that the work of the new committee will be cumulatively useful in easing our dollar position. Apart from important general decisions such as the lease-lending of civilian supplies to the Dominions, I am sure that many miscellaneous items, small and not so small, hard to specify in advance, will be caught up and dealt with by the new method, which would otherwise have gradually accumulated against us through the piling up of various unforeseen commitments with but little to offset against them. Thank you very much for initiating so helpful a procedure.

Yours sincerely,

J. M. KEYNES

To SIR HORACE WILSON, *2 July 1941*

My dear Wilson,

Thanks for your note brought by Bewley.[7] I certainly didn't expect to find myself still in Washington in July! The weather is horrible—nearly 100 this afternoon (the thermometer was still over 90 at half past nine yesterday evening) and very humid. However one lives mostly in air-conditioned rooms and I am quite well—merely uncomfortable. Phillips, who is in very good form, doesn't seem to mind a bit!

As I wrote to the Chancellor, if all goes according to plan, we shall have got more than we asked for. Morgenthau is full of smiles and helpfulness. If there is a hitch, which is still possible, it will not be the fault either of Morgenthau and the Treasury officials or of Hopkins and his lease lend boys. They are stretching their ingenuity and using up their time in trying to find ways to replenish our dollars. The trouble has been the statement to Congress by that blasted Director of the Budget who is insisting that his pledges should be literally observed. The U.S. Treasury people tell me privately that what he actually said was still worse and so hopelessly inconsistent with the facts that they had to cook his evidence in proof. He is a peculiar kind of animal, a real chimaera, half way between an official and a minister, and a sort of cross between the Controller and Auditor General, My Lords of the Treasury, and the head of the Prime Minister's personal staff. He and Morgie are often at cross purposes. M. tells me that the trouble all arose because he (Morgie) could not go to the Hill on that occasion, as would have been natural, because, having taken on himself the responsibility of allowing us to place orders during the interim, which was contrary to what the President had told Congress, and having given a personal pledge to Phillips that he would find the

---

[7] Bewley had come out to Washington from London to replace Sir Frederick Phillips who was to return to the Treasury for re-acclimatisation.

means of paying for our post Jan. 1 commitments, which he had no authority to do, he dared not run the risk of cross-examination. And the Director of the Budget took his place. So you will see how much we owe M. in spite of all the insults we have heaped on him (but he was very naughty about Viscose of which I have long been intending to send Catto an inside history). As I was given to understand that he would like to have a letter of interim gratitude to balance my previous persistent grumbles, I have to-day sent him something, of which I enclose a copy.

I am about to draw up a revised balance-sheet showing what our position is likely to be on the most optimistic hypotheses (Phillips would say on hypotheses much too optimistic, since experience shows that there are always all kinds of deductions and abatements to make). The revised statement should be read in this light, namely, that, if even the least thing goes wrong, an appropriate reduction must be made.

The turning point seems to have come after I sent Hopkins a grumble, of which I think I sent you a copy.[8] I had been told that it would be he and not Morgenthau who would be concerned with the rest of my business. On getting this Hopkins saw that it was going to be a frightful nuisance from his point of view and would involve him in just those sort of financial details which he loathes and always tries to avoid. So he felt moved to pass the buck back to Morgenthau, telling him that the whole job of satisfying us should be his business hereafter and that he, Hopkins, would endorse whatever was arranged. Morgenthau, on his side, jumped at this because it brought him back again into the war picture,

---

[8] This letter appears above, pp. 130–3.
Neither Hopkins nor Morgenthau reacted at all well to Keynes's letter as their telephone conversation indicated. It appears that Mr Bell, Dr White and Professor J. Viner convinced Mr Morgenthau that he should take it seriously. *Morgenthau Diaries*, Vol. 410, pp. 106–11, 119–29.
Jacob Viner (1892–1970), economist; University of Chicago, 1916–46, Princeton, 1946–60; Emeritus Professor, Princeton, 1960–70; Special Assistant to Secretary of U.S. Treasury, 1934–9; Consultant to Department of State, 1943–52.

from which he would have been largely excluded if Hopkins had stood on his full rights of lease lend authority. So M., having been given full authority for the whole issue, then sat down with enthusiasm to see what could be done, putting real steam behind it and engaging all his officials to do their best. So, for once, the personal issue was settled in the most satisfactory way and to our great benefit. Phillips and I have been working completely together over all this and there is nothing left to settle which he cannot do as well as or better than I. I should like to see what Morgie calls the McCoy (see the enclosed letter) finally determined, but, apart from that, there is nothing to keep me here on this particular score.

But there remains the question of 'consideration'. There we are completely at a standstill since the letter I wrote to the Chancellor for delivery through Peacock. I shall probably be writing another short letter in a day or so. But the President, whose health is not particularly satisfactory, has now been away from Washington for more than a week, so that it has been impossible for me to have the projected interview. When I have had that and I have reported, you will have to make up your mind what you want me to do. It might be, I think, that I would have a better chance of carrying through that particular negotiation than most people, if it is decided to bring it to a tangible conclusion at this moment. But, unless it looks practicable to get a genuine move on fairly quickly, it may be better to put the whole thing off at least for a time and let me come back immediately. I hope to be in a position to send some news by cable early next week, which should reach you before this letter.

The most tiresome thing which has happened lately is the re-opening of all the conditions of the Jesse Jones loan, which Peacock thought he had satisfactorily settled. When Peacock was handling it all was going exceedingly well, and everyone supposed that the thing was through. Indeed, I do not suppose that Peacock would have returned home unless Jesse

Jones had given him the impression that all points of principle were finally settled. But since Gifford took over everything conceivable has gone wrong. Phillips and I have had nothing whatever to do with it except to try to stiffen Gifford and give him a little advice, which he has been very reluctant to receive. Indeed, he has not spent a single night in Washington; —dashes here by plane for an hour or two and slips back again without even reporting to us what he has been doing. I cannot believe that this has been the best way of going to work. It is hopeless to try to tackle Jesse Jones, who, though extremely tough, is quite human, through the agency of his solicitor in New York, through whom most of the negotiations seems to have gone on. However, you will have had the benefit of the advice of Peacock. My own view is that the best thing you can do is to stand firm and give Gifford very little discretion to yield on any point where Peacock is satisfied that he had a gentleman's understanding. Gifford is so frightfully defeatist (of which his whole attitude to the Viscose negotiation was a signal example) and always sets out from the starting point that we have got to agree with a good grace practically to whatever the Americans suggest.

Yours sincerely,

J. M. KEYNES

Accompanied by the Ambassador, Keynes saw President Roosevelt on 7 July. The President did not want to go into the details of a 'consideration' agreement at that stage, as he thought that any general agreement would not become public until early 1942. However, as a result of the President's instructions, Keynes's talks with Mr Acheson now took a more serious turn, despite the restriction that Keynes should only concern himself with wartime rather than post-war matters.

To SIR KINGSLEY WOOD, *13 July 1941*

Dear Chancellor,

May I add a personal note to the enclosed report on my negotiations, which is intended to be the final one. Some time is likely to elapse before all the detailed arrangements covered by the enclosed are fully worked out in practice. But it is no part of my job to stop here for that. Phillips has played a major part in reaching the solution I report, and we have worked throughout in the closest harmony. He has been in charge of the particularly difficult task of getting direct relief from the old commitments and deserves to be very much congratulated that, at long last, this looks like reaching an unexpectedly favourable solution.

I have also carried the questions of American participation in the financing of surpluses and post-war Anglo-American co-operation in relief and reconstruction as far as is appropriate for me to take them. Dean Acheson's reply is being dispatched to Leith-Ross, and it will be for him to take the next step.

Thus, nothing remains except the negotiations about 'consideration'. I do not think that these need take long once we can get down to business. Here I am held back by the long interval between each move. It takes fully a week to get a reply to a cable; indeed that is only possible if no time at all has been lost at the other end. When Acheson and I have got a stage forward there is Mr Hull to be dealt with, whose attention is not easily gained, since he is in poor health and has, in fact, been away from Washington for several weeks with papers going down to him in the country. And, finally, there is the President, whom one cannot expect to attend to one except at his own leisure. I am praying that, in spite of this, not too much time will elapse, since we are all dreadfully homesick to return. But it is hard to say just how long it will take.

As you know, I saw the President again last Monday in connection with 'consideration'. He is not a sick man, but he is not exactly a fit one. I thought he was fundamentally weak and tired and using his courage and willpower to keep going and to deal with his task. Whilst I have been in Washington he has had three attacks of low fever with other minor symptoms. I am told by those round him that he is still suffering from more or less chronic sinus trouble which, as you know, is most painful. When the Ambassador and I saw him a few days ago he was complaining bitterly about the heat, and was clearly suffering from the humidity and discomfort of it. Indeed Washington at this time of year is not fit for human habitation. The White House as a whole is not air-conditioned since (so the Private Secretary told me) Congress would consider the necessary expenditure as too luxurious for the head of the State, though most hotels and cinemas are so treated. The President has one of those noisier *ad hoc* air-conditioning appliances in his own rooms, but much dislikes them and refuses to turn them on. Knowing the symptoms through having suffered so long from something of the same sort myself, I am perfectly convinced that he has a minor chronic streptococcal infection and that his vigour will be liable to deteriorate slowly, with eventual concentration of the poison in some weak spot, unless something is done about it. He is looked after by an old Navy doctor, and I gather that no bacteriological test has ever been made. I have begged several of those round him to try and see that the necessary steps are taken, at any rate to test what is the matter with him, but have naturally felt rather shy of saying much about this.

On top of that, Mr Hull has been away from Washington in poor health since 9 June, and is expected to be away at least another fortnight. The papers go to him, and he talks on the telephone, but no-one knows when his attention to a matter has really been gained, and I think that it is only on the major issues that he is concentrating his mind. Hopkins is pretty well for him and has not been out of action for some time, but he, of course, is not fit and cannot be regarded as having normal executive vigour. Stimson[9] is very old. Knox,[10] on the other hand, seems very vigorous indeed. So you will see that, as Lippmann expresses it, there is a certain atmosphere of invalidism very disadvantageous for waging a war. The will and the intention and the sentiment and the good heart are all that we could wish. But the executive drive and the organs of decision are defective.

That is particularly the case on the economic front. This country is running into economic perplexities of the first order of difficulty. There is no apparatus of executive decision having any adequate authority short of the President himself. Yet the President ought to be left free to concentrate on issues of strategy, diplomacy and politics without having to consider the pressing and difficult details of economic policy, which he does not really care for any more than our own Prime Minister does.

Yours sincerely,

J. M. KEYNES

P.S. As I am wanting to write to Mr Governor to-day, having not sent him notes hitherto, I am venturing to let him have direct a copy of the two enclosures to this letter.

To SIR KINGSLEY WOOD, *14 July 1941*

I attach a revised forecast of what our gold and dollar reserves are likely to be in the light of the latest arrangements to which Mr Morgenthau has agreed. This, I hope, will be my final report on the subject before I come home.

The final upshot is, as you will see, a more liberal provision

---

[9] Henry Lewis Stimson (1867–1950); Secretary of State, 1929–33; Secretary of War, 1940–5.
[10] William Franklin Knox (1874–1944); Secretary of the Navy, 1940–4.

than that for which we hoped when I left London. The broad
result can be accepted as reliable, but the estimates in detail
and particularly the estimates as at particular dates are open
to a wide margin of error. In particular, I may have under-
estimated the time lags in making effective the new arrangements for bringing supplies to the Dominions and also
certain other items under lease lend procedure. We can feel
some confidence that in the long run the position should not
be worse than what I have set out in the enclosed paper. But
for this calendar year it may prove that I have been too
optimistic. If, however, we set off the next six months against
the six months after that, the reliefs now arranged look like
being sufficient to cover the whole of the current items which
we have to meet out of free dollars, thus leaving us with a
net annual balance of $m500 ($m42 per month) in our favour,
out of which to meet the liability for old commitments.

This means that the request you instructed me to make
would have been met even if we obtained no further relief
from the old commitments beyond the $m300 promised to
Phillips. In fact we now expect something better than this. We
are being relieved of old commitments in a variety of ways,
with the details of which I need not trouble you. The negotiations have been intricate, involving several Government
Departments, and the final outcome is still not yet accurately
calculable. We have, however, good reason to hope that old
commitments having a gross face value of something like
$m600 will be taken off us sooner or later. This will be subject
to a substantial deduction in respect of the portion of the
contracts delivered before the transfer is complete and of
various items which will turn out in practice to be irrecover-
able. Phillips agrees, however, in the light of his experience,
that, if the full nominal amount is as much as $m600, the
actual relief to us should reach $m450 as the most likely
estimate, with $m500 as a bare possibility and $m400 as a safe
minimum.

The amount of the old commitments is a figure subject to constant revision for various reasons. It is sufficiently accurate to put the sum outstanding on 1 July at $m1,170. If we deduct from this a relief of $m450 as above in respect of contracts taken over and receipts of $m425 from the Jesse Jones loan, we are left with no more than $m300 to meet out of current income, spread over a period of more than a year. Since our estimated surplus income in gold and dollars available to meet this is at the rate of $m500 a year, we can hope to add $m450 to our reserves in the course of the next eighteen months. The major part of this addition should accrue to us in actual gold, our dollar receipts and balances being about enough to meet our dollar outgoings without further replenishment from newly accruing gold.

As we start out on 1 July of this year with a balance of about $m180, this raises the aggregate reserves to $m630 without making allowance for further windfalls such as sales of wool and additional South African gold.

Mr Morgenthau is not very good at remembering exact figures or at appreciating the precise relationship of the figures realised at some future date to the arrangements he has agreed to make. But the responsible statisticians of the U.S. Treasury, particularly Dr Harry White, definitely accept a free balance of $m600 as a proper objective for us to aim at. Before I leave, I shall, in thanking Mr Morgenthau, put it on record in writing that we expect the arrangements, which he has made for us, to lead to our having a free balance of at least $m600 in due course. By the time we have finished paying for the old commitments, we shall have a very new situation one way or the other, but I do not at present see much reason to fear a diminished liberality under lease lend directly intended to sap our balances. On the other hand, it will be quite natural that, if eighteen months hence no unforeseen contingencies have eaten into our reserves, so that they reach the full anticipated figure, the special and peculiar steps which are now being taken in various directions to relieve us will not longer be to easy to sustain. Indeed, it is reasonable that after our balances have been substantially restored exceptional ways of relieving us can no longer be expected; and we may be required to look after for ourselves an increasing proportion of troublesome miscellaneous items.

14.7.41   [copy initialled] J. M. K.

REVISED FORECAST OF BRITISH GOLD AND DOLLAR RESERVES

The following is an attempt to revise the estimates of our prospective cash reserves on the basis of the more optimistic assumptions which there is now good reason to make, though not yet quite conclusive.

1. My original request to Mr Morgenthau was for a margin from which annual payments amounting to $m325 could be made by us outside lend lease. Subsequently the estimate of our requirements was reduced to $m275, made up of the hard core of administratively difficult items $m150 and a further margin of $m125 for other items excluded from lease lend for one reason or another.

These estimates need some further revision in the light of the developing situation. In view of a telegram lately received from London, the hard core items can be reduced to $m100, and it is possible that ways will be found in due course of bringing the total below this figure. As regards the further margin of $m125 it now seems that the items excluded from lease lend for political reasons will be much smaller than we previously anticipated. On the other hand, the reserve required for various other items falling outside lease lend will be much more than we have estimated hitherto. There are first of all the cases where payments have to be made out of free dollars for reasons of urgency and to escape the delays of the lease lend procedure, which will be large in number but perhaps not large in amount. There is not yet enough experience to estimate the annual aggregate of these with any accuracy. The second, much greater, item is for various payments to personnel which, it is ruled, are expressly excluded by law from the lease lend procedure except where some special excuse can be found. Some of these items are very large. Payments under the air training scheme may be of the order of $m20 per annum; those in respect of the civilian technical corps, if it reaches its full figure of 30,000, might amount to $m1½ non-recurrent and $m23 recurrent. As time goes on and we receive more assistance from American personnel, there may be large additions to these items. On the other hand, the cost of ferrying aircraft, which might be as much as $m14, it is now thought can be lease-lent. The U.S. Treasury Committee is being very helpful in devising expedients to reduce these burdens on free dollars and it is possible that a way may be found of providing even for the cost of the civilian technical corps mentioned above. Thirdly there are tax payments in respect of old commitments which are being demanded of us by States, estimated at $m5–20 according to the amount which the U.S. Treasury, who are doing their best for us, can get us off. Thus, whilst the reserve of $m125 may prove sufficient, it would not be safe as yet to cut this figure by any significant amount. If we keep it at $m125, the total off-sets necessary will be about $m225 per annum altogether.

On present prospects the goods lease-lent for transfer to the Dominions etc. should reach $m250 per annum at least when the new scheme is in full operation and might exceed this figure if sufficient goods for export are available under priority. Equally, if the exports are not available under priority, the financial burden will be reduced just as much as if they were available and were then lease-lent. There is likely to be a time-lag of some six months before the new scheme is fully operative. On the other hand, there will also be a time-lag in the development of some of the items which this sum is needed to off-set.

There remains in addition the possibility of bringing certain payments to third countries under lease lend. Sugar and molasses from Cuba can very probably be dealt with. Sir Arthur Salter hopes to find a way of dealing with the Swedish, as well as the Norwegian, ships which will relieve us of expenditure under that head without diminishing the effective control of the Ministry of War Transport over these ships.

One way and another, therefore, we can regard the inevitable expenditure out of free dollars as being wholly or mainly off-set by the new items brought under lease lend, subject to a possible deficit during the interim period before the new arrangements are fully operative, off-set by a surplus at a later date. That is to say, the payments out of free dollars will be cared for *apart from any relief in respect of old commitments.* If, therefore, the relief in respect of old commitments exceeds $m300, the total relief we shall have obtained will be that much better than the request made by the Chancellor of the Exchequer which I passed on to Mr Morgenthau.

2. It is now probable, though not yet quite definite, that the amount of old commitments taken over on one heading or another will amount eventually to $m400 to $m500 instead of $m300, the minimum previously assumed. This is to be regarded as a net figure, after adding the additions to the old commitments due to modifications in old contracts which cannot be lease-lent and subtracting sundry old commitments which will have evaporated for one reason or another.

3. The Jesse Jones loan will be for $m425 instead of $m400.

4. There is a fair reason to hope that wool stocks in U.S.A. and Australia, valued at $m70, will be taken over by the United States Government. There may also be some sales of lead.

If allowance is made also for the additional South African gold expected in September, I calculate that, after the Jesse Jones money has been received, our free reserves of gold and dollars, excluding all Dutch and Belgian gold, should not fall below $m500 and should stand at the desired figure of round about $m600 at all dates except at the low point forecast for the first half of 1942. After the end of 1942 the reserve should rise steadily, the old commitments having been substantially paid off, and might reach $m1,000 within the year after that.

On the following assumptions:

(1) that we ignore the proceeds of sales of wool and lead and of the additional gold from S. Africa;

(2) that $m200 is received from the Jesse Jones loan in August and $m225 in September and no further receipts from marketable investments;

(3) that the old commitments (after allowing for a relief of $m450) mature as follows (monthly averages): July–December 1941, $m60; January–June 1942, $m50; July–December 1942, $m10;

(4) a favourable balance for the whole of the sterling area of $m42 a month, inclusive of gold and exclusive of the old commitments, the state of our reserves, excluding Belgian and Dutch gold, but including scattered gold and minimum working balances, will be

July 1, 1941	180	Jan. 1, 1942	497	July 1, 1942	479
Aug. 1	162	Feb. 1	489	Aug. 1	481
Sept. 1	344	Mar. 1	481	Sept. 1	513
Oct. 1	551	Apr. 1	473	Oct. 1	545
Nov. 1	523	May 1	465	Nov. 1	577
Dec. 1	505	June 1	457	Dec. 1	609

11 July 1941   J. M. K.

To SIR KINGSLEY WOOD, *15 July 1941*

Dear Chancellor of the Exchequer,

I received last night the instructions from the Prime Minister and yourself on 'consideration'. This was lucky, because I just had an opportunity to discuss them with the Ambassador and get his instructions before he left Washington for a ten days' trip in the West. Later in the morning I saw Acheson and have not thought it worth while to send a telegraphic report of what passed, since there is nothing further for you to tell me until I hear from him again. But I may as well put it on record in this letter.

I handed him a draft on the lines of my instructions and added to this a brief preamble, thus turning it into an aide memoire. This was because so jejune an agreement seemed to be better so described and also because the President had said that he thought the form of the document should perhaps be an aide memoire rather than a formal agreement. In the course of the discussion I slightly amended the terms of III as shown in ink on the enclosed copy, since otherwise this clause seemed to amount on our side to literally nothing.

Acheson's comment was that this document agreed to excuse us from any liability to deliver goods or assets whilst we, on our side, entered into no undertaking of any sort of description. This is undoubtedly true, but I was able to point out that the comparative lack of content seemed in line with the President's wishes as he conveyed them to the Ambassador, and that the Prime Minister was very strongly of the same opinion and pleased that the President was of the same mind as himself as to the undesirability of entering into details at this stage.

Nevertheless, it is obvious that Acheson thought it exceedingly unlikely that anything so one-sided would be agreed to and that any such suggestion would meet with considerable resistance from the State Department. I am afraid, as I indicated in my previous telegrams, that we shall not get the economic clause excusing us from the delivery of goods and assets unless we do at least something to meet them in other directions.

After pointing out that the document, which I had prepared under instructions, following closely what we took to be the President's intention, I added that if, on further reflection, the President had something he wanted to add, I would, of course, immediately submit it to London. I pointed out that I was handing in this document in the hope of helping matters on a stage, but in truth it was for them to offer us a draft rather than the other way round.

Acheson agreed with this. Indeed, he has a bad conscience, though it is none of his fault, that he has not handed me a draft hitherto. He promised that he and Sumner Welles would immediately work on the subject and themselves have a full discussion with the President with a view to letting me know at an early date whether the President agrees that something on the lines I have given them is in accordance with his intention or whether he has other ideas.

I told Acheson that I was very anxious to leave Washington by a plane due to depart on 23 July, and he promised to do his best to bring things to a head before that date. Failing that, I propose to come by a plane on 1 August, making that definitely my last date. I am quite sure that, if nothing definite is reached by then, it is much better I should come back and report. Indeed, I pointed out to Acheson that the Ambassador would be in London during August, so that, if points arose which required considerable further discussion, probably the best plan would be that I should take new proposals back to London rather than attempt to settle them on the spot.

Yours sincerely,

J. M. KEYNES

AIDE MEMOIRE

As reported by the President to Congress on 10 June 1941, discussions were entered upon between the Government of the United States and the British Government early in June with a view to an agreement to fix the terms and conditions under Section 3(*b*) of the Lease Lend Act, upon which the foreign governments receive the aid authorised by the Act.

After an interchange of views between the President and the British Prime Minister through the intermediary of the British Ambassador in Washington, it was agreed between them that it would be premature at the present time to give final definition to the terms and conditions which the President would deem satisfactory under Section 3(*b*) of the above Act, and that the President should reserve his position until in due course with the progress of events it was clearer to him what proposals it would be in the mutual interest of the two countries and of the world for him to make; but that it would be right and proper to declare and agree forthwith certain main purposes and intentions of the final agreement to be reached at a later date.

I

(1) A declaration of common purpose.

(2) A declaration by the President that the carrying out of this common purpose is the main object of the aid accorded under the Lease Lend Act and that the benefits thereby obtained are, in his judgment, the signal advantage secured by the United States under Section 3(*b*) of the Act.

(3) In respect of the balance of aid accorded under the Lease Lend Act not thus compensated no cash account shall be set up and no delivery of goods or assets shall be asked which would interfere with the normal economic relations between the United States of America and the British Commonwealth after the war or with the capacity of the British Commonwealth to purchase American goods and services.

II

The British Government agree to return at the end of the war so far as practicable all goods received under the Lease Lend Act which have not been destroyed or consumed in any case in which the President calls for their return.

III

The British Government will be happy to discuss with the United States Government in due course further measures of cooperation over a wider sphere.

Keynes's suggested amendment of III would have made it read as follows:

The British Government agree to discuss with the United States Government in due course terms and conditions covering further measures of aid and of co-operation over a wider sphere.

To SIR KINGSLEY WOOD, *20 July 1941*

My dear Chancellor,

This letter is to report the events of the last week, or rather perhaps an absence of events in the last week, in continuation of my last letter. Dean Acheson carried out his promise to prepare a memorandum on 'consideration', which he discussed and agreed with Sumner Welles. The two of them took this to the President and discussed it with him. He told them that he was not prepared to give them any decision there and then but wished to give further thought to it. It looked from this as though there might be a longish delay. Fortunately, however, the President gave his further instruction yesterday; and unfortunately, as I gather, this instruction was not in sufficiently clear terms to allow Sumner Welles and Dean Acheson to pass anything on to me. Acheson tells me that they are not sufficiently clear as to just what the President means and must get some further elucidation from him before they can get on.

There is just a chance that I may get this in time to catch next Wednesday's plane, particularly if next Wednesday's plane is delayed a day or two, which is not unlikely. But the State Department and the President are greatly engaged this week-end on the clarification of their ideas and the preparation of plans in relation to the Japanese situation. So Acheson doubts, very reasonably, whether he will be able to get the President's further attention to 'consideration' in time to discuss it with me on Tuesday. In reply to my question whether the document when it was communicated to me will be something which I shall just have to take back to London or whether he will wish to talk it over with me orally, he replied that he thought that an oral discussion would probably be helpful before I left and that he would like me to stop for this. In the face of this answer, I can hardly leave without the further discussion. So I am proposing, if necessary, to stay on for the plane a week later, though very greatly disappointed not to get off.

The final version of the Jesse Jones agreement is, in my judgment, by no means too bad. Phillips was extremely successful in restoring the atmosphere and in getting several quite useful concessions. He deserves, I think, considerable congratulations. The position he now has here in Administration circles is a very great asset to both Governments. Mr Daniel Bell, the Assistant Secretary of the Treasury, talked to me fully about this a day or two ago, as I shall be reporting when I get back.

There has, as you know, been a considerable to-do about American criticisms of our export policy on the ground that we are using lease lend to compete unfairly with American exporters. We have such a rock-bottom good case when we have a chance of explaining it that I feel some confidence that all this will die away in the end. The matter needs very careful and thorough handling. But I believe it would be a mistake to make any drastic change of policy unless it is quite clearly forced on us. I fancy Mr Harry Hopkins is raising the issue in London.[11] The whole thing is, of course, politics. It is a question of lasting out the next few weeks, when the new lease lend appropriations are being discussed, without surrendering anything important. In any action we take we have to remember the possibility of lease lend arrangements overrunning the end of the war, and it might prove very inconvenient to have entered into clear-cut undertakings about exports which would hamper us severely in the changing conditions. No legitimate complaint could possibly lie against what we are doing now. The State Department and the Department of Commerce, with whom we are in close touch, are perfectly satisfied with our conduct. The State Department entirely concurred in a plea which I made that it was for them to tell us what they wanted us to do, when we should, of course, do our utmost to find a satisfactory solution. Until they make specific requests to us it would be a pity to do anything merely in response to irresponsible clamour. The official statement which we gave the press on the occasion of my press conference was a conflation of a document which I had prepared and some paragraphs which the State Department themselves drafted for us.[12] It has been amusing to find that all the passages which have aroused criticism were taken verbatim out of the draft which was prepared for us by the State Department themselves, though we were not allowed to state that publicly! I [was] careful! But we hardly liked not to use the State Department's stuff when they had been so helpful as to give it to us, though we were not allowed to state this in public. So you will see what pitfalls there are in this country.

[11] Mr Hopkins was then in London discussing logistical and strategic questions with the British Government.

[12] Keynes had given a press conference on the matter on 14 July. He had also been interviewed by the *Washington Post* on the matter on 9 July.

All this is connected with an important issue, which may be coming to a head in the course of the next week. So far we have had no formal authority for the transfer of food or other raw materials and commercial goods out of Government hands into the hands of private distributors in U.K. Nor have we had any authorisation for transfers to Dominion Governments. The Ministry of Food and others concerned are carrying on solely on the basis of informal oral authority. We have thought it undesirable to drift any longer and have been trying to bring the matter to a head. It is all going to be rather difficult, particularly in the light of the political situation. They have not yet proposed any formula to us themselves. I append two documents, each giving a formula which Phillips and I think we might safely give. I certainly doubt if we shall get away with less. The problem will be to ward off something much worse. Nothing formal will be done about this without our seeking formal authority from London. But you may be glad to be warned that all this is going on, all these various matters being closely interconnected. As soon as an American official scents political difficulties abroad, he is apt to become extremely unreasonable.

I was very glad to get your personal letter of 5 July, which was delivered to me here on 14 July, though in fact the bomber mail ought, if properly organised, to be better than that. It presented rather an interesting contrast with the delays in cables. As it happened, you also sent me a telegram about my seeing the President on 'consideration' which reached the Embassy here the same day, namely 5 July, but was not delivered to me until after 5.30 p.m. on 18 July, four full days later than your letter. It lay in the Embassy undeciphered for eleven days, and it took two more days after that before I had a copy. Your other telegram to me of the 11th July was not delivered to me by the Embassy until the 19th July. It is worth noting that, in present conditions, telegrams which are not marked 'Important' or 'Immediate' are not delivered so quickly as letters. The disorganisation is said to be pretty severe. Last Sunday I was told that the Cipher Room at the Embassy was 30,000 groups in arrears.* The solution really lies in a drastic reorganisation and improvement of the bomber mail. If that were rapid and reliable and everyone knew just what the arrangements were, I believe that cabling, which is getting on to an altogether excessive scale, could be cut down by half.

Yours sincerely,

J. M. KEYNES

P.S. Since writing the above I have had a further discussion with the lease lend authorities about the formula for avoidance of private profit which they may require in the case of transfers to private hands. General Burns,[13] Mr Cox, Mr Phil Young[14] and Mr Brown,[15] Mr Harry Hopkins' four principal officials concerned with lease lend, were all present. They suggested that we should not at present take too seriously what Mr Morgenthau had pressed on Mr Purvis and the rest of us the other day. They said it related solely to articles obtained through the Treasury Procurement Division, which does not include food, tobacco or cotton. They thought that we should be well advised to await further developments and leave the Treasury to put forward a formula. Put bluntly, they implied that they doubted if Mr Morgenthau fully understood the bearing of what he was saying. They think, and in

---

* To-day (20 July) they are said to have reached 9 July telegrams, not marked important or immediate—i.e. 11 days in arrears and it will take them two more days to get the carbons distributed.

[13] Major General James H. Burns, Executive Officer, Office for Emergency Management, Division of Defense Aid Reports for Lend Lease programme, 1941; later involved in other aspects of Lend Lease administration.

[14] Philip Young (b. 1910); Assistant to Under-Secretary, U.S. Treasury, 1938–40; Assistant Executive Officer, Emergency Management, 1941; Lend Lease Administration, 1941–3; Foreign Economic Administration, 1943–4.

[15] Winthrop Gilman Brown (b. 1907); General Counsel Office, Lend Lease Administration, 1941; Executive Officer, Harrison Mission, U.S. Embassy, London, 1941–3; U.S. Lend Lease Mission to India, 1943.

this Mr Purvis agrees, that the best plan would be, not so much to offer a formula as to prepare a brief arguing that our present arrangements are perfectly satisfactory. Possibly this might await the return of Thompson and myself to London, when we can assist in its preparation with full knowledge of the difficulties to be met.

This is satisfactory, since the suggested formula attached to this letter is clearly difficult. I prepared it because, on the assumption that one had to take Mr Morgenthau seriously, we should certainly have got off with nothing less. I have, of course, not handed it in and it can be disregarded at present.

On the other hand, the formula about transfers to the Dominion Governments was approved by General Burns and his colleagues. A telegram will have arrived about this before you receive this letter.

Transfer of lease lent goods by British (or a Dominions) Government to fabricators or consumers shall be on such terms that no middleman or broker shall be permitted to take a profit and that no intermediary handling the supplies shall receive any return beyond the minimum reasonable remuneration for services actually performed.

Requests in detail received by the British Missions in Washington from the Dominions etc. will be strictly criticised from the standpoint of essential need in relation to the war effort before they are submitted with a view to requisition. It is proposed that the criterion adopted should be that the materials are either required directly in connection with the war or are so essential that the lack of them would impair the efficiency of the importing country's economy for the prosecution of the war effort as a whole; and that the formula allowing their transfer by the U.K. should require an undertaking by the British Government to this effect.

It was 28 July before Keynes received the American consideration proposals, which he took back to London with him the next day. He wrote
the following note on the meeting.

'CONSIDERATION'

MEMORANDUM OF CONVERSATION WITH

MR DEAN ACHESON OF THE

STATE DEPARTMENT, 28 JULY 1941

Mr Acheson handed me the attached document saying that
it represented what the President thought might form the
basis of satisfactory provisional arrangements, but it did not
represent a final commitment on the President's part. I
understand that it embodied ideas which had been approved
by the President in conversation, and that he had signified
concurrence with the wording of this paper read to him over
the telephone, but had not had it before him in writing.

I called attention to the following points:

1. I asked if Article II was intended to cover strategic
materials such as tin, and whether it should be interpreted as
introducing reciprocal lend lease arrangements. I expressed
the hope that it did not mean that any current supplies which
are now paid for in cash would cease to be so paid for. Mr
Acheson pointed out that the article contained no reference
to payment on lend lease terms but only to supplies. He
understood that it was not meant to disturb in any way the
existing de facto arrangements. But he said that if at some
future time the U.S. was having any difficulty in making
payment they might be free to raise the other interpretation.

2. I called attention under Article v to the fact that it might
be outside our power to make restoration where transfer had
taken place under Article III, for example to an ally. We
agreed that this could probably be dealt with, without
difficulty, by passing on the obligation to restore if called upon
to do so in all cases where transfer was approved.

3. Under Article VII I pointed out that the word 'discrimination' was ambiguous and might lead to difficulty. I asked whether our acceptance of this article would preclude a system of imperial preferences. Mr Acheson replied that he thought it would. I then asked whether it would preclude import and exchange control. Mr Acheson said it might be interpreted in that way. Some people might so interpret it, but he doubted whether anything so cut and dried or technical was in the President's mind. The President had in view the general approach to the economics of the post-war world, which should be one excluding special privileges or nationalistic or imperialistic arrangements. He was not thinking in technical terms. I was led to understand that the first part of this article in effect relieved us of any possibility of war debts. In return for so great a concession the President thought something definite should be required on our side. He reacted strongly against the entirely negative formula in response to such positive advantages which was contained in the draft I had been instructed to hand to him. He thought that we should not be left as free as air after the war to adopt any economic system we thought fit after he had foregone so much. Mr Acheson led me to think that suspicions had been a little bit aroused by our repeated rejections of, or at any rate our refusal to react favourably to, his proposals for Anglo-American conferences on this subject.

Obviously, there is a difficulty here, but I do not think it is an insuperable one. There may be doctrinaire persons who would like to force on us in this field something which we should dislike, but the President is not one of them. He *does* want us to commit ourselves to the spirit and purpose with which these post-war problems shall be approached, and to the approach being an agreed and joint one between the United States and Great Britain.

4. Articles III and IV are, I think, a mere recapitulation of terms of the Lend Lease Act.

18.7.41   J. M. K.

THE CONSIDERATION FOR LEND LEASE

Draft handed by MR DEAN ACHESON *to* MR KEYNES, *28 July 1941*

Whereas the United States of America and the United Kingdom of Great Britain and Northern Ireland declare that, with self-restraint and sober purpose, they are engaged in a co-operative undertaking, together with every other nation or people of like mind, to the end of laying the bases of a just and enduring world peace securing order under law to themselves and all nations;

And whereas the United States of America has extended and is continuing to extend to the United Kingdom aid in resisting aggression; defense of the United Kingdom against aggression is vital to the defense of the United States of America;

And whereas the United States of America has extended and is continuing to extend to the United Kingdom aid in resisting aggression;

And whereas the final determination of the terms and conditions upon which the United Kingdom receives such aid and of the benefits to be received by the United States of America in return therefor should be deferred until the extent of the defense aid is known and until the progress of events makes clearer the final terms and conditions and benefits which will be in the mutual interests of the United States of America and the United Kingdom and will promote the establishment and maintenance of world peace;

And whereas the Governments of the United States of America and the United Kingdom are mutually desirous of concluding now a preliminary agreement in regard to the providing of defense aid and in regard to certain considerations which shall be taken into account in determining such terms and conditions, and the making of such an agreement has been in all respects duly authorised, and all acts, conditions and formalities which it may have been necessary to perform, fulfil or execute prior to the making of such an agreement in conformity with the laws either of the United States of America or of the United Kingdom have been performed, fulfilled or executed as required;

The undersigned, being duly authorised for that purpose have agreed as follows:

ARTICLE I

The United States of America will continue to supply the United Kingdom with such defense articles, defense services, and defense information as the President shall authorize to be transferred or provided.

ARTICLE II

The United Kingdom will continue to contribute to the defense of the United States of America and the strengthening thereof and, (should circumstances arise in which the United States of America in its own defense or the defense of the Americas may require) articles, services, facilities or information, will provide such articles, services, facilities or information as it may be in a position to supply.

ARTICLE III

The Government of the United Kingdom will not without the consent of the President transfer title to, or possession of, any defense article or defense information transferred to it under the Act or permit the use thereof by anyone not an officer, employee or agent of the Government of the United Kingdom.

ARTICLE IV

If, as a result of the transfer to the Government of the United Kingdom of any defense article or defense information, it becomes necessary for that Government to take any action or make any payment in order fully to protect any of the rights of a citizen of the United States of America who has patent rights in and to any such defense article or information, the Government of the United Kingdom will take such action or make such payment when requested by the President.

ARTICLE V

The Government of the United Kingdom will return to the United States of America at the end of the present emergency, as determined by the President, such defense articles transferred under this Agreement as shall not have been destroyed, lost or consumed and as shall be determined by the President to be useful in the defense of the United States of America or of the Western Hemisphere or to be otherwise of use to the United States of America.

ARTICLE VI

In the final determination of the benefits to be provided to the United States of America full cognizance shall be taken of all property, services, information, facilities, or other benefits or considerations provided by the Government of the United Kingdom subsequent to 11 March 1941 and accepted or acknowledged by the President on behalf of the United States of America.

ARTICLE VII

The terms and conditions upon which the United Kingdom receives defense aid from the United States of America and the benefits to be received by the United States of America in return therefor, as finally determined, shall be such as not to burden commerce between the two countries but to promote mutually advantageous economic relations between them and the betterment of world-wide economic relations; they shall provide against discrimination in either the United States of America or the United Kingdom against the importation of any produce originating in the other country; and they shall provide for the formulation of measures for the achievement of these ends.

ARTICLE VIII

This Agreement shall continue in force from the date on which it is signed until a date agreed upon by the two Governments.

Signed and sealed at Washington in duplicate this day of   , 1941

ON BEHALF OF THE UNITED STATES OF AMERICA
(Title)
ON BEHALF OF THE UNITED KINGDOM OF GREAT
BRITAIN AND NORTHERN IRELAND
(Title)

Keynes's reactions to the word 'discrimination' in Article VII were much stronger than his memorandum suggests. In fact, he reacted so strongly that, in combination with his statements to Mr Hawkins in June, they became the object of considerable discussion in both American and British circles, both of which suggested that his comments had damaged Anglo-American relations.

Mr Acheson reported the relevant section of his comments as follows:

From a memorandum by D. ACHESON,[16] *28 July 1941*

Mr Keynes then raised Article VII, and stated that very serious considerations were raised by the provision that the final settlement should provide against discrimination in either the United Kingdom or the United States against the importation of any product originating in the other country. He asked whether this provision raised the question of imperial preferences and exchange and other trade controls in the post-war period. I said that

[16] From *Foreign Relations of the United States 1941*, vol. III, pp. 11–13.

it did raise these questions, but that the Article was drawn so as not to impose unilateral obligations, but rather to require the two countries in the final settlement to review all such questions and to work out to the best of their ability provisions which would obviate discriminatory and nationalistic practices and would lead instead to cooperative action in preventing such practices.

Mr Keynes then spoke for some time quite strongly about this provision. He said that he did not see how the British could make such a commitment in good faith; that it would require an imperial conference and that it saddled upon the future an ironclad formula from the nineteenth century. He said that it contemplated the impossible and hopeless task of returning to a gold standard where international trade was controlled by mechanical monetary devices and which had proved completely futile. He said that the only hope of the future was to maintain economies in balance without great excesses of either exports or imports, and that this could be only through exchange controls, which Article VII seemed to ban.

He went on to say that the language used in Article VII had a long history; that it permitted all sorts of cunningly devised tariffs, which were in fact discriminatory and prohibited sound economic monetary controls. Finally, he said that at the end of the war we will probably have a great excess of exports, the British would require a considerable excess of imports, and that the formula provided in Article VII was wholly impossible.

I replied to Mr Keynes that I thought he was taking an extreme and unjustified position and that it must be clear to him that no one would be less likely to impose a rigid and unworkable formula upon future developments than the President.

I said, and Mr Keynes agreed, that the proposal made by him had been wholly impossible, inasmuch as it provided merely that lease lend aid should be extended; that the British should return what was practicable for them to return; that no obligation should be created; and that they would be glad to talk about other matters. I pointed out to him that such a proposal could not possibly be defended in this country. To this he did not demur.

I then said that the purpose of Article VII was to provide a commitment which it should not be hard for the British to give that, after the emergency was over and after they had received vast aid from this country, they would not regard themselves as free to take any measures they chose directed against trade of this country but would work out in cooperation with this country measures which would eliminate discrimination and would provide for mutually fair and advantageous relations. I added that there was nothing narrow or technical about the provisions of Article VII, but that the British should realize that an effort of the magnitude of the lease lend program on our part imposed upon them the obligation of continuing good will in working out plans for the future and that they must consider our position as well as their own during that future period.

After some further discussion along these lines, Mr Keynes stated that he would take the proposal back to London and would discuss it there, and said that the British Government might propose some alteration in the language or might wish to have some further clarification on the Article.

He then said that there was considerable difference of opinion in London about future courses. There were some who believed that Great Britain should return to a free trade policy; there was a middle group, among whom he classified himself, who believed in the use of control mechanisms; and there was a third group who leant toward imperial policies. I said that I realized this and that we hoped that in his discussion of the Article he would not take a narrow or technical view regarding the language as a draftsman's product, to be carefully analyzed in order to see what might or might not be done under it, but would try to direct attention to its major purpose and attempt to get agreement in order that the major purpose should be achieved.

At the end of our talk he seemed more reconciled to the Article, but by no means wholly so. He insisted that he agreed with the broad purpose and believed that it could be worked out.

Keynes himself set out his views more fully in a letter from New York the next day, just before he left for home.

To D. ACHESON, *29 July 1941*

My dear Acheson,

I should not like it to be thought because of my cavilling at the word 'discrimination' that the excellence and magnanimity of the first part of that Article VII and of the document as a whole had gone overlooked.

I will do what I can to interpret the mind of the President and of the State Department to people at home and feel some confidence that a right conclusion will be reached.

The Ambassador comes on leave in about a fortnight and I dare say that the main discussions will await his return. So do not expect a reply in the very near future.

My so strong reaction against the word 'discrimination' is

177

the result of my feeling so passionately that our hands must be free to make something new and better of the post-war world; not that I want to discriminate in the old bad sense of that word—on the contrary, quite the opposite.

But the word calls up, and must call up—for that is what it means strictly interpreted—all the old lumber, most-favoured-nation clause and the rest which was a notorious failure and made such a hash of the old world. We know also that won't work. It is the clutch of the dead, or at least the moribund, hand. If it was accepted it would be cover behind which all the unconstructive and truly reactionary people of both our countries would shelter. We must be free to work out new and better arrangements which will win in substance and not in shadow what the President and you and others really want. As I know you won't dispute this, we shall be able to work something out. Meanwhile forgive my vehemence which has deep causes in my hopes for the future. This is my subject. I know, or partly know, what I want. I know, and clearly know, what I fear.

Sincerely yours,

J. M. KEYNES

Before leaving Washington, Keynes had also written to Mr Morgenthau.

To H. MORGENTHAU, *28 July 1941*

Dear Mr Secretary,

I am hoping to catch a clipper from New York early tomorrow morning and am very sorry that I shall not have an opportunity to take leave of you. There have been long delays in getting a draft from the State Department on the matter I mentioned to you. Your advice about this proved quite right! But at last to-day I have got something, and the best I can do with it is, I think, to take it back with me immediately for discussion at home.

I am very grateful for the good progress which has been

made and the essential help which you have given Phillips and myself in getting forward. The establishment of the committee[17] at the Treasury was a great idea and has made all the difference. I shall be able to report to the Chancellor of the Exchequer that he can now have full confidence in the adequacy of the financial arrangements which have been set up. Clearly it will take some time to work them out in detail, and it is not yet possible to estimate with any precision the total quantitative effect of the various measures under discussion. But we have now a sufficient margin to allow some of the reliefs (though not the biggest!) to fall through.

Our estimate is that the British dollar balances and the gold held by the Bank of England taken together should in due course attain the desired level of $m600, not too much to provide for contingencies but enough to afford relief from anxiety. We cannot estimate at what date this figure will be reached. Much depends on whether old commitment contracts result in punctual deliveries. Hitherto, as you know, we have been better off each month than we expected as a result of serious delays in delivery, and it is possible that the above figure might be attained temporarily in the latter part of this year. If so, it will fall away next spring when a low point is likely to be reached, recovering again by the autumn of 1942, after which our currently accruing income (the old commitments having been substantially cleared off) should exceed our outgoings apart from unforeseen developments.

These figures take account of our normal sources of income and our known commitments. They make no allowance for unforeseen outgoings on the one hand or for possible windfalls on the other hand. I believe that the Chancellor of the Exchequer hopes to receive late in the year a special receipt of gold of about $m120 from the South African Government out of which South African Government debt in London will

[17] The committee of American and British officials met regularly at the U.S. Treasury to discuss outstanding lend lease problems as they arose. Keynes had taken a regular part in the meetings while in Washington.

be redeemed, the stock being requisitioned from the British holders and handed to the South African Government for cancellation.

Thank you for your kindness and hospitality to my wife and myself. May we be remembered to your wife? We have stayed in Washington much longer than we expected. But it has been a valuable and interesting, and educative experience. I shall be able to give our Treasury in Whitehall a much truer picture of what Washington is really like;—and, I should like to add, the full story of what you did for us during the critical months at the beginning of this year without which irreparable delays might have been suffered by this year's war effort.

Yours sincerely,

J. M. KEYNES

Chapter 5

WASHINGTON, 1941: DISCUSSIONS WITH ECONOMISTS

In the gaps between his meetings on official business, during his Washington visit Keynes circulated widely in Washington. Of particular interest were his contacts with American economists, especially staff members of the Office of Price Administration and Civilian Supply. Although his views on hog price trends following a meeting of officials on 9 July and some of his private discussions are of only limited interest, some of his exchanges and comments on the subject of the American mobilisation of resources are of more general interest.

Keynes's first comment followed a meeting at the home of Dr Laughlin Currie on 22 May. No other record of it survives in the Keynes papers.

From a letter to A. P. LERNER,[1] *23 May 1941*

I have not yet dogmatised on the question of whether or not there is immediate danger of inflation in the U.S.A. I said that I thought it was a tougher problem here than in the United Kingdom and needed careful attention. As to what danger there is I am trying to collect evidence and find it pretty confusing. Last night I was present at a gathering of youngish economists in the house of Laughlin Currie, where we discussed this. They were taking the line that the risks were small, unemployment would continue, in spite of the defence programme, on a large scale, and that even the present spending programme would not produce anything like full employment owing to its being so much concentrated in certain particular directions. Quantitatively I was not entirely convinced by what they were saying, but they did open out to me possibilities in this country which I had not been appreciating.

[1] Abba Lerner (b. 1903); economist; Assistant Lecturer, London School of Economics, 1935–7; later positions at various American Universities.

Of course, there is the usual bother of what one means by inflation. What I am interested in in the present context is whether the equilibrium between savings and investment can be kept so to speak spontaneously without either the depletion of stocks or the rise of prices being called in to balance the position. My young friends last night were relying on a very high level of spontaneous saving as a result of the obstacles in the way of spending money on durable consumers' goods which they expect to be enforced before spending has reached its peak. I wish you had been there last night. I should have been much helped to have had your opinion. I have not been following American statistics with any closeness lately and, therefore, could only judge the plausibility of what I was being told on general principles.

On 10 June, he attended a meeting with a group of economists at the National Press Club. A note on the occasion was taken by Walter Salant.[2]

Mr Gilbert[3]
Don D. Humphrey[4] and Walter S. Salant
Dinner meeting of OPACS officials
  with J. Maynard Keynes
On Tuesday evening, 10 June, several OPACS officials had a dinner meeting with J. M. Keynes at the National Press Club. Those present were, besides Keynes, Leon Henderson, Sumner Pike, Lubin, Ken Galbraith, Joseph Weiner, Taylor Ostrander, David Ginsburg, Raymond Goldsmith, Calvin Hoover, J. M. Clark, John Cassels, and ourselves.
  Mr Keynes began the discussion by outlining the stages of rising prices as follows:

[2] Walter Salant (b. 1911); economist; research in Cambridge 1934; researcher, U.S.A. statistics, Treasury Department, 1934–6; Assistant Professor, Harvard, 1938; member, senior staff, Industrial Economic Division, Office of Secretary, Department of Commerce, 1939–40; Head Economist, Research Division, Office of Price Administration, 1940–5; Economic Adviser to Economic Stabilisation Director, 1945–6; Economist, Council of Economic Advisers, 1946–52.
[3] Milton Gilbert (b. 1909); economist; U.S. Department of Commerce, 1939–40; Chief, National Income Division, Department of Commerce, 1941–51; subsequently Economic Adviser, Organisation for European Economic Co-operation and Bank for International Settlements.
[4] Donald Dougan Humphrey (1908–1964); economist, in government service 1940–8; Professor at various American universities.

(1) At the first stage there is upward movement of prices as a result of speculative demands, inventory accumulation, anticipation of higher prices and costs, etc.

(2) In the next stage there is upward pressure on wages resulting from the competition of employers for labor, especially skilled labor.

(3) Wage increases resulting from union pressure.

(4) Finally, there is the large scale pressure on prices due to the general level of demand exceeding the value of output at existing prices. This 'gap' can be closed only by heavy taxation, a high pressure savings campaign, or rationing on a wide scale.

According to Mr Keynes, we are now in the first and easy stage where all one has to do is to put on a price ceiling.

We are probably going to get to the next stage very soon, if we are not there already, and at this stage the upward pressure on prices comes from a genuine increase in costs, not only of wage costs (which, incidentally, are not going to decline with rising output for much longer) but also with rising real costs due to use of rail transportation instead of shipping, necessity for more frequent shunting of freight cars as traffic gets heavier, and so on. These cost increases justify price increases and when they arise, OPACS will not be in a position to refuse a price increase without keeping down or causing a contraction of output. It is, therefore, necessary to begin now to eliminate competitive bidding up of wages. This so-called 'poaching' or 'pirating' presented a difficult problem in England. Measures were taken to stop it, but evasive devices of all sorts are developed by employers and it is only with some difficulties that it was stopped.

Pressure from labor itself to raise wages must be prevented by generating a public opinion on the part of labor against them. After a year of what appeared to be futile effort, the argument that since the supply of consumable goods could not be expanded, an increase of wages in one area of labor constituted a sort of robbery from other labor, suddenly became accepted.

Finally, with respect to the gap between demand and the value of output at existing prices, Mr Keynes referred to the discussion at Mr Currie's house. He said that when he first came over he was pessimistic; that the discussion at Currie's had made an impression on him but that he was leaning back again toward his former view because he thought the figures talked about at Currie's were too optimistic. (Presumably referring both to the capacity of non-durable consumers' goods and the extent of saving out of additional income.) He wondered whether those who took the stronger expansionist view at Currie's house did not forget that to increase the supply of consumable goods would not of itself eliminate the gap between demand and supply; one must take into account the fact that when the supply of consumable goods is increased, the incomes of those producing them are likewise increased and that the gap would be reduced only insofar as saving and taxes increase. He questioned whether, with a 25 or 30 billion dollar program the gap would close of itself before the point of inflation.

We stated that the increase of demand resulting from the payment of income to the producers of consumers' goods had not been neglected; that our figures involved no logical errors of double-counting and no neglect of anything that should be counted. Nevertheless, we said, the gap would be reduced. Further, we expressed the belief that if the gap did not disappear before the point of full utilisation was reached, special measures should be taken to close it. All we contended was that such special measures should not be taken long before the point of full utilization is reached.

To this Mr Keynes said that before we convince the public special measures are really needed, a year or more would elapse and consequently even if there were no need to close the gap now, 'it would not be intellectually dishonest' to begin now with the economic propaganda necessary to make the public accept the eventual necessity of much heavier taxation, etc., etc. In response to our statement that the gap should not be closed long before the point of full utilization is reached, Mr Keynes said something which neither of us understood: Why should it not be closed too early? This will not cause any contraction. We said that it would inhibit expansion.

At about this time the meeting broke up and the few remarks which we were able to get in along these lines were probably lost in the general melee. As the meeting broke up we asked if he would be interested in the figures. He said he would be and gave us his address, here and in England.

11 June 1941

Following this discussion, Salant sent Keynes an additional note and on 21 June Humphrey and Salant visited Keynes and left further statistics supporting their case. The resulting correspondence appears below without the supporting statistics.

From W. SALANT, *12 June 1941*

Dear Mr Keynes

Following our dinner meeting Tuesday night at the National Press Club, I thought it might be desirable to put down on paper exactly what I take to be the view which several of us expressed at Currie's house. I think that in a letter I can make our theoretical position clear in the belief that you will acquit us of logical errors.

As I understand it, you felt that those who met with you at Currie's house were too optimistic regarding the degree to which output of non-durable consumers' goods could be expanded, and that they assumed too low an expansion of consumer expenditures for a given stimulus of defense expenditure. In other words, you felt that we overestimate supply and underestimate demand, and consequently underestimate the danger of inflation. While these are in part quantitative questions, you asked if we did not neglect the increase in income which would result from an expansion in the output of consumers' goods via the multiplier. I should like to restate the position as I see it in the light of your comments.

1. We realize that the expansion in the output of consumers' goods will not reduce the discrepancy between supply and demand by the value of the additional output; that is, we do not neglect the expansion of income and demand which accompanies the expansion of supply. We realize that the discrepancy at existing prices will be automatically reduced only to the extent that the expansion of demand, including not only multiplier but acceleration effects, falls short of the expansion of supply at existing prices and without special measures.

However, we believe that there will be some considerable reduction in the discrepancy as income expands through (a) voluntary saving, (b) the high and increasing proportion of taxes which inhibit consumption. Under this head we are not double counting by including both the voluntary saving at old tax schedules and the increase in *all* taxes which we now expect. We are including only that increase in taxation which has the effect of inhibiting an expansion of consumption. (c) Shortages of durable consumers' goods will hold down the total increase in demand for non-durable consumers' goods because of the fact that only a part of what would have been spent on durable goods had there been no shortage will be diverted to non-durable goods when a shortage exists. (d) High amortization in connection with defense facilities. (e) The shift to profits.

2. Even if the discrepancy between demand and supply were not decreased by an expansion of output in the non-durable consumers' goods field, such an expansion of output would hold down prices at any *given* level of demand; that is, it would raise the level of demand corresponding to any given upward pressure on prices. This is desirable because (a) the additional output is valuable for its own sake; (b) it is extremely bad for morale to stop an expansion while there are still millions unemployed; (c)

the level of output which we reach during this defense program will in the future probably be regarded as a bench mark for comparison, just as 1929 has been until recently. It would be a calamity to have this bench mark at a level which is so low that it leaves millions of people unemployed; (*d*) in many industries which are adaptable to producing goods for military purposes, the larger their capacity and the more people they are training the greater the possibilities of diversion to military uses, should such diversion prove necessary.

3. We do not say the expansive effects of the defense program upon income will die out before full utilization of all capacity is reached. If there is a 'gap' at the point of full utilization (or in practice somewhat before that point is reached), we are perfectly willing to take whatever special measures are necessary to close it. But we are strongly opposed to taking those measures long before full utilization is reached. Such a policy would retard further expansion. The only incentive to expansion is the ability to sell additional output. Some pressure of demand at existing prices is required. No doubt it is difficult to get just that amount of pressure which will induce expansion without getting so much as to cause a rise of prices. If the choice were between a 50 percent rise of prices and several hundred thousand unemployed, no doubt we would regard the latter as the preferable alternative. I think, however, that the actual alternatives for 1942 are closer to a 15 percent rise of prices or 6 million unemployed. Faced with that choice we prefer the former alternative.

I am enclosing tables showing the relation of net saving to net national income, and the relation of two concepts of gross saving to gross national product. They show that the amounts we assume will be saved are not inordinately high in the light of past patterns. If they seemed incredibly high to you, perhaps you were comparing our estimate of the ratio of future gross saving to gross product with past ratios of net saving to net product.

I believe that the facts show that we do not overestimate the potential output nor underestimate the expansion of demand which will result from a given increase of defense expenditures. We are assembling this material and are most eager to have you consider it. Mr Humphrey or I shall take the liberty of telephoning you in the hope that a discussion of our methods and results can be arranged.

Sincerely yours,

WALTER S. SALANT

To W. SALANT, *9 July 1941*

Dear Salant,

When you and the others visited me what is now nearly three weeks ago, either you or Humphrey (I forget which) left two interesting papers showing the components of change in gross national product between 1940 and 1941 and 1941 and 1942.

It would interest me to know from which end, so to speak, you arrived at your forecasts. I follow pretty well the estimate of investments etc. Have you arrived at total income and its division between consumption and savings by estimating, e.g., the probable non-durable consumption and so discovering the total you arrive at?

Or have you approached it the other way round, estimating the propensity to consume at different levels of income, having reached, as a pure inference from this, the amount that non-durable consumption will have to be if the investment is on the scale assumed?

You will see that I am at my old point, namely, that unless you make some peculiar assumption about perfect elasticity of supply, there is not necessarily any solution on the assumption of stable prices. But, apart from this, I should like to know which of the items in the calculation is arrived at, so to speak, by the method of difference. In other words, which of the figures has a reasoned estimate behind it and which of them comes out in the wash as what is required to produce a consistent picture?

Apart from that logical point, I find the statistical assumptions surprising, at any rate on British experience. As between 1940 and 1942 you are assuming that only 44 per cent of the increase in national income will be consumed, and as between 1941 and 1942 only 37 per cent of the rise. This presumes an extraordinarily low marginal propensity to consume.

All this is only repeating what I said before, but those papers you left with me give me a convenient text for bringing the issue to a head.

Yours sincerely,

J. M. KEYNES

From W. SALANT, *15 July 1941*

Dear Mr Keynes,

In answer to the question which you asked in your letter of 9 July, our forecasts of income and its components are based essentially on estimates of the propensity to consume. We infer the amount of non-durable consumption from investment, rather than by estimating the probable non-durable consumption directly. I say 'essentially' because some of the investment components are also derived.

I believe our general method is made clear in the enclosed memorandum. On pages 2 and 3 you will find a statement of which factors are parameters and which are deduced, and on page 10 a list of the relationships used. This memorandum, which is a revision of one that was sent to you, differs from our forecasts only in the fact that it does not allow for any lag in the adjustment of income to changes in investment.

Of the two tables I left with you to which you referred in your letter, the one showing the components of change in gross national product from 1941 to 1942 had a slight overstatement of the increase in plant investment and a slight understatement of the increase in consumption. A corrected sheet is enclosed. The increase in consumption is 39 per cent instead of 37 per cent of the increase in national income.

The low level of the marginal propensity to consume is accounted for by (1) an assumed lag in the reaction of consumption, (2) by the effect of shortages of consumers' durable goods upon the propensity to consume and (3) by the effect of increased tax rates. The attached Table 1 shows the effect of the second and third factors on the marginal propensity to consume. (This table is made up to show the investment and other 'offsets to saving' separately. Gross national product is derived from total offsets to saving.) According to this table, if there were no shortages or tax increases, consumption demand would increase by 56 per cent of the total increase in income. This figure is quite consistent with the past relationships, shown in Table 2, particularly when one considers the accelerating yield of taxes at the high level of national income before any increase of rates.

188

With shortages and higher tax rates the marginal propensity to consume is cut down to 39 per cent. Consumer dissaving in the form of increased instalment credit alone is reduced by $3.3 billion as a result of these shortages. This constitutes an autonomous reduction in the propensity to consume. It is based upon the assumption that only the down payments will be diverted to other consumption. We think it reasonable to assume that people will not go into debt to purchase non-durable consumers' goods to any further degree than normal merely because they cannot borrow as much to buy durable goods.

Sincerely yours,

WALTER S. SALANT

To W. SALANT, *24 July 1941*

Dear Salant,

I have found the further tables you sent me with your letter of 15 July very interesting and instructive. You make your assumptions pretty clear. I like your way of estimating the effect of the various disturbing factors.

But I come back all the same to your fundamental assumption of (*a*) no rise in price of durable consumers' goods in spite of perfect *in*elasticity of supply, and (*b*) no rise in price of non-durable consumers' goods in virtue of perfect elasticity of supply. Both these assumptions seem to be unjustified and in plain conflict with the obvious facts. Yet it is only by virtue of making them that you are able to reach a determinate solution. In the past I have always regarded the *price* factor as the flexible element, which would be forced to suffer whatever degree of change is necessary to restore equilibrium. That is why I began by thinking when we first talked about this that there was a *theoretical* difference between us. For it did not occur to me that you could have made such extreme assumptions about elasticity of supply.

When price-fixing is introduced, we have to depend on the effect of shortages on the propensity to consume as the flexible element. When this is not enough, which is the case in U.K., we have to supplement it by rationing. The equilibrium of our whole system now depends on the effect of shortages and rationing on the propensity to consume. We are driven on from one type of rationing to another, and the extent to which we can *avoid* rationing is the measure of the success of our fiscal policy coupled with appeals to patriotic duty.

Whether your assumptions about the marginal propensity to consume are correct is another matter which experience will test. I should predict that you might reach your figures with the aid of price rises (relatively to wages) but not without them.

Yours sincerely,

J. M. KEYNES

P.S. I am expecting to go home next week.

Since writing the above I have had a further discussion with Gilbert. I understand from him that you have *not* assumed stable prices. But I find no indication in the paper *what* assumption you have made about this.

If

$f(p, s+c)$ is the demand for consumers' goods when their price is p and income is $s+c$

and

$Q(p, s+c)$ is the supply of consumers' goods when their price is p and total output is $s+c$, where s is output of consumers' goods, c other output, equilibrium requires that

$$f(p, s+c) = s = Q(p, s+c)$$

There is, in general, only one price level at which this will hold.

At the end of his visit to America, Keynes made two comments on the American economists he had met.

The first came in an exchange with Professor J. M. Clark[5] after a meeting on 24 July.

From PROFESSOR J. M. CLARK, *24 July 1941*

Dear Professor Keynes

On the subject of yesterday's conference, I've been writing more than I've been talking, and several things are about to come out. (1) An article, in words of one syllable, in the August *Survey Graphic*, (2) Further comments on the inflation-symposium, to appear in the *Review of Economic Statistics*, August, (3) An essay in a collaborative volume on Defense Economic Policy, edited by E. S. Mason.

It was only after writing these that I actually read your *How to Pay for the War*, though of course I knew its main ideas, and I find similarities in points which I had not known about, such as to suggest plagiarism on my part; for which I hope to be forgiven. As to the *Survey* article, the editors had a feeling that it was expedient to treat the question as one of current American fact rather than as one of borrowing a foreign device. Your remark of last evening, *re* question in which direction error is more dangerous, you will find paralleled in my note in the *Review of Economic Statistics*.

With best wishes
Cordially yours
J. M. CLARK

P.S. It has seemed to me that what I call the 'income-flow analysis', of which yours is the most noted presentation, has done something which has not been done in comparable degree since Ricardo and Marx: namely, constructed a coherent logical theoretical system or formula having the quality of a mechanism, growing directly out of current conditions and problems which are of paramount importance and furnishing a key for working out definite answers in terms of policy. On this a 'school' has grown up. All that has tremendous power; and is also exposed to the dangers of too-undiscriminating application, from which 'classical' economics suffered, and of which I think the Gilbert–Humphrey attitude is one illustration.

I am myself enough of an 'institutionalist' (whatever that may mean) to have more than a lurking distrust of formulas and equations! But not

[5] John Maurice Clark (1884–1963); economist; Professor of Political Economy, University of Chicago, 1922–6; Professor of Economics, Columbia University, 1926–51; National Resources Planning Board, 1939–40; Office of Price Administration, 1940–3.

enough of an institutionalist to ignore their importance: merely to want to think all round them and reckon with the imponderables that modify their action; and the other factors which no single formula can comprehend —for instance, the long-run incidence of continued large deficit-spending!

Yours

J.M.C.

To PROFESSOR J. M. CLARK, *26 July 1941*

Dear Professor Clark,

I have much appreciated getting your letter. There is a quantity of stuff in my *How To Pay For The War* which is now common ground amongst many economists, and I certainly cannot claim it for myself alone. I shall be very interested to see what you write and will be grateful if you can send me any off-prints,—to King's College, Cambridge, or to the Treasury, Whitehall, where I expect to be returning in a few days. As you will have gathered the other evening, I agree with what you say about the danger of a 'school', even when it is one's own. There is great danger in quantitative forecasts which are based exclusively on statistics relating to conditions by no means parallel. I have tried to persuade Gilbert and Humphrey and Salant that they should be more cautious. I have also tried to persuade them that they have tended to neglect certain theoretical considerations which are important in the interests of simplifying their statistical task. I am afraid I have only partially succeeded, though I expect the results of the argument will sink in. I am very sorry to have differed from them in opinion, because I have a high appreciation of their gifts and of the work they are doing. I like Gilbert's persistence and indomitableness. They are so much on the right side of things and thinking so well and clearly that one need not be afraid perhaps of criticising them.

I felt in our discussion the other day that underlying the superficial differences of opinion there really was a wide measure of general agreement, and nearly all of us would have found ourselves united in any contest with the outside world. And that is as it should be between colleagues and economists.

Yours,

J. M. KEYNES

The second came in a farewell letter to W. S. Salant.

To W. S. SALANT, *27 July 1941*

Dear Salant,

Thank you for sending me your article on Income Velocity.[6] I am leaving Washington tomorrow and will take this away with me to read on the journey home.

Farewell greetings to yourself, Gilbert and Humphrey. I have greatly enjoyed our discussions. Do not think because I have been in a critical mood that I do not appreciate the value and significance of the work you are all doing; I sympathise with it infinitely more than I criticise.

But it is when I come across stuff which is on fruitful lines that I feel most critical, if only for the reason that it is worth criticising.

I have no doubt that you will all suffer a great deal of frustration in the coming months. Nevertheless, I should not be surprised if, when a year is past and you are able to look back, you will find that you got much more of your way than you were realising at the time. There is too wide a gap here in Washington between the intellectual outlook of the older people and that of the younger. But I have been greatly struck during my visit by the quality of the younger economists and civil servants in the Administration. I am sure that the best hope for good government of America is to be found there. The war will be a great sifter and will bring the right people to the top. We have a few good people in London, but nothing like the *numbers* whom you can produce here.

Yours sincerely,

J. M. K.

[6] 'The Demand for Money and the Concept of Income Velocity', *Journal of Political Economy*, June 1941.

Chapter 6

LONDON, 1941: FINAL STAGES OF NEGOTIATING THE FUNDAMENTALS OF LEND LEASE

On his return to London, Keynes continued his involvement with the subjects of his Washington discussions. On 2 August he prepared a covering note on the matter of Consideration, a copy of which went to the Prime Minister.

'CONSIDERATION'

I attach the document handed to me by Mr Dean Acheson on 28th July, and behind it a memorandum of my conversation with him which I prepared immediately afterwards. I left copies of both these documents with the Ambassador.

The proposed agreement is on the formal lines, which was originally intended. The preamble sets out the declaration of common purpose in language which echoes the Declaration of Independence. Except in Article VII substantially all the detailes are postponed for a subsequent date.

Articles I and VI raise some points of detail which I mentioned to Mr Acheson, but I think that no substantial point arises here which cannot be dealt with easily. The agreement has been padded out by quoting verbatim or in substance portions of the Lend Lease Act.

The substantial issues are reserved for Article VII.

The first part of this is not quite so clear or so satisfactory to us as the form of words I had drafted. But it is meant to say, and it does in fact say, that there will be no war debts. That is to say, no deliveries of cash or goods having merely economic significance. It is of enormous importance for us to get this settled now and not leave us to the mercies of different conditions and very possibly a different President.

194

But the second part with the undertaking against 'discrimination', whatever that may mean, is of an awkward character and is not made less awkward by the elucidations of the meaning of this which I obtained from Mr Acheson in conversation.

My opinion is, and Mr Acheson as good as admitted it, that the State Department have taken the opportunity to introduce their pet idea in language which they mean to be technical; whereas, the President himself had nothing so definite in view, and meant only to require that we should agree to co-operate and to do so in a certain spirit and with a certain general purpose.

In our rejoinder we can take any of three lines:

(1) the wording of the document might be accepted as it stands and a covering letter might be added in which we explained what we meant by 'discrimination', stating that it is not used technically and does not commit us to any particular technical solution;

(2) we might offer an alternative wording in the document itself; or

(3) we might attempt to replace the latter part by the old suggestion of an Anglo-American Conference or Commission, which was suggested by Mr Acheson at an earlier stage but discouraged by London.

I fancy that this bit was put in to bring things to a head in view of the discouragement of the Commission or Conference but nevertheless I do not think it is necessary for us to return to the Conference proposal if that is thought to be premature. On the whole, the first alternative might be the best. I will, if instructed, prepare a form of words.

The general purport of this form of words would be to explain that by the absence of 'discrimination' we meant the absence of international arrangements, the object of which was to exclude a particular country from general advantages, and that it did not mean that we were cut off from specific technical solutions of the problems of the post-war world. In particular, it did not necessarily mean complete freedom of trade and absence of all currency and other restrictions between each separate country and political unit in the world. For this we should have to envisage the post-war world in enough detail to be confident that this would be the right solution. For example, it would not preclude currency systems and tariff systems embracing more than one political unit but covering less than the whole world. In short, it would be an indication of spirit and intention, not a commitment, which would be wholly inappropriate in a document of this kind, to a particular technical solution of hypothetical post-war economic and currency problems. I could put it better than that, but that would be the up-shot.

[copy initialled] J. M. K.

Keynes also discussed the results of his mission with the Exchange Control Conference on 6 August and the Foreign Secretary on 12 August.

On his return to London, he also became involved in the discussions of British export and distribution policies with regard to lend lease supplies. As noted above (p. 167) Keynes had given a press conference in Washington in July where he drew attention to the decline that had already occurred in Britain's export trade, the need for such trade as was continuing in paying for essential imports (e.g. Argentine food) and the cancellation of several South American export contracts which involved goods similar to those going to Britain on lend lease.

During the rest of July negotiations had continued in Washington for an exchange of letters between General Burns, the Lend Lease Executive Officer, and Mr Purvis, the head of the British Purchasing Commission. During these, the Americans accepted the principle of substitution,[1] and the importance of Britain's foreign exchange needs while the British agreed to restrict exports of materials similar to those received on lend lease to the absolute minimum necessary for the successful prosecution of the war.

[1] Where supplies from the United States formed a much smaller proportion of total supplies than the proportion going into war production, they would be deemed to have gone into war production irrespective of their final use.

These negotiations resulted in a draft letter, sent to London on 1 August.

However, at this stage, Mr Winant entered the field with a proposal for immediate action through a unilateral British undertaking, which he presented to an unprepared and unbriefed Chancellor. The resulting draft, which conceded many of the Americans' demands, came to Keynes for comment.

To E. W. PLAYFAIR, S. D. WALEY *and* SIR R. HOPKINS, *5 August 1941*

EXPORT POLICY

This memorandum [not printed] strikes me as carefully drafted, subject to one ambiguity, and not likely to do much harm in practice. The ambiguity relates to the question of exports to the sterling area. At the end of 3(i) it is explained that *existing* contracts for export to the sterling area are not interfered with by the formula. It is left ambiguous whether this also applied to future exports. I hope it was intended that 3(i) should be applicable throughout only outside the sterling area. The words should have been 'will be used in export outside the sterling area with the exception of the following special cases'. If that is meant, as I rather presume, is it too late to get the words inserted? With that ambiguity removed, the formula seems to me to be likely to be fairly innocuous in practice.

On the other hand, I am rather worried about the procedure. I do not believe that Mr Winant was acting on any instructions from Washington and that he had been put up to it by Mr Harry Hopkins. This means that it echoes the situation which existed about three or four weeks ago, since when much water has flowed over the dam. On the day before Mr Harry Hopkins left Washington he had an interview with Mr Purvis in which he went off the deep end about this whole matter, said that he had discussed it with the President and that the President was much concerned. I fancy that he repeated this to Mr Winant, which would be considered sufficient authority to invoke the President's name in the matter. But meanwhile the consideration of the question was being continued through the proper channels with the heads of Mr Hopkins's department.

In order to make clear what we were doing, it is important to emphasise the exact technical position. Under Clause 4 of the Lend Lease Act we only have the right of transfer outside Government hands with the express approval of the President in each instance. But so far we have never succeeded in getting such approval in writing. The only urgent case which has arisen in practice is that of food, and there we have carried on under oral authority that we could as an interim arrangement continue to act as though we had authority in writing. As, however, all sorts of other cases were becoming actual, I started about a fortnight ago pressing strongly to get the matter settled. It was agreed on all hands that this was now essential. The only proper course is for the lend lease authority to propose a formula which we shall have to sign on each relevant occasion. It is for them to determine the conditions, not for us. But General Burns, who is acting for Mr Hopkins in his absence, agreed that it would be better for us to see this in draft. Mr Cox, who is next in command after General Burns, and acts for Mr Hopkins on the U.S. Clearing Committee, was strongly in favour of a formula embodying the doctrine of substitution. Subsequently I discussed the details with him in his own office. General Burns, on the other hand, thought a rather more general formula was desirable. General Burns told Mr Purvis that he would let him see any draft that the General intended to send. This draft actually arrived on July the 25th. I have a copy of it in my pouch, which ought to have arrived by now, but of course has not. This draft was discussed on July the 26th at two meetings. First of all between Phillips and myself, [and] Chalkley[2] and Stirling as representing the Board of Trade,

---

[2] Sir (Harry) Owen Chalkley (1882–1958); Consular service and other commercial counsellor posts 1916–31; commercial counsellor, Washington, 1931–42.

and afterwards between Phillips and myself with Mr Purvis, Monsieur Monnet and Mr Brand representing the Supply Council. We thought that the general formula was fairly satisfactory, but Mr Purvis was asked to make certain suggestions to the General without pressing them too strongly. He was to see the General the day after I left Washington. The general upshot of the General's formula was that we were to concentrate on our specialities (which he exemplified by whisky and Harris tweed, a combination which we thought was incomplete without haggis and not perhaps quite an adequate foundation on which to wage a war and we substituted fine textiles as an example instead of Harris tweeds), and we were only to have exports of other categories in so far as they were essential to provide us with necessary exchange. It was ambiguous whether or not the latter referred to foreign exchange outside the sterling area, and one of our suggestions was to make this clear.

What happens now I don't know. The General's purpose was, I think, to have a formula agreed with us beforehand which he (General Burns) could produce during the forthcoming lend lease appropriations debate in Congress if he was cross-examined on the subject. I suppose he might be persuaded to substitute the present memorandum. I do not know whether the memorandum has been telegraphed to Phillips and Purvis or whether they are still continuing in blissful ignorance on the basis of the General's own proposal.

Generally speaking, the whole thing looked rather dangerous some three or four weeks ago. It was rumoured that Mr Hoover was going to take it up. But in the last fortnight the agitation seems to have died away completely. The Department of Commerce, the State Department, the Treasury and the Lend Lease Administration are all on our side and were busy concocting a formula which will satisfy Congress and will be the least hampering possible. It is quite likely that they will be as happy with this new formula as with the one they were preparing themselves.

DISTRIBUTION OF LEND LEASE GOODS IN U.K.

This was raised more particularly by Mr Morgenthau. But Mr Cox of the Lend Lease Administration was anxious to make it clear to us that nothing which Mr Morgenthau said had any relation to food, which does not fall within his domain, but only to the other miscellaneous raw materials etc. which are obtained through the Treasury Procurement Division.

Mr Morgenthau has recently sent to London for a temporary visit to the Embassy Mr Frank Coe,[3] a young economist in whom he has confidence. The last stage of the discussion at the Treasury Committee was that on my return to London I should suggest to Mr Coe that he should prepare a report to Mr Morgenthau as to what our arrangements actually are and that the relevant Departments should put the necessary material at Mr Coe's disposal. I have been intending to do that; and perhaps it would be well to carry out this suggestion as arranged. I should like to add that the storm which Mr Morgenthau momentarily created about this was probably due to a complete misunderstanding and that he meant something quite different. He is extremely suspicious of our purchasing departments in U.S.A. on the ground that they are trying to preserve vested interests and old channels of trade and even that there may be concealed commissions knocking round somewhere. It is the nature of our arrangements on the other side rather than on this which is really under fire. I would prefer to explain orally what lies behind this.

5.8.41   J.M.K.

---

[3] Frank Coe (b. 1907), economist; adviser on war finance, National Defence Council, 1940; special assistant to U.S. Ambassador and Financial Attaché, London, 1941; Executive Secretary, Joint War Production Commission, U.S.A.–Canada, 1942; Assistant to Director, Board of Economic Warfare, 1942–3; Adviser, Mexican–American Committee on Economic Co-operation, 1943; Assistant Administrator, Foreign Economic Administration, 1943–5; Director, Monetary Research, Treasury Department, 1945–6; Secretary, International Monetary Fund, 1946–9.

As it happened, the 'Winant draft', which had caused the confusion, was a red herring and the Burns' exchange of letters was still very much alive. This draft was open to the objections that it could be held to prevent the export of any materials similar to those obtained under lend lease and that it drew no distinction between those materials whose use in the United States was restricted on supply grounds and other goods. Professor Robertson also objected memorably to the characterisation of Britain's traditional exports.[4] Throughout August, discussion continued, Keynes preferring the Burns draft, and ministers and Mr Winant preferring the unilateral British draft.

In the end, after further difficult negotiations, the unilateral Winant alternative was adopted. The U.K. published it on 13 September in the form of a White Paper. In the agreement Britain agreed to refrain from any opportunity to apply materials similar to those received under lend lease to enable exporters to enter new markets or to extend their trade at the expense of U.S. exporters, and to refrain from using any materials, however obtained, for exports in other than a few specified cases, if the use of such materials was subject to restriction in the United States owing to supply shortages. The memorandum also set out conditions for the transfer of lend lease goods into private trade.

During this period, discussions also continued on Article VII. The Acheson draft of 28 July raised the problems of Imperial Preference, a policy close to the hearts of many ministers and officials, established in agreement with the Dominions as the basis for important trading relationships, and the post-war international economic position of the United Kingdom. The British opponents of Article VII won a brief victory in August when they

---

[4] *From* ROBERTSON *to* PLAYFAIR, *19 August 1941*
I do hope that we shall not accept delivery of this insulting document.

The solid arguments against the formula were set out in Apurs 511. But apart from them the whole impression which the formula seeks to convey is false and ridiculous. It is an impression of a picturesque little nation whose trading reputation depends on a few specialities popular in fashionable circles in Boston and New York, but which had presumptuously, under the temptations of lend lease, gone outside its 'traditional' field to try its hand at real industry like metallurgy and the staple textile trades, and has now humbly promised to draw in its horns again. 'Traditional articles', indeed! Shades of the great textile inventors, iron-masters, railway contractors etc. of the nineteenth century!

Could the British Supply Council present General Burns with an outline of the economic history of nineteenth-century Britain?

I do not attach much importance to long-term arguments as a rule in wartime, but what chance have our Board of Trade negotiators of trade treaties and the like if we once accept this caricature of the character of British trade?

defeated an American attempt to add the words 'without discrimination' to the fourth point of the Atlantic Charter,[5] but this had not abated State Department efforts on Article VII. Nor had it meant the end of attempts amongst British officials and Ministers to make the Article more acceptable.

Keynes took an active part in these discussions, emphasising throughout that Britain had to take the American drafts seriously; despite his sympathy with H. D. Henderson's comment on 12 August, 'I am profoundly convinced that the new wine of planning and Socialism that we shall increasingly have to drink cannot be put in the old bottles of the gold standard, Free Trade, the most-favoured-nation clause, and the open door; and I have the gravest misgivings as to the wisdom of giving assurances that the refurbishing of these old bottles will be our aim and purpose.' Perhaps his strongest statement concerning the need for an agreement that was more than a vague form of words came in August as the drafting continued towards the formula Lord Halifax delivered to the Americans in October.[6]

To LORD CATTO *and* SIR RICHARD HOPKINS, *28 August 1941*

1. In my judgment it would be worse than useless merely to offer a recapitulation of the 4th and 5th points of the Atlantic Declaration. These points are in fact extremely vague and commit us to very little. But, apart from that, they are something we have agreed to already and would represent no *quid pro quo* at all.

To make a derisory offer which, when analysed, means no concession whatever to the American point of view would, I think, be most injudicious. We have tried it on once already with the effect of producing a definite stiffening of the terms

[5] The form of words adopted ran 'they will strive to bring about a fair and equitable distribution of essential produce, not only within their territorial boundaries, but between the nations of the world'.

[6] The important section of this draft ran, 'they shall provide for joint and agreed action by the United States and United Kingdom, each working within the limits of their governing economic conditions, directed to secure as part of a general plan the progressive attainment of balanced international economies, the avoidance of harmful discriminations, and generally the economic objectives set forth in the joint Declaration made by the President of the United States of America and the Prime Minister of the United Kingdom on the 12 August, 1941 [the Atlantic Charter]'.

beyond what was previously in draft. If we make another derisory offer, we shall find the terms going up against us again.

The President and the State Department have two objects in view. First, to get some assurance that we shall pay a considerable amount of attention to their point of view in post-war arrangements. Secondly, to have something plausible to offer Congress when the document is published. The President did not contemplate publishing it immediately on signature, but thought he would probably be forced to do so within about six months. A mere recapitulation of the 4th and 5th points would be considered a bad joke from both these points of view.

2. Nor do I think that Mr Amery's suggested amendment with reference to 'our established economic policies' would be serviceable. For it is precisely a change in our established economic policies that the Americans are asking for.

I sympathise with Mr Amery's criticism of the most favoured-nation obsession. But I think he underestimates the reasonableness of the State Department if we will go at least a little way to meet them. They have always regarded the Ottawa Agreement as our riposte to the Hawley Smoot tariff. They have it fully in mind to make large concessions on their side in that tariff of the order of 50 per cent as a *quid pro quo* for the modification of Ottawa. The concessions they contemplate are even more important to the Dominions, particularly to Australia, than to us.

It is clear that we cannot commit ourselves to abandon the system of Imperial Preferences in principle. And for that reason we cannot accept the original wording. But, if we are prepared to discuss the whole issue in the spirit of meeting the American point of view, I do not think we need be unduly afraid of their unreasonableness in detail. It should be possible to work out new arrangements as satisfactory to the Dominions as to ourselves, which might gradually abate the extent of the Imperial Preferences in practice without abandoning them in principle, but only in return for valuable concessions. I do not see how we can expect faithful Anglo-American economic cooperation on any lesser terms than this.

The revised formula suggested by the Chancellor certainly would not commit us to abandoning the system of Imperial Preference in principle. It only commits us to work to the best of our ability in the direction of reducing such special arrangements as much as possible. I repeat that less than that we can scarcely do if we are to meet the Americans at all. I should, therefore, urge that the revised formula, amended, however, in the light of the criticisms of Lord Catto and Mr Henderson, should be retained. This runs, you will remember, as follows:–

They shall provide joint and agreed action by the U.S. and U.K., each working within the limits of their governing economic conditions, directed to the progressive attainment of a balanced international economy which would render unnecessary policies of special discrimination.

3. It would, I believe, be of real assistance to obtaining an agreement if Mr Greenwood's suggestion were followed up, by adding another clause providing for an early and authoritative discussion of the matters lying behind clause VII. By 'early' I do not mean next month. It is essential that we should first of all clear up our own ideas. But the interchange should take place not later than next spring.

I should have thought it was desirable in any case that we should enter into authoritative discussions next spring. But whether that is so or not, I doubt if it is avoidable. We can if we like do it in a more hole-and-corner way as a by-product of the discussions on surpluses.[7] But, where the matters at issue go far beyond the interim period, I question if this is a convenient framework in which to proceed.

[7] There had been discussion in London of the growing surpluses of primary products in many of the British colonies as a result of difficulties of shipment and of the serious repercussions on the finances of the countries concerned. See also *JMK*, vol. XXVII.

We may do serious harm to post-war prospects if we burke full and early discussion. There are enormous difficulties in the way of Anglo-American economic cooperation. No one can be more sensible of these than I am. I should like sometime to write a note on just what I feel about this. But it would be a great mistake to argue from these lurking difficulties that the members and officers of the Administration with whom we shall be dealing are either unfriendly or unreasonable. The truth is that they are enormously ignorant of our particular difficulties and problems. For this reason it is of the first importance that we develop our case in great detail and at great length,—on a scale which anyone over here except an academic economist would think very boring. Our only hope of getting a satisfactory agreed solution is by being extremely forthcoming with all relevant, and even irrelevant, information and extremely patient in endless discourse.

The President is, I believe, already piqued by our apparent reluctance to enter into discussions. Thus an additional clause providing for such discussions might increase the acceptability of our revised draft.

4. The general tenor of the papers below suggests to me that the precise character of the position we find ourselves in is not fully appreciated. We are no longer completely free agents in this matter—'free as air', as the President expressed it. And that is what he feels entitled to bring home to us.

We have accepted assistance under the Lend Lease Act in full knowledge of the terms of this Act. This Act entitles the President to require from us 'payment or repayment in kind or property or any other direct or indirect benefit which the President deems satisfactory'. In the last resort we are in his hands. So far, as a purely interim arrangement, he has agreed to goods being handed to us under the Lend Lease Act with our merely tacit acceptance of the terms of that Act. The point has now come when he asks us to put our signature to a paper by which we recognise in express terms our obligations under the Act. He is tender of our susceptibilities and does not wish to put it, or attempt to put it, in the form of an ultimatum. But there is nothing to prevent him from asking for assets in any part of the world, for deliveries of tin and rubber over a period of years, or many other advantages. We have two alternatives before us. One alternative is to omit Article VII of the proposed agreement, leaving the President free to ask for economic 'consideration' hereafter, but leaving us unfettered in respect of post-war economic policy. If we do this, we leave the matter to be settled at a later date when President Roosevelt may be no longer in office and when the Americans will be far clearer than they are now about what they want. To-day we have the advantage of a just and friendly President and of the fact that the Americans are not yet at all clear in their own minds what it is they do want. The just and friendly President is agreeable to sign away for himself and his successors any right to demand merely economic 'consideration', which would be the equivalent of war debts. In return he asks us to meet him, at any rate to some extent, in the matter of post-war economic policy.

If we are prepared to agree to nothing, which is what the recapitulation of the points of the Atlantic Declaration or Mr Amery's amendment would amount to, we stand the risk of losing the waiving of war debts and gain, as it seems to me, almost nothing on the other side. For the President has many other weapons which he can use, apart from the 'consideration' agreement, to force us into line in economic matters. If we refuse to play at this stage, it is in the character, both of the President and his advisers, to take a very different and a much stiffer line next time these issues arise.

I hope, therefore, that the War Cabinet will think twice before putting up a derisory offer or refusing any concession whatever to the American point of view. We have an opportunity to-day which may not recur. I have more anxiety than have some of my more optimistic colleagues about the future development of Anglo-American cooperation, and I am more tenacious than they are of our future freedom to mould our economic system in accordance with what will be our post-war needs. I am greatly afraid of those who think our best course is to agree with a grin to whatever the Americans suggest. But to fly to the other extreme and refuse to move an inch in their direction is even more dangerous. I am always alive to the fact that the optimists have one tremendous force on their side. For who would save his life must lose it or be prepared to, and it may well be that if we approach the post-war world in that spirit we shall have been well inspired. Rightly or wrongly, I am disposed to take a more cautious course. But I should prefer the policy of faith to a refusal to meet the Americans at all.

5. May I add a word on the question of procedure? Lord Halifax is now in this country. He will be charged with the later stage of this negotiation. Is it not important and desirable that he should be brought into council at this stage and should have the opportuinity of expressing judgment on the papers in this file before we go any further?

6. I append another paper dealing with certain points of detail which emerge from the papers below.

28.8.41   [copy initialled] J.M.K.

In the course of September, Keynes also commented on a State Department characterisation of the views he had expressed in Washington and their view of the post-war world contained in a memorandum from Mr Hawkins to Mr Acheson.

To SIR HORACE WILSON, *19 September 1941*

Broadly this is a very fair account of the course of the discussions. The only passage I question is that marked 'A' on page 3, which I do not recognise as like anything I said. But this is not a material point.

Nevertheless, the memorandum does not give quite the right impression because it neglects the following aspects.

(1) The context of these discussions was a request to us,

partly in connection with the trade negotiations and partly in connection with the 'consideration' discussions, to agree beforehand to a formula which would tie our hands and cut us off from such a solution as is discussed in these pages. I was arguing, not necessarily that our policy would follow bilateral lines, and certainly not that this was the most desirable solution, but simply that we might be forced to move along these lines unless some other comprehensive solution was found and, therefore, that it was unreasonable to press us to cut ourselves off from such solution before such comprehensive solution had been explored. I expressed myself strongly in favour of common discussions on this subject, bringing in economists and Treasury experts to deal with aspects with which the State Department was necessarily less familiar. Throughout, my emphasis was on the unreasonableness of asking us to commit ourselves to the contrary *before* a solution had been found.

(2) The paper shows that the State Department is still thinking in terms which prevent them from seeing that no solution is possible until the United States itself becomes a balanced country and that this must involve a reduction in their exports relatively to their imports. They seem to think that some satisfactory international contraption could be erected which would enable them to go on having unlimited exports irrespective of what they were importing. My difficulty was that the State Department would think in terms of particular trade arrangements instead of directing their attention to the solution of this underlying problem. Nevertheless, economists who are advising the Administration, such as Professor Hansen[8] and Professor Viner, are fully alive to the major problem and so, I think, is the Treasury. Unfortunately they did not take part in these discussions,

[8] Alvin H. Hansen (1887–1975), economist; taught at University of Minnesota, 1919–37; Chief Economic Analyst, Department of State, 1934–5; Special Economic Adviser, Federal Reserve Board, 1940–5; Littauer Professor of Political Economy, Harvard, 1937–56.

which, I should add, were of the most informal character and were never brought to any satisfactory conclusion, being broken off half way through because both parties were too busy on other matters.

(3) Not the faintest hint is given in this paper of what lines an alternative solution might take. Nevertheless, it is progress, I think, that they should at least have realised vividly in our minds that there is a considerable problem.

So far from its being my opinion that the bilateral arrangements to which the Americans object are the ideal solution, I have been spending some time since I came back in elaborating a truly international plan which would avoid these difficulties. I have, as you know, now reduced such a plan to writing, though it has not yet been subject to criticism or is fit for circulation outside the Treasury. This document reinforces my feeling that we should do well to start from some such proposal as that which I have prepared or a variant of it, even though we may feel that it is probably too international and too Utopian to take form just in that shape in the real world. If it is agreed that there is nothing disadvantageous to this country in my Utopian plan, at any rate nothing disadvantageous if it is accompanied by other plans and is not regarded as a complete solution by itself, then let it be for the Americans to raise objections. Let us start constructively, offering them something which would give them all they ask, provided they are really prepared to be truly internationally minded. If they reject it as it stands, it is then their responsibility either to propose amendments or to put forward an alternative. I do not myself see how there can be any alternative except either a variant of my international scheme or a variant of my bilateral scheme, as briefly and very incompletely set forth in this paper. (I have not yet put in writing the details of what a bilateral scheme might look like if we were to be forced back on this expedient.) Possibly you may wish to send a copy of this to Lord Halifax and Mr Eden so that they will at least know that we are trying to make progress on this matter. We shall have to be ready with something by next spring if the proposed Anglo-American Conference materialises. But, as I have said above, we are not yet ready to circulate material or have discussions outside the Treasury.

19.9.41   [copy initialled] J.M.K.

During the period following his return to London, Keynes also kept a watchful eye over the progress of his understandings with Mr Morgenthau. On 16 August, Sir Frederick Phillips sent a cable to London outlining a gloomier financial climate which threatened the 'settlement' on the old commitments and, through the possible delay in another Lend Lease Appropriation bill, the curtailment of future British orders and the scale of Dominion inclusion in the scheme.

Although Keynes was away from the Treasury resting after the labours of the previous months, he did contribute a minute.

To S. D. WALEY *and others, 22 August 1941*

It is very possible that we now have more information relating to the subjects of Phillips's gloomy telegram 3829 of the 16th August. But it may save time if I put in writing my first reflections on that telegram prior to my returning to my room next Monday, 25th August.

(1) What Phillips reports is excessively out of key with what one reads in the newspapers about the increased and more urgent assistance which the President is promising us.* It also bears little relation to Mr Harry Hopkins's famous broadcast. It is, I suppose, very possible that Lord Beaverbrook is not acquiescing in this situation and, therefore, it may be that there will be yet another change of plan, this time in the right direction.

(2) Nevertheless, it is a good example of what I previously emphasised, namely, that one can take nothing whatever for

* But I see from some observations of Walter Lippmann quoted in to-day's *Times* that the President has in fact seriously lost control of Congress.

settled in U.S.A., for the sufficient reason that the Administration, not being in control of Congress, is not in a position to enter into commitments on anything. We shall have to bear this in mind in all the negotiations for Anglo-American economic co-operation. What our representatives say binds the British Government. What the State Department or the Treasury or the Departments of Commerce or Agriculture may intimate in the course of our conversations with them can and does bind no one. Thus every bargain can, and very likely will, be overthrown by Congress. It is one thing to make concessions for a definite *quid pro quo*, another one to make them for promises which evaporate in practice. We shall, therefore, have to be very careful in tying up our side of the bargain with theirs and making the one definitely contingent on the other.

(3) Nevertheless, whilst Phillips's report is most disappointing, it is perhaps rather too pessimistic. In particular, it may be a question more of delay than of getting nothing ultimately. Whilst the old commitments are gradually slipping out of our control as the result of deliveries, this process is a slow one, and even four months hence there will be quite a lot left capable of being cared for. Unless U.S.A. is going to fall away completely from her promises, it is quite certain that very large further appropriations will be required fairly soon, both for her own Departments and for us. It may be that we are having to survive a bad interim period. I am sure it is important that Phillips should persist in the face of every discouragement, keeping our demands in the forefront of the picture, whilst acquiescing in inevitable delays, never accepting 'no' for an answer and only agreeing to temporary postponement until the state of the available funds is better. The whole system of appropriations is fantastically inapplicable to war conditions. I spent much time arguing with the Americans how judicious they would be to cut away from this system altogether. I know many of them would like to and at long last some better system will be worked out.

211

They could not possibly have devised anything more adapted than the present system is for the maximum tiresomeness of Congress.

(4) It is also possible that he is a little too pessimistic about bringing Dominion requirements under lend lease. The different brackets under the old lend lease appropriations are in very different degrees of exhaustion. The maximum diversion from funds under one bracket to funds under another permitted under the law has already taken place. The miscellaneous bracket for war materials, out of which the Dominions will have to be satisfied pending new appropriations is, or was not long ago, fortunately one of the least exhausted of the brackets. Provided we are careful in not placing other orders unduly ahead of the needs of the case, I think there ought to be a margin for Dominion requirements which we shall be placing during the next few months. At any rate, so long as the lend lease appropriations are adequate when they do arrive, the worst that can happen is a very short delay.

(5) On the other hand, the postponement of the new Lend Lease Appropriation Bill now indicated by Phillips looks to me quite intolerable on some headings. As I mentioned above, some of the brackets are still unexhausted. But others had already been used up to the hilt early in July. I should have thought that so long a postponement would involve so much hindrance to the war effort as to be quite intolerable unless Mr Hopkins and the President are capitulating to an overwhelming wave of isolationism. Phillips certainly suggests that the decision to adjourn Congress is final, and I suppose we must accept that. But it might have the result, and the President may even foresee and like that result, of meaning that the Bill will have to be rushed through within a week when Congress re-assembles. It is not reasonably possible to wait until a date after 15th October.

(6) I do not know whether you think it worth while to bother Phillips with any suggestions until he makes a further

report. It would really be telling him nothing which he does not know already, but might possibly be useful in emphasising in his mind points which he already knows.

22.8.41   [copy initialled] J.M.K.

Further telegrams from Phillips increased the pessimism in Whitehall, as Keynes told Frank Coe of the American Embassy.

To F. COE, 2 September 1941

Dear Coe,

We have now heard from Phillips exactly what it was that Congress did over the appropriations. You may be interested to hear the up-shot, if it has not already reached you direct.

The changes effected by Congress against the recommendation of the Administration fall under three heads, namely:

(*a*) The War Department appropriations were reduced by nearly $600 million net.

(*b*) The previous unlimited contract authorisation for armoured force supplies contained in the previous Act of the 13th June was repealed.

(*c*) The power to lend-lease vessels under the new Maritime Commission appropriation was withdrawn. The appropriation under this head was limited to the power to lease vessels which must remain United States property.

The effect of all this on what we were discussing with Mr Morgenthau is rather disastrous. The effect of (*a*) is to reduce the funds available to the War Department to buy the old commitments, which it was proposed we should transfer to them. The effect of (*b*) is that the contract authorisation for tanks, etc. is no longer open-ended, so that the previous proposal to take over old tank contracts from us is made difficult. The effect of (*c*) is that the Maritime Commission cannot take over the Todd ships and hand them back to us except on lease. The Maritime Commission feel a difficulty in defending the purchase of this particular kind of ship for their own account.

Thus, out of the previous dollar relief to the British Treasury contemplated by Mr Morgenthau, only half now remains intact, which falls far short even of his ancient commitment to Phillips to find $360 million. Mr Morgenthau returns this week from a fortnight's holiday, after which I dare say we shall hear more.

If this information has not already reached you, perhaps the Ambassador may be interested in it.

Yours sincerely,

[copy initialled] J.M.K.

However, this was only the beginning of the process, and the first of many Keynes comments on fluctuations in American opinion and their effects on what the British considered firm understandings. In the end, the 'old commitments' taken over by the Americans in May 1942 came to $290 million.

October brought an additional problem, as the lend lease authorities passed supposedly confidential figures concerning Britain's external financial position to Congress. Over the succeeding months, this resulted in three Keynes notes on the subject taking up the position that the Treasury later tried on the American authorities early in 1942. The last of these notes appears below.

To LORD CATTO *and* S. D. WALEY, *31 December 1941*

PUBLICATION OF INFORMATION AS TO OUR GOLD RESERVES

(1) I agree with Robertson that such information as is published should be accurate and should be made available in this

country at the same time as in U.S.A. But I feel that we want to ponder more carefully the major issues of policy involved in publication before agreeing to continue with anything like what we have drifted into in the course of the last year.

(2) To begin with, there is the distinction between communicating relevant information to the U.S. Treasury for their confidential guidance and making the figures public to Congress and to Parliament and consequently to the whole world. Now that the United States is at war, I should have thought that it ought not to be impossible to persuade the U.S. Administration that future communications to Congress should take a different form and should be to the effect that the necessary information has been communicated to the U.S. Treasury, that they have satisfied themselves that the lend lease appropriations asked for are reasonable in the light of this information but that, for reasons of war policy, publication to the world at large, and incidentally to the enemy, is considered inadvisable.

It must be borne in mind that even in peace-time we did not think it safe from the point of view of our credit to publish up-to-date information at frequent intervals, the gold in the Equalisation Fund being disclosed only six months in arrear. It is highly unreasonable that we should be expected to disclose the whole position to the world at large and to the enemy quite up to date and in full detail at frequent intervals. Why should we give up the idea of persuading the U.S. Administration that this is a reasonable point of view?

(3) In raising the matter with the U.S. Administration and, if necessary, in the explanations given to Congress, it should be pointed out that the relevance of such figures to lend lease appropriations is not what it was in the early days. At the outset of the lend lease system we had substantial assets in hand.

The United States Administration reasonably wanted to assure themselves and to assure Congress that we should make a proper use of these in liquidating our pre-lend lease commitments. In fact we slipped into a situation which was more onerous to us than the U.S. Treasury intended through misunderstandings with Congress. However that may be, the position now is quite different. By far the greater part of the assets that we had in hand when the lend lease system came into operation either have or shortly will have been disbursed to meet the old commitments and other obligations not covered by lend lease. Any assets which we may build up in the next year or two as the result of having got to the end of our old commitments will only be collected by entering into much larger obligations in other directions. They will not represent any net improvement of our position but, on the contrary, will be a very small off-set to a far greater deterioration of it. We are exploiting our credit throughout the world to finance our obligations outside the U.S.A. We cannot do this unless some modest proportion of the liabilities we are incurring is off-set by liquid reserves available to the Bank of England. It is altogether unreasonable that the amount of these reserves should be disclosed and the liabilities against which they are held should not be disclosed; or that the amount of such accumulations should be taken into account in voting future lend lease appropriations. There is a vital distinction from this point of view between our pre-war assets, which were still in hand a year ago, and future reserves, which we deem it prudent to keep in hand as a percentage of new obligations we are incurring. The appropriate amount of such new reserves depends on the amount of the liabilities against which they are held, which are almost entirely outside U.S.A. They no longer have any important connection with our dollar outgoings taken in isolation.

I feel that it is most imprudent of us to acquiesce in the old assumptions instead of getting the realities of this new position recognised by all whom it may concern. And now is the time for a change when the actual facts and figures are not much altered from the last disclosure rather than later on.

(4) If the amount of our sterling obligations was common knowledge relatively to our free reserves, we might have great difficulty in persuading our overseas creditors to allow further sums to accumulate in sterling. In any case, there is always the risk that we shall find it difficult to make them go on as freely as they have in the past, when the sums to their credit (and therefore fully within their own knowledge) get bigger and bigger. It is, therefore, only common prudence for us to do our utmost to accumulate a free reserve, not utterly disproportionate to the amount of such liabilities. We cannot explain this in detail to Congress without exposing our weakness to the whole world. It is not even advisable that we should disclose the complete position to the U.S. Treasury. But I should have thought that we could fairly easily convince the U.S. Treasury of our *bona fides* in this matter and of the reality of our difficulties, and that they would appreciate the vital importance to our credit of drawing a veil over such disquieting facts. At any rate, we should try. There is no predicting just how embarrassing continuance of the present position might prove to be in some at present quite unforeseeable circumstances. We simply cannot afford to disclose to Congress and to the world at large the real justification for our raising our free reserves somewhat higher than they are now.

(5) We are faced with the dilemma that, if the reserves we publish are very low, this will be highly damaging to our credit in the outside world; whilst, if they are not very low, they will give a weapon to isolationists or any other opposition elements in cutting down lend lease. Surely the U.S. Treasury can be made to see that we should not be presented with this dilemma.

(6) My recommendation would be that we should agree to give complete and accurate figures of our own gold reserves

and dollar balances to the U.S. Treasury for their strictly confidential information, with an absolute undertaking from them that there will be no publication. I should also be in favour of letting them know in general terms any changes in the position of our obligations outside U.S.A. But I should not give them particulars of this, and should only go into further details if they were turning troublesome as a result of our free reserves gradually becoming rather larger than they are now.

(7) I am not in general an advocate of secrecy; far from it, I was far from convinced that we could not have been more open before the war about our position. But in time of war the position is changed. We cannot afford the risks to our credit, which might be very serious indeed in the event of the war taking a serious turn the wrong way, which might result either from a partial disclosure of our position and still more from a complete disclosure of it. From one point of view, partial disclosure is worse; from another point of view, complete disclosure is worse.

31.12.41   J.M.K.

The entry of the United States into the war on 8 December 1941 after Pearl Harbor raised, for a time, the possibility that the financial arrangements embodied in lend lease would change considerably. Keynes distrusted proposals for radically new arrangements, as these would require fresh dealings with Congress that might prove disadvantageous to Britain. Rather, he suggested that matters should remain within the lend lease framework, with the addition of British mutual aid which had evolved in an informal way during 1941.

In the middle of January 1942, while Mr Churchill was in Washington, Keynes set out the way in which opinion had developed and events were developing to Sir Frederick Phillips.

To SIR FREDERICK PHILLIPS, *14 January 1942*

My dear Phillips,

Your letter of 18th October, now long ago, was greatly appreciated. I circulated it with comments to all those concerned at the time and prepared myself to send you a reply worthy of it. But one thing or another always intervened, and the news which I had got hot for you always turned out stale, or incorrect, or irrelevant, or unnecessary. So that and the immense amount of time elapsing gave me the discouragement we all feel about correspondence when weeks elapse between reply and rejoinder.

The fact of my failing to write to you a real proper letter also held up all sorts of little things on oddments. I see the only sensible thing is to push along anything that is ready. So now I am reforming my ways. Please forgive me and send me more letters. You have no idea how much they add to the atmosphere here and how much they are studied by all concerned, even though they seem to get no response.

I am answering a batch of letters on special matters. But you may like to know a little more on the general impression.

As soon as America came into the war all other Departments began innocently to assume that the financial position was competely transmogrified and that there would be some over-all pooling which meant that we need bother no more about exports or gold supplies or anything else. As soon as it was known that the Prime Minister was going, we here had to be a bit careful as to what we said, as we had not the foggiest idea what might be in prospect. But we did have to answer that, so far as we were aware, nothing revolutionary had happened. We hoped for a more liberal interpretation of lend lease etc. but no fundamentally new basis.

Whilst the Prime Minister has been away we have had practically no news except from you, nor has the Ministry of Supply. Both of the big boys being in Washington, there was,

I suppose, no one in London worth telegraphing to. It is, therefore, conceivable that when they get back they will have something startling to tell us. But we are not expecting it. The impression seems to be that, not only has no financial matter been given a minute's consideration, but even questions of administration have scarcely come into the picture. It has been a question of buddies sitting around writing large numbers of tanks and planes on paper and talking about high strategy.

It was this doubt as to whether anything important was going on which led to an even greater fluffiness than usual in our recent telegrams to you about policy in relation to the new appropriations. But in truth it was clear that there was nothing to be done except to accept your excellent advice. I felt all along that our only wise course was to urge you along the path which you obviously wished to tread,—using the new atmosphere to escape from the maximum amount of old commitments possible and see that there would be enough appropriations in future to cover marginal cases and Dominion demands. If you could accomplish all that, we should not be too badly off, in spite of diminished prospects from rubber, tin etc. There has never been any other practical policy. So that is in the end what we have fired off to you, and there was really no reason why it should not have been put crisply from the start. Best of luck in carrying it all out. I could not have agreed more with all your recent communications than I have.

But that is not the end of the story, and you may like to have a little bit of low-down on the mysteries in the last paragraph of our last telegram, talking about policies on a new and wider basis. The Bank of England is very insistent, and Catto has much sympathy with the objects of the proposal, though not the form of it, that we ought to press now for some far-reaching pooling agreement, by which in effect U.S. meet in cash any ultimate deficit we may find ourselves faced with in U.S.A., excluding the use of any of our gold. I too am entirely sympathetic to the idea underlying all this, if it is practical politics. But I am not myself at present persuaded (and in this I agree with Waley, Bewley and Playfair) that it is easy to concoct a plan which would have much chance of getting through and be at the same time sufficiently serviceable to our purposes.

The general idea underlying such a scheme would be an extension of reciprocal lend lease, by which we supplied free of charge all services and expenditures of U.S.A. in the sterling area and all their imports from the sterling area; they on their part to go on lend-leasing us everything that was suitable to the lend lease machinery, to take over the whole of the financial responsibility for the old commitments and meet any cash and other outgoings we might have in excess of our own dollar cash receipts. This would be on the basis of the sterling area retaining the whole of its current gold production.

Obviously, on grounds of general principle, there is a great deal to be said for this. It is all more decent and proper in point of form. My difficulty is that it would not, so far as I can see, put us materially better off than we could be under a liberal administration of the existing arrangements, whilst it would mean approaching Congress with all the sore points which, at present, it is possible to keep under cover.

For, if U.S.A. is now ready to treat us more liberally, there is no reason why they should not take over all the old commitments through the existing machinery. If this is done, and if there is maximum liberality towards marginal cases and Dominion requirements also under the existing arrangement, I see no reason to suppose that we should not be substantially as well off as under the proposed pooling arrangements. Indeed, if a point comes, as it well may, when U.S.A. has heavy outgoings in the sterling area, we might quite possibly find ourselves substantial losers. Also, I feel that the transition from war to peace conditions might be still more difficult to handle; though on this I suppose two opinions might be held.

Meanwhile, we should be having to face Congress with just those points which hitherto it has seemed most unwise to emphasise. They would have to agree to meet those of our cash outgoings which are not susceptible to OLLA control; they would have to agree to leave our gold output out of account; and we should be very nearly, if not quite, re-introducing the dollar sign. All this would be difficult to explain, it seems to me, unless there were some compelling reason behind it and great pressure from the No. Ones. U.S.A. would think they were giving us a much more generous deal than in fact they probably would be. So, is it all worth while?

I am far from having reached a clear conclusion on the matter. Nor is any concrete scheme yet drafted in a fit state to be criticised. But I think it might help you to have some inkling of the vague talks which are going on.

There is another matter, much more urgent in my judgment, partly mixed up with the above, but largely independent. The growth of balances in favour of other parts of the sterling area is now becoming unmanageable. One hopes that the discussions, going on as I write this letter, in regard to Canada will clear that out of the way for the time being. But India remains an appalling problem, with Egypt as a good example of the minor difficulties. The more the war moves to the East, the more we spend in the Middle East, India, etc., with the result that, under the existing financial arrangements, Egyptian and Indian balances rise at a feverish rate. The Indian position is changing so quickly; it is difficult to estimate, but we are told that in the course of February alone our payments to the Indian Office will be so gigantic that Indian balances will rise in the course of the month by £42 million. We hope this is above the monthly average. But the average seems to be over £20 million and may approach £30 million. We have already vested practically all the Indian securities available.

The way in which this is mixed up with the American position is that we could get some mitigation if we charged India, Egypt, etc. for all they get under lend lease. I have always thought there was a strong case where civilian supplies were involved. But, if the amount of money were to be a real relief, we should have to include military supplies also. It would be extremely useful to have your opinion whether, if the whole situation were exposed to the Americans, they would be ready to approve a new principle, by which the value of all re-transfers to the Dominions from ourselves should be charged up against them and inure to our benefit. We should couple this with readiness to lend lease ourselves to any Dominion which had a balance the wrong way, as might, for example, be the case with Australia (though they look to be pretty well balanced on the current year). At any rate, our real problem is the financial arrangements with the sterling area—at least so I think—rather than with U.S.A.

The question whether or not we should have a wages policy simmers along with rather acrimonious interchanges between the Chancellor and Bevin.[9] But Bevin's last rejoinder was a formidable document, and most of us think that there is really quite a good case for drifting along as we are now, unless the situation takes a decidedly worse turn. The internal financial position is really surprisingly good. The price fixing policy has held and is costing us less than we expected. Small savings are not bad at all. It is arguable that the under £250 group are saving twice as much now as they were a year ago. The Revenue returns are extraordinary. In spite of there being apparently nothing to sell, the receipts of the Purchase Tax constantly exceed expectations. We can get as much more out of beer and tobacco in the next budget as we choose to ask. And so on under almost every head of revenue.

The Tax Reserve Certificates are a great success, and in the

9 For more on these matters see *JMK*, vol. XXII.

short time they have been opened £40 million have been subscribed, though this is the lean time of year for them. We expect the total subscription to reach at least £200 million, and I should not myself be surprised at more.

The chief trouble is about income tax on weekly wage earnings, the system of taxing them on their incomes in arrear does not work well. The question whether any change is possible is under active consideration.

Yours ever,

[copy initialled] J. M. K.

The period after America's entry into the war also saw renewed discussion of the 'consideration' issue, this time on the basis of the State Department's counter proposal for Article VII of 2 December.[10] Initially the Foreign Office, in the new era of a common effort, repeatedly urged acceptance of the American view. However Keynes was horrified at the idea of easy acceptance as a means of getting Britain's own way in the long run. The following handwritten comment on one Foreign Office proposal sets out his views briefly.

Minute on N. BUTLER *to* S. D. WALEY, *30 December 1941*

The theory that 'to get our own way in the long run' we must always yield in the short run reminds me of the bombshell I threw into economic theory by the reminder that 'in the long run we are all dead'. If there was *no one* left to appease, the F.O. would feel out of a job altogether.

31.12.41   J. M. K.

---

[10] The relevant segment of the American revised draft ran: 'To that end, they shall include provision for agreed action by the United Kingdom, open to participation by all other countries of like mind, directed to the expansion, by appropriate international and domestic measures, of production, employment, and exchange and consumption of goods which are the material foundation of the liberty and welfare of all peoples; to the elimination of all forms of discriminating treatment in international commerce, and to the reduction of tariffs and other trade barriers; and, in general to the objectives set forth in the joint declaration made on the 12th August, 1941....'

What will arouse suspicion will be our agreeing to unreasonable demands against our better judgment and then *inevitably* having to find some way of slipping out of our ill-advised words.

J. M. K.

With the New Year, Mr Churchill's visit to the United States, and the assumption that lend lease would remain the basis of Anglo-American financial arrangements, discussions were renewed on Article VII. As before, the issues of Imperial Preference and Britain's post-war economic position loomed largest. Keynes's contribution took the form of a note of 12 February.

To SIR HORACE WILSON, *12 February 1942*

LEND LEASE CONSIDERATION

Everything in the attached paper by Mr Waley is perfectly sound. But I should be a little inclined to approach the Prime Minister and other members of the Cabinet with a more simplified argument on rather different lines, such as the following:–

We can safely assume from now on that financial considerations will not be allowed to interfere with supplies from U.S.A. during the war. It is also most unlikely, whatever happens now, that we shall in fact pay for goods supplied under the lend lease arrangements. Nevertheless, if no agreement is reached, the position may be used as a continuing source of pressure on us later on, and we may find ourselves put into a somewhat humiliating position before we can escape.

It is not, however, anxiety on either of these headings which is the main ground for attaching importance to arriving at a friendly settlement if we can do so in any reasonable way.

There are two important purposes which would be served by an immediate settlement of the financial matters which Mr Morgenthau has put up before the President and are now lying on the President's table in conjunction with Article VII of the draft consideration agreement.

(1) The first of these is that, if these arrangements go through, it would be financially possible for us to undertake reciprocal or 'reverse' lend lease arrangements for the United States forces operating outside U.K. For munitions proper this would be necessary in any case. But, if we are strong enough financially to settle marginal cases on liberal lines, it may considerably facilitate the pooling of supplies and services on the physical side. If we can keep all accounting between us and U.S. to really important cases and to the minimum when our Forces are operating in the same theatres of war, sources of friction and possible delay will be avoided. If we have to go on fighting for our dollars day by day, these advantages will be lost.

(2) A primary purpose of the Treasury negotiations is to preserve some measure of financial independence in the immediate post-war period. That is at the same time the force of our case and the weakness of it. Mr Morgenthau is believed to have advised the President, provided article VII is settled satisfactorily, to take over from us the finance of the old commitments, estimated to amount to $800 million. These supplies have been physically pooled. It is, therefore, reasonable that they should be pooled financially also. This proposal is coupled with an offer on our part, if it goes through, that we ourselves will furnish the United States with all munitions from the sterling area on the same lend lease terms. Obviously it is most desirable that this settlement should be reached. On the other hand, if it does not go through, we shall not be actually short of dollars for the immediate purposes of the war. That is the weakness of our case. We need not suppose that the United States will interfere in the least

with war supplies. They are, however, in a position to make us pay for them to our last dollar or ounce of gold. If the settlement we hope for is arrived at, from now onwards our gold reserves will increase steadily from an exiguous figure, and we may hope to end the war with a reserve possibly as great as £250 million. Even this sum will be extremely small, since our inevitable adverse balance of trade in the first year after the war will be fully equal to that figure. But it will be enough to give us some measure of financial independence. If we emerge from the war with almost non-existent reserves —far less to bless ourselves with than France or Holland or even Belgium—this financial weakness is bound to reflect on our authority and influence in other spheres. The Americans will see us through the war all right. But it would be unfortunate that we should have so managed our affairs during the war as to have parted with the foundations of independent action immediately afterwards.

Again, although we may confidently rely on the continuance of lend lease arrangements during the period of hostilities, it is of the greatest importance to us that they should not suddenly cease so far as food and raw materials are concerned when the war is over. It is at that date that the consequences of a bad settlement to-day will show themselves.

If the danger to which we were supposed to be exposed by withholding an agreement to Article VII is the interruption of lend lease supplies or having to pay in cash for those we have already received, we could afford to ignore any such suggestions, since a threat on these lines is surely empty. But financial arrangements which would hamstring us after the war are of more real danger.

Finally, there is the risk of highly undesirable publicity. Lord Halifax's last telegram indicates that, if there is a breakdown at this stage of the negotiations, the U.S. State Department will acknowledge this publicly. They will publish to

Congress the offer they have made and inform Congress that we have refused it. This might result in the worst possible consequence, namely, that Congress itself would take out of the hands of the State Department future negotiations on 'consideration'. If that happens, there will be reason to despair of a sensible arrangement.

12.2.42 [copy initialled] J.M.K.

On the same day as the previous minute, President Roosevelt, who on 5 February had urged Britain's acceptance of the revised State Department draft since 'further delay...will be harmful to your interests and ours', cabled the Prime Minister that the document did not imply the trading of imperial preference for lend lease. All he was asking for was 'a bold, forthright, and comprehensive discussion looking forward to the construction of what you so aptly call "a free, fertile economic policy for the post-war world" excluding nothing in advance'.

On this assurance, a British proposal for an exchange of notes qualifying Article VII disappeared. After consulting the Dominions, Britain signed the agreement on 23 February.

Chapter 7

WORKING WITHIN LEND LEASE, 1942–43

The continuance of lend lease in its earlier framework, with the addition of the Combined Boards, did not remove the problems of the 'old commitments', the level of Britain's exchange reserves and the disclosure of the reserve levels to Congress. Nor did the signing of the Mutual Aid agreement settle the position regarding reverse lend lease, where the principles applicable to the overseas sterling area became entangled in the problem of Britain's rising overseas indebtedness.[1]

The negotiations concerning the 'old commitments' dragged on until May, finally resulting in American concessions worth $292 million. Although this amount was well below that which Keynes had attempted to obtain in Washington in 1941, it effectively removed the problem of dollar inadequacy in so far as Britain's immediate needs were concerned. However, it did not resolve the problem of the appropriate level of Britain's reserves, given her growing liabilities and prospective post-war needs, nor the problem of how best to present the existing situation to the Americans so as to avoid the twin dangers of political pressure for cuts in lend lease and possible distrust of sterling and a consequent unwillingness to continue accumulating sterling balances elsewhere.

Keynes's 1941 attempts to prevent publication of Britain's reserves which culminated in his memorandum of 31 December (above pp. 214–18) led to instructions to Sir Frederick Phillips to try the case on Mr Morgenthau and Mr Bell. When they intimated that any concealment from Congress was politically impossible, the British agreed to provide the figures in the traditional gross form with a qualifying statement.[2]

Although there were to be various alarms concerning gold shipments and exchange resources in the winter and spring of 1942, the possibility of

---

[1] For an early Keynes reference to the problem, see above p. 222. For a fuller discussion of Keynes's involvement and proposals see below pp. 262–3, 276ff.

[2] 'British holdings of gold and U.S. dollars are not held solely or specifically against our liabilities in the U.S., but constitute a partial cover for obligations and responsibilities of great magnitude and worldwide character. Gold currently acquired differs from our original stocks in that it can be acquired only by further increasing our overseas indebtedness.' 5 February 1942.

Britain's reserves actually rising came to the fore and with this the problem of informing Congress arose in a new guise. Keynes reopened the discussion on 20 April.

To LORD CATTO *and* SIR RICHARD HOPKINS, *20 April 1942*

THE PUBLICATION OF OUR RESERVE POSITION TO THE CONGRESS

We have to remember that we are still a long way from happy about this and must raise it with Phillips when he is here on his next visit. I am making this note as a reminder to be brought up for discussion when he is here.

If Cobbold's[3] policy of not exporting gold is successfully held to, we may expect to have a holding of £m200 or more by the end of this calendar year, increasing steadily thereafter. If this position has to be reported to the Americans *sans phrase*, I do not see how we can hope to avoid difficulty. Yet, in spite of this respectable increase in our reserves, we shall in fact, taking everything into account, be further down the drain at the end of this calendar year than we were at the end of last.

We must, therefore, find a form of publication to the Americans which makes this clear and does not isolate gold as past statements have. The Americans do not really want gold as such. Nothing is more useless to them. They want merely to be assured that we are not sponging on them unnecessarily and that we have a legitimate need for the assistance which they are giving.

I suggest, therefore, that there are two principles which we should endeavour to establish:–

(1) that the figures for gold are not given separately;

(2) that absolute figures are not given henceforward, but an accurate comparison of the deterioration or improve-

[3] Cameron Fromanteel Cobbold (b. 1904), 1st Baron 1960; entered Bank of England as Adviser, 1933; Executive Director, 1938; Deputy Governor, 1945; Governor, 1949–61.

ment of our position compared with what it was last time we reported.

The first principle is necessary in order to give a correct over-all picture; the second is necessary in order not to give away to the whole world the weakness of our total net position, as it would be if absolute figures were provided. Comparative figures should surely be sufficient proof to the Americans as to whether we are gaining or losing ground as a result of their assistance.

I believe that it would be a useful first step, both statistically and in our own minds, if the monthly report, with which the Bank of England have been providing us relating primarily to the Exchange Equalisation Fund, were drastically revised hereafter, so as to conform to the realities of the situation as they have now developed. The emphasis on the Exchange Equalisation Account as such is partly a mere piece of accounting arising out of the fact that it is a separate determinate fund; partly it is a survival of the time when these were the only figures of which we had accurate information at the end of each month. Chiefly, I suppose, it is a survival of the days when there was a sharp distinction between hard and soft currencies. For these historical reasons it is now an amalgamation of gold, U.S. dollars, our Canadian position and a bunch of minor currencies, most of which are frozen. The result is that the final outcome is not intelligible or significant as it stands, and in present circumstances it entirely leaves out the accumulation of our more dangerous liabilities.

Hitherto a more comprehensive picture has been compiled in rather an amateurish way for the purposes of the White Paper and the aggregate of overseas disinvestment. The Bank of England is now engaged in a much more professional compilation. The figures up to the end of March should be available before very long. This might be the opportunity for considering the form for a revised statement, relegating the Exchange Equalisation Account as such to the accountants.

I need not burden this note with attempting to make precise suggestions as to exactly what this new statement should contain. My immediate purpose is to suggest that it should form the starting point of a new kind of return to the Americans. We shall have, incidentally, the good excuse that it will embody new information which has not hitherto been available in any very accurate form.

When we have such a statement as the above, we can easily see how it best lends itself to reproduction for use in America in a form which is at the same time accurate in neither overstating nor understating the change in our true position and is fairly innocuous in not divulging embarrassing details. We have a good excuse, and not merely a good reason, for not isolating our gold reserves from every other form of reserve. Some of our liabilities are definitely in gold; some of them are potentially in gold; nearly all of them can be discharged by gold; and, indeed, when peace comes there are few of them which can be definitely protected from becoming a gold liability except by some version of blocking. Thus the general idea would be to show, say, at six months' intervals, the increase in our overseas liabilities, the liquidation of our pre-war capital assets and the increase of our reserves in the shape of gold and various foreign currencies.

This is not a bad date at which to institute such a statement, since, whilst our liabilities will be increasing four or five times as rapidly as our reserves, they will not be increasing at quite so indecent a rate as hitherto, as a result of the more complete operation of lend lease and the Canadian gift.

22.4.42   [copy initialled] J.M.K.

When Sir Frederick Phillips was in London on one of his periodic visits, after a preliminary discussion with Mr Waley and Mr N. Young,[4] Keynes raised the issue in more general terms.

[4] Norman Egerton Young (1892–1964); entered Treasury, 1919; Financial Adviser, British Embassy, Paris, 1939–40; British Government Director, Suez Canal, 1939–45.

THE FINANCIAL DEAL WITH U.S.A.

1. Even though we have to give up the prospect of getting take-outs for the air contracts, we are in no serious risk of running short of dollars. Our gold reserves are likely to increase steadily and, in the course of time, fairly substantially from now on. Thus any increase in our dollar resources will appear to be in excess of our needs, and the prospect of this has, no doubt, played a part in the difficulty of getting the air contract take-outs.

2. This difficulty is accentuated by the form in which the statistics of our financial position are given to the U.S. Treasury and to Congress. From now onwards we shall appear to be getting richer and richer the longer the war lasts; whereas in actual fact very much the opposite is the truth.

3. In short, it is now quite out of date to regard our dollar problem as the essence of our financial difficulties. That is a hangover from the pre-lend lease and early lend lease days. No doubt we should be quite glad to get a further margin against contingencies; but substantially that problem is solved, and we need not from now onwards bother our heads about it unduly.

4. But that does not mean that all our financial troubles are over. It merely means that their centre of gravity has shifted. What now alarms us is the steady growth of our sterling liabilities to really enormous dimensions, with great prospective embarrassment to our post-war position.

5. This growth in our overseas financial burdens outside the dollar area calls attention to the fact that there has been no fundamental revision of financial responsibilities for the war between ourselves and the United States since they en-

tered the war. The principle still is that, whilst they help us with dollar expenditure, we are responsible for all miscellaneous financial outgoings in every other part of the world. This was the only possible arrangement when we were fighting the war alone. Today it is an indefensible survival of the fiction that obligations incurred in the sterling area, which happens to cover the whole area of hostilities, cost us nothing.

6. Our principal financial need today is, therefore, a revised arrangement covering our respective financial obligations overseas which does not add to our dollar assets (which is no longer necessary), but reduces or sets a limit to the growth in our sterling liabilities.

7. This can only be brought about by an arrangement which causes some part of the growth of the external balances of various overseas countries to take the form of dollar balances instead of sterling balances. A re-arrangement of this kind would have in fact considerable advantages from everyone's point of view. The overseas countries in question have already got more sterling balances than they care about and would much prefer that at least some part of any addition should take the form of dollar balances. In the revival of post-war trade it will suit the United States that these countries should not be so overwhelmingly in possession of sterling, as distinguished from dollar, resources. From our point of view it will be immeasurably easier to regulate and control the outflow of these liquid sterling resources if our creditors have separate dollar funds and are under no pressing necessity to turn any part of their sterling into dollars.

8. In what follows I apply this general principle in the first instance to the Middle East area, for which it seems specially suitable. But there is no reason why we need stop there. It might apply to certain neutral countries and perhaps eventually to India. On the other hand, there is no reason why it need apply to the Dominions or to the Colonies.

9. The principle would not apply to the pay, food and

lodging either of British or American troops, which would remain the separate responsibility of whichever of the two governments was concerned. But all other outgoings, e.g. in the Middle East area, retrospective to the date of the United States entering the war, would be shared equally between the United Kingdom and the United States.

10. The following are illustrations of the kind of headings under which the outgoings in question would fall:–

(1) Expenses for the improvement of transport and communications in the Middle Eastern countries.

(2) Assistance to the Free French in Syria or elsewhere.

(3) Assistance in any shape or form to the governments of the Middle Eastern countries, either by loan or from free services or otherwise, including Egypt, Ethiopia, Palestine, Syria, Turkey, Iraq and Iran.

(4) Expenses incurred in these countries for prisoners of war.

(5) Subsidies in these territories, part of which would overlap with (3) above, such as the subsidy to the Negus, the subsidy to Ibn Saud, and any other such.

(6) Expenses of civil administration of occupied areas.

(7) The costs of supporting or supplanting local currencies.

11. The responsibility thus assumed by the United States should not take the form, as it would if nothing were done to the contrary, of supplying these countries with more dollars, which they would then turn over to the sterling area exchange control, thus at the same time increasing British dollar balances and British sterling liabilities. It should take the form of the Middle Eastern countries in question acquiring, directly or indirectly, dollar balances in place of sterling balances, which would become available to them for use after the war.

12. It would be premature to discuss the most convenient technique to adopt. The object aimed at is clear enough,

namely, that an appropriate part of the unspent liquid balances of these countries should take the form of dollars instead of sterling.

13. Some of the recipients are not in a position to accumulate dollars. Retrospectively, therefore, adjustment could only be made by the U.S. taking a proportionately larger share in respect of those countries which are accumulating balances. But there need be no difficulty in carrying out this general principle, once adopted. Take, for example, the case of Ibn Saud. He accumulates no balances, but receives a monthly subsidy in the shape of gold. Henceforth, under the above arrangement, half this subsidy would be provided by U.S.A.

Doubtless a project such as this would have to be raised in the first instance at a high level. The completion of reciprocal lend lease arrangements would provide a suitable opportunity for raising it. I doubt whether the fact of our sole financial responsibility for the miscellaneous cost of the war in all areas of hostilities is properly appreciated by the higher powers. We are not, so far as I am aware, getting any credit for carrying this oecumenical burden.

9.6.42   [copy initialled] J.M.K.

At that point, the issues raised by Keynes simply contributed to the general climate of opinion in London. However they soon became known, at least in part, to the Americans when Mr Stettinius[5] visited London in July and August. In the course of his visit, Mr Stettinius met Keynes on three occasions. On two of them, Keynes wrote notes on what transpired.

[5] Edward R. Stettinius (1900–49); member, Advisory Committee to Council of National Defence, 1940; Chairman, Priorities Board, and Director, Priorities Division, Office of Production Management, 1941; Lend Lease Administration and special assistant to President, 1941–3; Under-Secretary of State, 1943–4; Secretary of State, 1944–5.

To LORD CATTO *and others, 22 July 1942*

NOTES ON CONVERSATION WITH MR STETTINIUS, 21 JULY 1942

Present: Mr Stettinius   Lord Catto
               Mr Winthrop Brown   Lord Keynes

The conversation began by my giving the general background of our financial requirements in various parts of the world. I explained that, if our U.S. dollar requirements were taken in isolation, existing lend lease assistance was probably fully adequate, and we were not likely to run short of dollars. Moreover, in view of the probable receipts from American troops in the sterling area, it was now unlikely that we should have to supplement our dollar resources by the shipment of any gold. I had the impression that Mr Stettinius was not alive to the very large sums in dollars we were likely to receive through the presence of American troops in the sterling area. He clearly had no figure in mind and had not been told the average sterling expenditure per head which would be paid for by dollars and not by reciprocal aid. I gave him a general hint of what this would amount to.

I went on to say that in asking for anything more we were laying ourselves open to the accusation of being greedy; having regard to the dollar position alone. On the other hand, taking our requirements in other parts of the world, our financial impoverishment was progressive. I gave him some general facts about this with particular reference to India and the Middle East, which seemed to be completely news to him. I do not think he had any idea whatever of our disbursements in these quarters. He was ready to appreciate the difficulty of our acquiring funds from India, at any rate in present circumstances, as compared with the rest of the Dominions. I touched more lightly on the neutral countries. I explained in broad outline the Canadian position and pointed out that it might be necessary to sweeten the position there with a view to a second grant by providing them with some gold or dollars meanwhile.

I had the impression that Mr Stettinius fully recognised the force of the case, and he then went on to ask what we should do with increased resources, if we acquired them. I replied that, so far as gold was concerned, we should try to raise our gold reserves to the level of a billion dollars, with a view to the post-war situation, and we should also like to end the war with a reasonable amount of free dollar balances. During the war we should make use of any increased financial ease to pay out gold or dollars to neutral countries or others who were reluctant to allow their sterling balances to increase without limit; that we might help the Canadian position; that there were a number of blocked or semi-blocked American holdings of sterling which we should like to release freely; and we should also then feel that we could go ahead with reciprocal aid on the most liberal lines without any feeling of embarrassment.

In that case, Mr Stettinius said, what are the concrete ways in which you think I could help? Naturally I adverted first of all to the air contracts. He made it clear at once that he was on our side in that matter and was of the opinion that that was the major assistance that we could, and should, have. At a later stage in the conversation, after we had joined Mr Waley, he said in so many words that he was wholly on our side in that matter, that he had not given up the battle, that he intended to fight it vigorously on his return to Washington, and one of his purposes in coming was to gather evidence and information which would assist him in the task. He then went on to suggest that perhaps he might help us over the hard core of miscellaneous items by arranging for a free credit in cash up to (say) $2 million a month, out of which we could meet bits and pieces. I welcomed this on administrative grounds and added that, if this procedure was once adopted, it might save both of us a great deal of trouble to bring under the new procedure various oddments which are at present subject to lend lease.

On his asking about further measures to help, I said that there were still directions in which lend lease could be liberalised and instanced in particular supplies to our Caribbean possessions and the distinction of combatant and non-combatant areas in the Colonies, which had the effect of discriminating against West Africa as compared, for example, with East Africa. Although this ancient bone of contention has been the subject of innumerable telegrams, he seemed to have the dimmest acquaintance with the problem, and I was doubtful whether he was even aware that his Department had ruled against us. At a later stage in the conversation, when this matter was explained in more detail, he immediately said that he would see that the position was revised in our favour. Not a great deal of money in this, but it will save much friction with the Colonial Office.

Mr Stettinius then changed the subject and said that he personally was giving earnest consideration to the question of putting matters on a different basis with Congress, in particular getting rid of the term 'lend lease' and some of its inconvenient associations. He said that the President's Fifth Lend-Lease Report, which went a very long way in the liberalising direction, had had an excellent press. (I had the impression that Mr Stettinius had either written this or had at least contributed to it.) He said that speeches by Mr Sumner Welles and Mr Acheson in the same direction had also had a good press, and he thought that in the autumn the political atmosphere might be ripe for a further step forward.* Could we help him in suggesting a better name? He had had in mind

---

* On this part of the conversation Lord Catto adds as follows: Mr Stettinius told us that in the minds of many in Congress lend lease had still its old meaning, i.e. that something would come back, and in fact that there should be consideration. He mentioned that when he gave evidence before Congress last time, he was asked why we did [?not] give Bermuda as consideration; but his view was that all this must be changed now. Since America came into the war, there had been a marriage and he was anxious to see a pooling of resources as indicated in the last paragraph of the President's Fifth Lend-Lease Report.

something like 'United Nations Reciprocal Aid', but obviously felt this was a bit clumsy.

Lord Catto and I warmly welcomed this and went on to point out that, if the lend lease association were got rid of, it might help us considerably on the knotty problem of the keeping of records. Reciprocal aid had brought this to a head. The keeping of proper records would use up uselessly thousands of clerks and soldiers and would be a shocking waste of manpower. Could we, if we got rid of the description of 'lend lease' also greatly mitigate the obligation to keep records and give instead descriptions of the kind of services required, rather than meticulous lists of every single individual operation. Mr Stettinius thought this very desirable and was obviously as much opposed to records as we were, on the grounds of the unnecessary administrative labour and inconvenience caused.

At that point Mr Playfair joined us, and we went to Mr Waley's room to continue the conversation, which covered partly the same ground as the above.

Mr Stettinius talks of visiting the Treasury again in about a fortnight's time, when we might perhaps think of some further points it would be worth putting to him. No one could be more helpful and quicker at taking up points. Mr Winthrop Brown adopted, rather usefully, the position of devil's advocate. Once or twice he gave me the impression of thinking, perhaps rightly, that his master was moving a bit too fast and giving us too much encouragement. After I had explained why we wanted to build up gold and dollar reserves, in spite of our immediate U.S. dollar position being secured, he remarked that, in substance, our purposes were entirely post-war and would, for that reason, not commend themselves to Congress at the present stage of things. I replied that substantially there was a great deal of truth in this. On the other hand, if we were starved of free resources, felt our current obligations growing to an unmanageable weight and were unable to eke out the immediate position, e.g., by help to Canada or by making part payment in gold or dollars to neutral countries, our war-time efficiency was definitely impaired. Also, if we felt free to interpret reciprocal aid on the most liberal lines, if we wished to, that also would certainly assist efficiency. I added that, in so far as our purposes were post-war, there was nothing indefensible or unreasonable in that. We were carrying the whole financial burden of the war in the Middle East and many other parts of the world, and it was wholly reasonable that we should be free to accumulate gold and even dollars as an off-set to the much greater liabilities we were incurring in the common cause in those parts of the world. Mr Brown did not dispute these contentions and said that he only wanted to bring out the other side of the matter, because that was certainly what Mr Stettinius might be called on to answer when he went home. I pointed out that one certainly would not put the case to Congress as having primarily a post-war importance, since there were fully adequate reasons for the assistance in question on grounds arising entirely out of the war.

Mr Brown also raised more than once some of the more controversial issues relating to South America, in particular to the sale of our South American investments and the question of our exports to South America. There was a suggestion on Mr Stettinius's part of their giving us greater assistance in that direction on the basis of our diminishing our activities and our possessions in that part of the world. This was dangerous ground, and I left Lord Catto to take up the tale and explain some of the perplexities of it. Mr Brown was much more persistent on this subject than Mr Stettinius, who became quickly aware, I think, of the underlying difficulties and did not press the point.

22.7.42   J. M. KEYNES

To E. PLAYFAIR, *6 August 1942*

At a farewell meeting this morning Stettinius raised again the question of sending out to him a brief which might help him in supporting the case for the abolition of records, at any rate so far as reciprocal aid is concerned. He asked to be supplied with some good specimen cases of the waste of time and manpower which would be involved by a contrary policy. Could you undertake this?

Salter, who was dining with me last night, I found to be very much up in arms on the same side, but being under the delusion that it was the Treasury which was insisting on records. He gave the example of conveying American troops by the Queen Mary and the task of working out in terms of money just how much more expensive the Queen Mary was to run than a more ordinary transport, not in order that we should charge the Americans the sums which were arrived at, but purely for record. He also instanced the case of oil bunkers, where he had found his staff trying to arrive at a figure worked out by averages, some of the oil having been bought at one price, some at another price, a third lot lent-leased and, therefore, chargeable at nothing; the freight and storage of each consignment having varied and some of that freight having been lent-leased; the completion of the whole task accurately being a most formidable undertaking. Stettinius was impressed by these examples and said that, if you could give him a certain number suitable for him to produce when challenged when he is on stand before Congress, he would be very grateful. This is well worth doing, for it may be the thin end of the wedge for getting the money values out of the debit side of the account as well.

I mentioned to Stettinius that in the last version of the Reciprocal Aid Agreement which had reached us the reference to records had tacitly disappeared. I gather he was inclined to claim some of the credit for this. He told us that, after his meeting at the Treasury the other day, he had cabled both to Acheson and to Morgenthau pressing the case against records, and he had reason to believe that he had made progress in convincing them.

I mentioned above that Salter was under the belief that it was the Treasury (the usual whipping boy) which was insisting on wasting the time of his staff in preparing these statements. As soon as the position is cleared up with the Americans, it might be well to notify all our departments in no uncertain terms what our actual policy and preference in this matter is.

6.8.42   [copy initialled] K

Keynes's change of signature will be noted. He had been made a Baron in the birthday honours list of 1942.

Britain's current and prospective international position continued to worry Keynes and led to several more notes and memoranda before the end of the year. Two notes in September, supplemented by a note of a conversation in October and Treasury discussions with Mr White and Mr Morgenthau in November, although they did not lead to immediate changes, brought several changes in policy in 1943 after considerable Treasury and Bank discussion and further American pressure.[6]

OUR PROSPECTIVE DOLLAR BALANCES

I. *The Statistical Position*

At the end of July the Bank of England estimated that our E.E.A dollar balances at the end of the year might be expected to stand at about £m50. They have now revised this to £m69. Net gold at the end of June was £m112 (£m179—25 Belgian —36 special a/c and Swiss registered gold liability—6 U.S.

[6] See below pp. 316–47 for events and thinking in the Middle East and India. For reciprocal aid, see Sayers, *Financial Policy*, ch. XIII.

registered sterling). South Africa is now selling gold to us at a very slow rate, but, even assuming the continuance of this, net gold should be not less than £m131 on 31 December; or (say) £m200 in gold and dollars.

This is already within striking distance of the $m1,000 which is the latest figure we have mentioned to U.S. as our aim. Yet it is probably a very conservative estimate. The best (or the worst, according to how you are looking at it) might be much higher for the following reasons:-

(a) Receipts from U.S. troops in the sterling area might be higher. The Bank estimates assume a receipt of £m21.6 in the calendar year 1942 in respect of troops in the U.K., of which £m15 had been already received by 7 September, so that the estimate assumes no material increase in the rate of receipts during the last third of the year compared with the first two thirds.

(b) The Bank has put in a figure for the 'unidentified' sources of income at the equivalent of only three-quarters of the actual receipts of the June quarter; and similarly in the case of 'other receipts' for the rest of the sterling area. If the June quarter experience was repeated for the rest of the year, our receipts (including the rest of the sterling area) would be £m16 above the estimate.

(c) Nothing is allowed for possible further concessions under lend lease such as the air contracts; and the special receipts from sale of planes, capital facilities etc. in the second half of the year are put at the moderate figure of £m16, which might be exceeded.

(d) Purchases of gold are put very low above and assume that there is no further vesting of South African securities or any improved settlement with South Africa in other respects.

(e) There is no allowance for receipts from Russia.

Thus it is not beyond the limits of possibility that the aggregate dollars and net gold might reach the $m1,000 by December 31 or soon after. When we get into 1943, with

B[ritish]P[urchasing]C[ommission] outgoings wilting, the time-lag in lend lease to the rest of the sterling area overtaken, and increased U.S. troops in the sterling area, the figure will rise substantially and cumulatively—perhaps by something between £m3 and £m4 a week for dollars and gold taken together, so that the total might cross $m1,500 before the end of the year, of which about half might be in dollars. If South Africa accepts the Bank of England's policy about gold sales, it is possible that the total reserves might reach $m2,000 by the end of the year.

The above is on the assumption that none of the off-setting measures suggested below have been taken.

II. *The Adequacy of the Reserves*

This increase in our liquid assets does not mean an improvement in our net position—very much the contrary. Currently our liquid assets may be increasing by £m1–2 a week, and next year, perhaps, by £m3–4 a week. But our gross liabilities (or loss of assets), against which this has to be set, are increasing at the rate of more than £m10 a week. The point is that the centre of gravity of the problem has changed hemispheres. The increase in our gold and dollar reserves is an indication of this, and *not* of our being too greedy and of the Americans (and Canadians) being too liberal. Nevertheless this development carries great dangers with it. For the increase in our gold and dollar assets is (so far as the Americans are concerned) in the shop-window, whilst the increase in our liabilities is a carefully guarded and well-preserved secret.

One may doubt, moreover, whether it is sufficiently appreciated in U.S. or anywhere else that the dollar balances of the E.E.A. represent the consolidated dollar reserves of the whole of the sterling area and can scarcely be regarded as the private property of the U.K. at our sole disposal. The position in this respect is anomalous. The sterling area has pooled its dollar reserves in our hands, but not its gold reserves. This lies behind the decision of South Africa to keep the whole of their reserves in gold. But the rest of the sterling area, whilst not reducing their gold reserves, are not increasing them, and the whole of it, including South Africa, adhere loyally to the pooling of dollar reserves (though there have been some recent reports of indiscipline by the Belgian Congo). We now obtain a monthly report of the working balances of the other sterling area controls, which they hold to their separate account in terms of dollars. These have lately been declining and now stand at low figures. At the end of June Australia held a little less than $m5; South Africa's holding was only $m1.7, India's $m1.8, Egypt's $m2.5, and all the sterling area controls outside U.K. held in the aggregate less than $m12.

It is indeed preferable that the dollar balances of the sterling area should remain pooled in our hands, provided this does not lead to misunderstanding on the part of U.S.A. and hence to a reduction of the aggregate which it is thought reasonable for us to hold. Otherwise it might be better that the reserves should be a little more widely distributed.

If we in the U.K. intend to regard the entirety of our gold and dollar reserves as at our own free disposal for our own future expenditure, well and good. If not, we ought perhaps to face the position more frankly both in our minds and in discussions with the U.S. Administration. At present we are running into the position of accumulating reserves which are grossly insufficient to our total liabilities and yet of appearing to accumulate reserves which might be regarded as excessive for our own requirements, seeing that they are gained entirely at the expense of someone else's liberality. (I sometimes notice even amongst ourselves a suggestion of guilty conscience for trying to get from U.S.A. more than we need; whereas we ought to have a guilty conscience for not making still more strenuous efforts to accumulate reserves more adequate to the liabilities we are incurring. We are repeating our policy of accumulating large liquid overseas liabilities against insufficient reserves which was the cause of our downfall before we abandoned the gold standard.)

How are we to protect ourselves against the risk that too marked a growth of our dollar balances might cause a reversal of the present trend of the Lend Lease Administration towards liberality, and (incidentally) criticism of Mr Stettinius as the reward of his friendly attitude towards us? Even if it is true that any serious reversal of the principles of lend lease is unlikely during the war, especially now that we have reached the era of Reciprocal Aid, it may be quite another matter when we get to the immediate post-war period. Obviously, with the state of public information about these matters what it now is, our position is liable to be judged by the amount of our gross reserves, and not by the relation of these to our gross liabilities. If we hold £m400–500 in gold and dollars, we shall be expected to contribute more to world relief and suffer a more abrupt termination of lend lease to ourselves than we can well afford; and it may be no defence that we owe three times this amount and that, even apart from this and as a result of the loss of overseas assets, our own adverse balance in the first two years after the war will be liable to absorb the *whole* of these reserves, unless something is done about it. It will not be appreciated that our reserves at the end of the war will, in reality, belong to the rest of the sterling area except in so far as we block our liabilities; and they will, therefore, be treated as our own private wealth.

Unless we can discover some better and clearer manifest, we, who will in fact have borne the brunt of the financial sacrifice of the war and *literally alone* amongst the Allies will have suffered a serious reversal of our overseas financial position, will appear as having, on the one hand, played a nasty confidence trick on the rest of the sterling area, and on the other, as having deceived our American friends into putting up more money than we really required. That is how we shall look and be represented.

This is the major problem, for which it is not the purpose of this paper (it might be the subject of another one), which has a more limited scope, to find the safest and most honourable solution. I turn, rather, to some relatively minor suggestions by which we might perhaps avoid aggravating the dangers and suspicions facing us, on the assumption (at present indisputable) that we cannot neglect appearances. The fault of these is that they do avowedly deal with appearances, whereas greater frankness all round—with ourselves, with the rest of the sterling area and with the U.S. Administration—may be what is most needed.

III. *Gold Reserves* versus *Dollar Reserves*

An increase in our gold reserves is probably safer politically than an increase in our dollar balances. It is now well accepted in U.S. that it is no longer suitable to the relations between the two countries to expect us to ship gold to U.S. But the U.S. Treasury might find it difficult to justify to Congress a considerable growth in our dollar holdings, even though they themselves accepted the reasonableness of an increase in our total reserves in relation to our liabilities. Thus where we have the alternative—as we often have—of meeting expenses in dollars or in gold, we should prefer the former. This requires a conscious reversal of policy. For during the long period in which we were acquiring, or might have to acquire, dollars through the perilous shipment of gold, we naturally preferred the other alternative.

For example, if we cannot avoid making some cash payments to Canada, it is better that we should make them out of our dollar, than out of our gold, reserves. In negotiations with Switzerland, Portugal, Persia, etc. we often have the opportunity of choosing which suits us best.

I have heard it suggested that we cannot freely act in this way without the previous approval of the U.S. Treasury and that they might be reluctant to agree. Assuredly there should be no concealment from them and we have to carry them with us in any general policy we adopt. But the U.S. Treasury have never claimed, so far as I know, that our dollar balances are in any sense blocked, and it is most important to maintain the position that they are at our unrestricted disposal. In our relations with the U.S. Treasury any claims on our part for increased assistance should always be made on the basis of our *aggregate* reserves of gold and dollars in relation to our liabilities and our requirements.

There is, moreover, an extra reason in the new situation which is now developing why we are entitled to act freely on the lines suggested above. An important part of our dollar income will arise from the expenditures of the American Army in the sterling area, which in turn involve us in expenditures in all parts of the world. Dollars thus accruing should obviously be at our free disposal for any necessary purpose.

The Russians are entitled to pay what they owe us in gold or dollars at their option. At first they paid us in gold; more recently in dollars. We might encourage gold by offering cheap and acceptable terms of delivery. (The Russian payments deserve a special footnote. They paid us £m10 in gold, then $7 in dollars for supplies from this country. They have paid us $m3 in dollars and owe us another $m25 in dollars for supplies from U.S.)

As a minor point of statistical presentation; in giving the net figure for our dollar assets, the amount of U.S. registered sterling should be deducted from the gross amount of our dollar balances and not from our gold reserves. For in fact our liability is to find dollars, and not gold, for them. At the end of June 1942 U.S. registered sterling amounted to about £m6.

IV. *Quick Assets other than Gold and Dollars*

It is better not to melt quick assets into cash before we need. The following are examples:-

(i) The Bank estimates assumed that we shall receive a further £m6.2 from the Jesse Jones loan before the end of this year. Should we not postpone taking up this final instalment until we need it which (apart from the considerations I am chiefly concerned to emphasise) costs us interest?

(ii) We should not sell vested U.S. securities if we can possibly help it.

(iii) We should not vest South African Government securities against gold and, if we have to agree the transaction in principle, we should put off its consummation as long as possible.

(iv) We should not seek to transfer stock piles to American ownership but should, on the contrary, prefer to hold them ourselves. This applies particularly to wool, including current sales of wool. But it also applies generally to all stock piles. It also means that we should no longer be eager to get payment in advance or at the earliest possible date for supplies purchased by us on U.S. behalf. All this also requires a conscious reversal of policy, since hitherto we have been urging the Ministry of Supply in precisely the opposite direction.

V. *Is it advisable to borrow yet further in order to increase reserves?*

When dollars were acutely short, it was our policy to seize every opportunity to increase them at the expense of increasing correspondingly our sterling liabilities. Is it advisable to continue this in the new circumstances? Or should there be, here again, a conscious reversal of policy?

(i) We have spent three years educating every Government Department and all our officers overseas who are honestly seeking to serve the purposes of the Treasury, that the whole object of our financial policy is to obtain gold and dollars even at the cost of increasing our liabilities in sterling (as though the latter were no serious embarrassment). When lend lease came in, some people expected us to reverse it. We had to explain that we could not yet do so, because the problem of the old commitments had not been satisfactorily solved. But now, we not only can, but should, reverse this policy. The dollar problem, as such, having been solved, and the growth of our sterling liabilities having become our chief anxiety, it is now important *not* to swell our dollar resources unduly at the cost of still further increasing our sterling liabilities.

The process of de-education will be long and difficult —especially as we shall not be in a position to explain ourselves very fully and frankly to all those concerned. Our representative in Persia has recently provided a good example. He found that the Americans were providing themselves with Persian currency by selling dollars to the Bank of Persia, and he naturally thought that he would be serving our purposes by suggesting that *we* should provide the Persian currency against dollars, thus swelling our dollar balances and increasing our sterling liabilities to Persia. This is what we have been teaching everyone to do in all parts of the world.

(iii) The release of the blocked film balances and the discharge of certain other oddments of liabilities to U.S. which Mr Cobbold has proposed.

(iv) A greater willingness to allow gold or, preferably dollar payments to special account and registered sterling countries which are making difficulties about increasing their holdings of special sterling.

To sum up, I would rather hold gold and dollar reserves totalling £m250 whilst retaining quick assets and discharging our more embarrassing liabilities to the tune of £m250, than raise the reserves to £m500 at the cost of parting with such quick assets and incurring yet further liabilities. I do not believe that we shall succeed, whatever the realities of the situation, in persuading the United States that we are in serious financial straits if we are found with upwards of £m500 in gold and dollars about our person.

10.9.42   KEYNES

SUPPLEMENTARY NOTE ON OUR PROSPECTIVE DOLLAR BALANCES

I have received notes on my previous memorandum from Professor Robertson (2), Mr Waley, Mr Playfair, Mr Grant[7] and Mr Rowe-Dutton;[8] nothing so far from Sir Frederick Phillips. The following supplementary reflections are in the light of comments received in these notes:–

I. *Statistical Position*

Broadly speaking, Professor Robertson confirms the figures previously given. He thinks that by the end of this year we may hold £m130 in gold+£m95 in dollars = £m225 = $m900. By the end of next year his forecast is £m150 in gold+£m225 in dollars = £m375 = $m1,500. He regards my possible maximum of $m2,000 by the end of next year as improbable, but not impossible. Since his estimates do not take any account of windfalls from U.S.A. in respect of old commitments, etc. or any exceptional transactions in gold, this conclusion does not

[7] Alexander Thomas Kingdom Grant (b. 1906); Lecturer, Department of Political Economy, University College, London, 1938-9; joined Treasury, 1939; Under-Secretary, 1956; Under-Secretary, Export Credits Guarantee Department, 1958-66; Secretary, Faculty of Economics, University of Cambridge, 1966-71; Senior Research Officer, Department of Applied Economics, 1971-3.

[8] Ernest Rowe-Dutton (1891-1965), K.C.M.G. 1949; civil servant, Inland Revenue, 1914; transferred to Treasury, 1919; Financial Adviser, British Embassy, Berlin, 1928-32, Paris, 1934-9; Principal Assistant Secretary and Third Secretary, Treasury, 1940-5; Under-Secretary, 1946.

appreciably differ from mine. Please note that, whereas his figure for gold is nearly 50 per cent higher than his figure for dollars at the end of this year, his figure for dollars at the end of next year is, on the other hand, 50 per cent higher than his figure for gold. (But his figure for gold is based on the current rate of receipts in South Africa rather than on the higher figures which may result from recent discussions.) He points out that the figures I gave (page 3) [above p. 246] for sterling area dollar reserves should be *pounds*, not dollars as stated.

II. *General Principles*

(i) I should agree with Professor Robertson that one's position is strengthened on general banking principles by adding equal sums to one's assets and to the liabilities against which they are held. My whole point is that, unless we are careful, it will not be a question of adding equal sums. We might get into a position in which our liabilities would continue to increase, but the rate of increase of our assets would fall short of our hopes because of the outward appearance that we did not need further accretions. The whole weight of my emphasis should be taken to have been on that. The same comment also applies to a passage in Mr Waley's comments.

(ii) Professor Robertson points out that we need not feel particular anxiety about some part of our liabilities which are not likely to be withdrawn suddenly. He concludes that perhaps we are not justified, in view of this, in pressing the Americans for any further assistance. Mr Playfair is inclined to arrive at the same conclusion on somewhat different grounds. He doubts the psychological wisdom of continuing to appear as suppliants. He thinks that, if we take a more free and easy line, we can rely on their seeing us through hereafter. I cannot agree with these comments. That part of our liabilities which is liable to be withdrawn is substantial.

But the probability of the withdrawal both of the more dangerous and of the less dangerous portion of our liabilities is greatly bound up with the general state of our credit. If we are strong they will not be withdrawn. If we look weak they certainly will be. Moreover, our existing liabilities are not the complete story. It is the further increment to these during the remaining period of the war—quite unpredictable; and, perhaps worst of all, our prospective adverse balance of trade in the two or three years after the war. (For it is then we shall be under the greatest pressure both from withdrawal of existing balances, from our current adverse balance of trade and from there being no longer war reasons for assistance from U.S. and the Dominions.) Nor do I think it safe to rely on American generosity hereafter. They are very liable to reactions of mood for all kinds of unpredictable reasons. As soon as we show ourselves in a less pressing mood, even our best friends will enthusiastically take the line of least resistance, that is of abating their assistance.

Moreover, 'trusting the Americans' in the post-war world is an entirely different proposition from trusting the friendly Americans with whom we are constantly working and with whom we have developed relations of mutual trust. On the other hand, I do entirely agree with Mr Playfair that we should as soon as possible reach the point of saying that we are satisfied with the existing system of lend lease and ask no more. It seems to me that we shall have reached that point as soon as the old commitments and other capital questions have been finally cleared up. It is a great pity that they were not cleared up a year ago, but that is not our fault. When they have been, and certain other matters of lend lease procedure have reached a conclusion, I agree that we should move the closure on any attempt to get more.

(iii) Mr Waley and Mr Playfair both emphasise the importance of increased frankness. I agree with this. The question is how far it takes us. It is one thing to be frank and intelligible to the U.S. Treasury; quite another thing to expect Congress and the big public to understand the story. The latter seems to me quite hopeless. Many contingent and hypothetical considerations have to come into the picture, and a wide knowledge of the principles of international finance must be presumed. Our intimate financial relations are not a proper subject for popular debate, and could not expect to receive rational and unprejudiced consideration. I emphasise, therefore, that, however frank we may endeavour to be, it will still remain true that we cannot afford to disregard appearances. The object of greater frankness with the U.S. Treasury would be *rather to justify than to obviate* the steps we are taking to preserve appearances. Moreover, even if the position is understood—and this applies perhaps even to the U.S. Treasury—does it follow that we can rely on unlimited post-war good-will, especially when it means political difficulties and administrative frictions and is very much the opposite of following the line of least resistance? I do not believe that any amount of practicable frankness will produce a position where it is safe for us to run up reserves of $m2,000 in gold and dollars, but mainly in the shape of dollars, without exciting criticism and reaction.

(iv) Gold versus Dollars. Here I have apparently not been very successful in persuading those who have read the memorandum that it is safer to hold gold than dollars. So I return to this question. My reasons are the following:–

(*a*) Our holdings of dollars are much more regularly and evidently published, since they appear in the quarterly or half-yearly returns of the Federal Reserve Board. This does not apply to our gold, publication of which is more sporadic, more confidential and, if we are successful, might be almost got rid of altogether in absolute terms.

(*b*) The Americans regard our holdings of gold acquired from the rest of the sterling area as only indirectly their concern and are much readier to regard it as a domestic matter between us and those from whom the gold is obtained. Our dollars, on the other hand, they regard as the direct offspring of the assistance they give us. There is indeed an element of truth in this. The element of truth is diminishing, partly because the dollars accrue from American military expenditure in the sterling area, partly because it is often a matter of convenience whether we meet a given expense in the one or in the other. But the detailed background of all this, which Congress can never be expected to know, will not affect the general conviction that our gold reserves are primarily our affair and our dollar reserves, if not primarily, at least significantly, theirs.

(c) Mr Waley thinks that dollars are a more liquid form of currency than gold, or might be in some circumstances. The opposite is at least equally true. There seems no reason to doubt that we can meet our sterling liabilities in gold. But there is an increasing tendency on the part of the U.S. authorities, having once learnt the technique, to regard dollars as something which can be blocked. (Mr Waley suggests that, in the case of Russia, it would be a case of risk of transport to ask them for gold rather than dollars. Is this correct? If the Russians pay us dollars, they have, I believe, to replenish their reserves by shipping gold. Once the gold has reached Vancouver, or whatever port it does reach, it is just as easy to ship it to Ottawa as to anywhere else.)

III. *Details*

(i) I agree with Mr Waley that the process of re-education must be very cautious and gradual. It is easy for those who are not seeing the picture as a whole to confuse the cases where to incur dollar liabilities has the effect of avoiding extra sterling liabilities and those cases where the dollar commitments, if incurred, would be a net increase to our liabilities. Provided those in the Treasury and a few key officials elsewhere have an up-to-date picture of the situation as a whole, the required results can probably be reached sufficiently.

(ii) I strongly agree with Mr Waley that we should now return the Belgian gold. I should like to take up that point again with the Bank of England.

(iii) I agree with Mr Rowe-Dutton that any relaxation in the use of dollars should be for the general interest and not for particular interest and that there should be no change in exchange control practice which would leave some individuals in a better position than others.

(iv) I believe that our readiness to be the owners of stock piles may in the course of time have a fairly wide field of application. The following case, where the Ministry of Supply are moving in the right direction spontaneously, is an illustration:

INDUSTRIAL DIAMONDS

The United States Government are anxious to accumulate a substantial stockpile of industrial diamonds. In order to meet this desire the Ministry of Supply have tentatively suggested a scheme whereby ten or fifteen million carats of industrial diamonds from roughly assorted stocks of producers would be shipped to the United States but kept in the ownership of the producing companies until required to meet a possible shortage. This would give the United States assurance of the physical possession of the diamonds and overcome many difficulties of sorting, avoid the artificial creation of apparent shortages due to depleting working stocks and give security against overloading the market with unwanted material at the end of the war—*Anglo-American Weekly Notes, No. 3*. Week ending 12th September, 1942

(v) Mr Playfair has given some examples of where our financial relations with South America can be made easier by a greater willingness on our part to put up gold or dollars.

(vi) Lord Catto has made a suggestion to me which deserves consideration in some shape or form, namely, that the other sterling area exchange controls should be encouraged to hold larger dollar balances of their own so as to emphasise the reality of the position, i.e., that the reserves standing in our name are really the reserves of the sterling area as a whole. I hesitated to suggest this because it might appear to weaken the concept of the sterling area. But there is a great deal to be said for it. Another example of the same line of action would be to allow the Currency Boards under the control of the Colonial Office to hold part of their reserves in dollars or gold. It seems to me very possible that the U.S. Treasury would welcome development along these lines. It will be an embarrassment to them if the other parts of the sterling area have no dollar balances whatever after the war. On the other hand, this would be too easy a way by which we could divest ourselves of our reserves without having consolidated our liabilities. I prefer, therefore, to think of these ideas in connection with some such larger plan as that which I briefly outline below. Mr Grant has also made an interesting proposal of a somewhat similar kind, namely, that instead of showing reserves as such, we should split up the figure in such a way that we showed several figures, some of them ear-marked for specific purposes. Like Lord Catto's suggestion I think this leads on to a consideration of the wider problem towards which I make first tentative essay below.

IV. *Has the Time come for a Larger Plan?*

I have been asked to develop the hint in my previous memorandum that some plan of wider scope might deserve consideration. I offer, therefore, the following first thoughts on this subject:–

The prospective improvement in our gold and dollar position naturally encourages the hope that we can arrive at some settlement affecting our overseas liabilities, by which we can get through without unilateral action and without any measure which could be properly criticised as a default. The question is whether it may not be premature to consider anything of this sort at the present stage. But perhaps it will make somewhat clearer the line of thought to which the earlier part of the memorandum is intended to lead if a possible line of approach is suggested.

By the end of this year our banking liabilities will have reached the exceedingly dangerous figure of £m1,500. They will have grown further before the end of the war, and we anticipate a serious adverse balance of trade in the first two or three post-war years. Against this we have a possible prospect of reserves of some £m500 in gold and dollars. Looked at in terms of these globular totals, the problem looks somewhat hopeless. But it is not so hopeless if the components are broken up into their several parts. A considerable part of these balances we may hope to retain for a more or less indefinite period, provided our general credit and banking position is maintained. As a rough estimate of the total of £m1,500 which our banking liabilities will reach by the end of this year, perhaps not above £m500 can be regarded as potentially dangerous so long as our general credit position is intact. If, however, the attempt to deal with this was to deplete our reserves excessively, then a considerable part of the remaining £m1,000 might also become dangerous. It is only by dealing satisfactorily with the dangerous part that the less dangerous can be expected to remain less dangerous.

The major problems, apart from the running deficit in the post-war years, appear to be India, Egypt and those Crown Colonies such as Malaya and Hong-Kong, which will have heavy post-war requirements for reconstruction. The rest of the British Commonwealth does not present any unmanageable task. The position in South America is deteriorating, but we still have the major part of our capital assets in that continent intact. This does not mean that any formula of solution which was found applicable to India and Egypt should not have a wider extension. But it does mean that, if we could find a formula for them, we should have gone a long way towards consolidating our position.

Perhaps the key to the solution of war debts is to be found

in the general principle of our paying the capital sum over a period of years, not unduly prolonged—(say) 15 years or, at the outside, 20—without the payment or accumulation of interest on the unpaid portion. This could be a principle of all-round application. It would apply to any loans made by ourselves which are still subject to interest (we have already made some progress in accepting the non-interest principle), e.g. Australia, New Zealand, Russia, the Free French, or any other Ally which is incurring liabilities towards us. It would apply also to existing loans which carry, actually or prospectively, a rate of interest, such as the Jesse Jones and the Canadian loans. A complete cancellation of all indebtedness arising out of the war might be difficult to carry and might not always operate very fairly. A compromise by which capital sums are repaid but no interest accrues on any obligation arising out of the war might be more readily accepted by those expected to make the sacrifice and might commend itself to world popular opinion as proper and legitimate. I believe that this would be a sufficient concession to give us the amelioration of our liabilities which we shall require. Let me take its application in one or two particular cases.

Recent discussions indicate that it would be far easier to deal on this basis with our obligations to India than to propose outright cancellation or outright grants on their part. Particularly after the shaking up which they have received recently, would it be too much to expect the Government of India to agree to a general settlement on some such lines as the following (in some respects this follows Sir J. Raisman's own suggestions when he was here):–

(a) All Government obligations and guaranteed loans to be vested.

(b) The remaining sterling reserves of the Government of India to be divided into three parts (the proportions of the three parts would have to depend on the absolute amounts involved). The first portion would be funded without interest and repaid for capital development purposes over (say) fifteen years, beginning 3 years after the end of the war, the amount being repayable at earlier dates by mutual agreement. The second portion would be transferred to the Government of India's currency reserves in gold or dollars. The remaining portion would continue to be held *quasi* permanently in the currency reserves in the form of Treasury Bills, with a general understanding that these would not be drawn on except by mutual agreement until after that part of the reserve which had been constituted by the above transfer of gold or dollars.

Or, take the case of Egypt. This is more difficult than the case of India because by no means such a large proportion of the sterling reserves are held on Government or National Bank account. Here it may be a necessary preliminary that the bulk of the reserves should be transferred to Egyptian Government ownership, they becoming the holders of their nationals' external foreign currency, replacing these external holdings by local currency which would only be transferred abroad in accordance with the current exchange control regulations. If such a transfer had taken place, or if the statistics were to show that a sufficient corpus of the reserves was under Egyptian Government control for such transfer to be unnecessary, then a formula similar to that proposed for India might be equally applicable.

A combination of settlements on the above lines, with vestings in proper cases, would bring our gold and dollars down to a figure appropriate to our own national purposes, whilst at the same time consolidating our overseas liabilities. The question is whether any such settlements can help us in our immediate problem. We might perhaps make some transfers of gold and dollars into the reserves of the rest of the sterling area, subject to some general understanding that account would be taken of these in a final settlement on the above lines in advance of implementing the final settlement in all its details.

Another alternative to the above would be the use of the Clearing Union. If the Clearing Union were brought in, the principle of non-interest bearing loans repayable over a period could be retained. But, in that case, it might be unnecessary to interfere with the immediate liquidity of the balances in the hands of the holders, which would appear, in their eyes at least, as an additional justification for the non-payment of interest. I mean that the Clearing Union might take over all liabilities incurred as a result of the war, making them immediately available in liquid form to the creditors and requiring repayment from the debtors by annual instalments over a period of (say) 15 years without interest.

30.9.42   KEYNES

To LORD CATTO *and others, 9 October 1942*

THE PROBLEM OF OUR DOLLAR BALANCES

I had lunch to-day with Mr Winthrop Brown and Mr Charlie Noyes[9] of Mr Harriman's office on this side and OLLA on the other side. They both of them took the initiative in pressing on me the urgency of considering the problem of our growing dollar balances. They said that this was already standing in the way of Mr Stettinius in obtaining for us the various concessions he had discussed when he was here. When he was endeavouring to have contracts transferred, obligations met, old commitments taken over, or better arrangements for hard core, he was met with the contention that we had no need of the dollars, as the growing state of our account clearly showed. They went so far as to say that they thought that, if the increase went on cumulatively, it might very well result in a demand that the United States should

[9] Charles Reinold Noyes (1884–1954), economist; Director, National Bureau of Economic Research, 1940–50.

be allowed to obtain raw materials from the sterling area on the principles of reciprocal aid.

They themselves, particularly Brown, since he was present at the conversation Lord Catto and I had with Mr Stettinius, were aware that we were building up these balances, not to meet commitments in the United States, but because of our growing liabilities in other parts of the world. They were themselves in favour of the additional aid, which Mr Stettinius was trying to get for us. But they said that they knew far too little about all this, or at any rate knew it in far too indefinite a form, to be in a position to answer their critics. Very little was known about the working of the sterling area, very little about our financial arrangements with the different Dominions, and next to nothing of what I had told Mr Stettinius when he was here about our growing indebtedness to India and Egypt.

They pressed on me that all this needed really urgent attention. I told them that it was very much in our minds, that we had in fact been giving thought to it and that we were only now waiting for the arrival of Sir F. Phillips to discuss it further.

Mr Noyes mentioned incidentally that the position vis-a-vis South Africa was the subject of constant criticism on the other side (he is just returned back from Washington). OLLA were being asked what justification there was for affording lend lease aid to South Africa when South Africa was visibly piling up great quantities of gold and clearly had no need of any such assistance. Why not, it was asked, expect her to pay for everything by transferring gold to the United States? I could only reply that there were strong political reasons, of which they were not unaware, for going gently with South Africa and that the amounts involved were comparatively trifling. In principle I admitted it was in present circumstances difficult to produce a convincing answer.

Mr Brown and Mr Noyes are, of course, not at the top of

the machine or very high officials, but they are good, understanding friends and are in a position to know the atmosphere in OLLA and elsewhere in Washington with which Mr Stettinius has to contend. They left me with the impression that the question of the dollar balances was even more immediately important than I had previously realised.

12.10.42   KEYNES

1943 saw a continuation and intensification of many of the concerns of the previous year. The November 1942 Congressional elections had resulted in a House of Representatives and a Senate much less favourable to the Roosevelt Administration than their predecessors and left Executive officials feeling more exposed. In these circumstances, the rise in Britain's reserves caused more concern, especially in the light of a Presidential ruling on 1 January (but unknown to the British until late in the year) that the permitted range of fluctuation for the reserves should be $600–1,000 million. At the end of December 1942 the reserves slightly exceeded $1,000 million. The upshot was pressure from the Americans to increase British deliveries under reciprocal aid and to remove items from lend lease. Early in the year South Africa was asked to pay for all non-munitions supplies and civilian tobacco disappeared from lend lease to Britain. Representations to Mr Morgenthau and Mr Stettinius failed to alter these decisions given the American political climate. The fears Keynes had expressed since 1941 were confirmed.

The earlier part of the year brought various suggestions from Keynes and others for a reallocation of war expenses, but it soon became clear that such an approach to the Americans would not get anywhere. Thus attention turned to the use of the reserves to minimise liabilities and reduce American pressures.

On 3 May, Keynes made a series of suggestions directed towards this end. After some discussion, he revised his document on 13 May, the revisions occurring in sections IV and V to cover areas other than India.[10]

---

[10] As already noted (above pp. 216, 222–3) Indian and Middle Eastern sterling balances had been a source of worry to Keynes since 1941. For more details on the problems in these areas see below pp. 316–47.

THE USE OF OUR GOLD AND DOLLAR RESERVES

I

We are faced with two major issues:–

(1) Progressive inflation in the Middle East and India on a scale which is now dangerous. For the last fifteen months prices have been rising at a rate of 2½ to 5 per cent a month, and confidence in paper currency as a form in which to hold hoarded resources is disappearing. As a result of this a new inflationary force, namely the hoarding of commodities, is superimposed on that of our large military expenditures (most of which is uncompensated either by taxation or loans). We are spending nearly £m200 a year in the Middle East and £m400 in India. Since we are making no attempt to adjust the exchange value of the local currencies to their purchasing power parity in terms of sterling, every 5 per cent of inflation costs us £m30 a year extra. It follows that even a *small* slackening of the rate of rise will pay us handsomely. And not less important than the financial aspect are the political and social consequences.

No remedy, which lies within our own control, is proposed to us from any quarter except the injection of gold. *All* the local experts think this will produce *some* effect.

Their arguments for expecting a favourable result fall under three heads:–

(*a*) Wheat and other commodities are not conveniently hoarded and are only taken up as a *pis aller*. If gold is available, that will take their place to some extent as a store of wealth and the hoarded stocks will be brought back to the market.

(*b*) Gold hoarding is, in these parts of the world, an attractive alternative to spending. To make gold available is, therefore, the most plausible means of encouraging saving.

(*c*) The mere rise in the price of gold as such tends to raise the prices of other commodities sympathetically. We are told, for example, that in Trans-Jordan and Syria (where prices have now risen to six times pre-war) it is now common for traders to go so far as to keep their books in terms of gold. Thus a fall in the price of gold may be expected to have a sympathetic effect on prices generally. In other words a falling, and eventually stable, price for gold will restore the prestige of the paper currency and prevent the widespread flight from the currency (i.e. an ever-increasing velocity of circulation) of which there is now a serious risk if we do nothing about it.

The argument, which we have been expounding in telegrams that it will have the opposite effect (i.e. that the injection of gold will cause an increasing *distrust* of the paper currency), is greeted with derision both by Sir F. Phillips and by those to whom we address it.

To these a fourth argument in favour of the course proposed is added. The par value of gold is about £8 per oz. The price in the East is from £16 to £20. We do not intend or expect that gold will be worth more than £8 per oz. after the war. If, therefore, we could dispose of (say) 5 million ounces at a price of (say) £12, we should make a clear profit of £20 million as well as using our gold to very good purpose for the prosecution of the war. If, in addition, the injection of this amount of gold causes prices to rise in the course of the year by even so little as 5 per cent less than they would otherwise, we should save ourselves nearly another £20 million; whilst the optimists would hope for *much* better results than this.

These arguments appear to be indisputable. The most one can say against them is that their advocates may exaggerate their quantitative effect. It is impossible to tell until one tries.

(2) Our second major problem arises out of the tendency of our gold and dollar reserves to rise to a figure which attracts suspicion in congressional circles and leads to a reduction of the lend lease aid afforded to us. If this increment

of our reserves represented a net increase in our resources, such action by Congress would be justified. But it does not. It arises because we have set up a system under which all the dollar earnings of the sterling area are accumulated into the reserves held in our name. The surplus of the sterling area thus accumulating we have to borrow, thus increasing our sterling liabilities by an equal amount and incurring an implied liability to convert this sterling liability back again into dollars, should our sterling area creditor have a legitimate need for them at a later date. In addition to this we have to borrow other large sums, so that, one way and another, our external liabilities are increasing at several times the rate of the increase in reserves.

We have tried to bring this home to Washington and to persuade them to adopt a formula of 'adequacy' for our reserves which takes account of our increasing liabilities. In this we have failed. All we have managed to do is to defer the crisis and to obtain some kind of unreliable promise against sudden action. It is only a question of time before the problem will again arise in an acute form unless we do something about it. We have promised Sir F. Phillips that we will try to find a solution, which means finding a way of using some part of our reserves to offset some part of our more pressing liabilities. For it is only in this way that a picture, which even approaches the reality of our financial position, can be successfully portrayed to Congress.

Indeed we have not succeeded even so far in staving off losses. The Americans owe us $176 million for old-commitment aeroplanes for which we have paid out dollars of our own, but of which they subsequently took delivery. We are told that it is useless for us to press this claim so long as we are so flush of dollars as we are now; and if the claim is left in abeyance too long, it will surely go stale. In addition tobacco has been taken off lend lease chiefly on the ground that we could afford to pay for it. This is costing us some $80 million in the current year and is recurrent. Here, therefore, already we have suffered a major loss of net external resources.

During 1942 our gold and dollar reserves increased by £108 million. (But the liabilities against which we hold them increased by £750 million.) In 1943, according to Prof. Robertson's estimates, they will increase by about a further £100 million. (But the liabilities against which we hold them are expected to increase by £700 million.) These estimates are, admittedly, highly conjectural. There are several factors which might cause our reserves to increase by substantially more. There can be no doubt that we should be in a much sounder position if we were to employ £50 million to £100 million of our reserves to offset a corresponding amount of our more onerous liabilities.

We have already explored the minor methods open to us, and nothing much more is to be hoped for except by some major method. The alternatives are limited to the following:-

(i) To pay off, in whole or in part, (*a*) the Jesse Jones loan, (*b*) the secured Canadian loan, or (*c*) the Portuguese holdings of sterling.

(ii) To hand back to certain members of the sterling area some part of the dollars which they have allowed us to centralise in our name but which, failing such action, we shall not be allowed to offset against our corresponding liabilities to them and may, therefore, finally lose altogether.

(iii) To use some part of our gold in the Middle East and India, which would not merely reduce our liabilities but also support the conduct of the war.

It does not follow that the adoption of one alternative need exclude the simultaneous adoption of either or both of the others. To alternative (i), however, there are some weighty objections. To repay the Jesse Jones loan would uncover the direct investments, and it is better to wait for our market securities to rise to an attractive selling level. Similarly to repay the Canadian loan would expose the security held against it as an available asset next time we need aid from Canada, but the conclusive argument against this course is that it would expose Canada to exactly the same position we are trying to escape from, namely curtailment of U.S. aid on the ground that they had enough gold and dollars to do without it. To repay a reasonable part of the Portuguese sterling balances in gold would not carry us very far, and would not (I think) help our statistical position vis-à-vis Congress as (in a foot-note) we already deduct the Portuguese balances as being a contingent gold liability in calculating our net reserves. Moreover, all these three methods must strike any informed observer as unnecessary and a deliberate emptying of pockets. None of these liabilities are pressing either now or in the early post-war period. We should be using our resources to reduce as little as possible our initial post-war anxieties, and, at the same time, doing nothing to help on the war.

Alternative (ii) deserves serious consideration. Prof. Robertson estimates our net dollar receipts from the rest of the sterling area in 1943 at about $m20, which is about two-thirds of our total increment of gold and dollars, of which India's share will be not less than $m100. If, therefore, we were to allow India to retain their net receipts of dollars instead of selling them to us against sterling, our problem would be greatly reduced. We must require as a condition of this that, if the dollar balance of trade moves against them subsequently, they will use these accumulations first before asking us to provide them with any dollars against their sterling balances. This change of procedure would, in fact, greatly strengthen the sterling area convention by making it more acceptable and much safer for the other participants. We cannot hope to maintain the present position just as it stands after the war. It would suit both us and the U.S. that these countries should have some dollar reserves of their own. The present arrangement is a hang-over from the days before lend lease when we had to use every possible expedient for bringing dollars into our coffers. Today it is not necessary; it causes an entirely misleading picture of our real position to be built up; it cannot last; and it much increases the dangers of our future position if the alternative to this moderate measure of dispersing some part of our reserves is (as is probably the case) that we should lose them altogether.

Alternative (iii) has the great advantages that it helps the war and, in addition to reducing our liabilities, may actually reduce the net costs of our operations. It should be entirely unobjectionable to the Americans. We can truthfully represent to them that we have carried to breaking point the policy of financing the war in India and the Middle East by printing paper money, whilst failing to increase comparably, and indeed actually diminishing, the goods to be purchased; that our experts on the spot are unanimous in advising us that the position can be held no longer without a sweetener of gold to regain confidence; and that we are, therefore, proposing to meet about 10 per cent of our expenses by selling gold bullion as a commodity.

II

The simple-minded reader of the above may be led to conclude that the sensible course is to kill each of these major issues with the other. The solution of the first requires that we should part with some gold; so does the solution of the second. Perhaps the simple-minded reader would be right.

Why then do we hesitate? Our substantial reasons are, I gather, two:–

(i) The dispersal of gold or dollars within the sterling area would be detrimental to the conception of the sterling area which, in the early days of the war, we laboured to impress on those concerned.

(ii) We might be led into a policy which would require ultimately more gold than we can spare, especially in the case of India, to which may be added that it would be premature to let India have such gold as we can spare, without using this inducement to secure a general settlement.

The answers to these objections are, in my judgment, the following:–

(i) The answer to this has been already given in part above. This particular version of the sterling area looks backwards to our early war difficulties and not forwards to our post-war problems. We have not a hope of sustaining it hereafter,—for example, we cannot reasonably expect that India will after the war lend her whole dollar surplus to us in return for sterling which cannot be used to acquire gold and the use of which is tied up with all our post-war economic uncertainties. The quadriga of the sterling area will soon get out of hand if we do not drive it on a lighter rein than this. On the other hand, the compromise suggested above may sustain much of the substance of the sterling area conception by making it more tolerable.

(ii) The amount of gold which we can spare is in fact large. During 1943 our gold and dollar reserves are expected to increase by £100 million and might (in my judgment) easily increase by more. Thus we could afford to disperse, with actual advantage to ourselves, at least £60 million this year. This is likely to be a recurrent position so long as the existing financial war-time set-up continues. This amount is, I think, considerably larger than our advisers in the East at present contemplate. But if in the result the policy looks good but needs for its fulfilment more gold fodder, we can expect to invoke American aid with considerable confidence. At one time I thought that we might seek American partnership in this enterprise from the outset. Probably, however, that presents too much practical difficulty. We had better start by ourselves and try out the policy unaided. If it succeeds but needs more support than we can give it, surely American aid can be relied on. Mr Morgenthau has already indicated, I believe, that he will not let us be embarrassed in financing Indian expenditure merely by lack of gold. Unilateral energy on our part might indeed prove to be the right first step towards the Anglo-American partnership in financing the local expenses of the war in the East which is sure to be necessary when the last phase of the Japanese war is approaching.

It is essential that we should first reach a clear decision on these questions of principle. The technical methods of carrying out the decision will be far from simple, and can easily be obstructed and defeated if there has not been a clear decision loyally accepted.

III

If it is agreed in principle that gold is to be used in the Middle East and India, how can it be injected to the best effect? The answer is not easy. I submit the following principles for discussion—a variant which is broadly similar to, but not altogether the same as, the Cairo recommendations of the Minister of State.

(i) Gold shall not be made available as currency or as a currency reserve. It shall be made clear that for all currency purposes the value of gold remains at £8 per oz., and that no government will acquire gold except for disposal under this scheme, at any price in excess of £8 per oz.

(ii) It shall not be bartered for commodities but shall be sold against local currency to provide an acceptable medium for hoarding, preferably not in coin but in small bars.

(iii) The gold shall be put at the disposal of the local administrations to the extent that they are willing and able to dispose of it under the conditions contemplated, and shall be sold to the public either by them or by us acting as their agents.

(iv) The local administrations shall pay us for it with their local currency at the par equivalent of £12 per oz., and the local currency thus obtained shall be used by us solely to meet war expenses within their area. Any profit from selling gold above £12 per oz. shall belong to the local administrations.

(v) Any other country holding gold, e.g. U.S. or S. Africa, and having war expenses to meet in these countries is, of course, free to follow the same policy; but it is suggested that, in this case, action should be taken jointly.

(vi) The amount to be made available by us in the first instance shall be 750,000 oz. of gold, to be allocated as to 375,000 oz. to the Middle East apart from Egypt and a further 375,000 oz. to Egypt if they wish to follow the same policy. A similar offer, up to (say) another 750,000 oz. should also be made to India, if it appears that the Government of India desire it. Ceylon will also have to be considered.

(vii) After three months' operations the policy shall be reconsidered. Further instalments of gold, up to a considerably larger amount if necessary, will be made available if the policy is thought to be successful.

The justification of the £12 price would be found (a) in the war costs of freight and insurance, (b) in the present purchasing power parity of the local currencies concerned in terms of sterling and (c) in the desire to encourage hoarding in terms of paper instead of gold.

It will be observed that the gold would be offered to India on exactly the same terms as to the other countries. At present the Government of India is opposed to selling gold in the bazaars. Unless, therefore, they change their minds, they may not be interested in the offer. We should be adamant against offering gold to India on any different terms from the others. (See IV (iii) below.)

It is possible that S. Africa will demand to share in the profit.

But it will be observed that she is allowed in on level terms in any area, e.g. Egypt, where like us she has local war expenses to meet. We should stand firm on this position. It is also possible that America may prefer to sell her gold at £8, which might be an embarrassment. If, however, we are pressed to let the local administrations have it on the same terms, we should firmly resist this also. At the very worst, if under pressure we have to surrender to others the difference between £12 and £8, we should only lose this element of well-deserved profit available towards meeting the expenses of the war in these areas; and we should not forfeit the other advantages of the scheme. If anyone were to be allowed to buy gold from us at less than £12 or to sell it for more than £8, they must ship it at their own risk and cost uninsured by us. This should also apply to any gold owned by others (e.g. Persian gold) which they may choose to ship.

IV

We might let India have gold for her currency reserve during the year 1943 to an amount equal in value to the surplus she earns in terms of dollars as from 1 January, 1943, subject to the conditions mentioned below, and, if possible, as part of a larger agreement. This is a very large concession and one for which India is eager. It is, therefore, a move to which we should expect her to respond, and the conditions should be as follows:–

(i) The amount of gold released to her would be based on an approximate calculation of her favourable balance with U.S. on all heads. It would be understood that, if at a later date the dollar balance were to turn against India so that the calculated amount became negative, she would hand back an appropriate quantity of gold to meet this deficit.

(ii) The arrangement should be subject to a maximum of £50 million.

(iii) India should agree to raise no difficulties against our selling gold locally as bullion at £12 as under proposal III.

The reasons for suggesting that we should let India have gold rather than dollars are:–

(*a*) There is no reason why the U.S. Treasury need be unduly interested in letting India have some gold, which is a consequence of the unwieldy level to which India's sterling balances will rise in the course of this year. If we were to let India have dollars it would be more directly a matter of interest and concern to the U.S. Treasury.

(*b*) Other members of the sterling area already possess independent gold reserves and this would not therefore be an innovation from the sterling area point of view.

(*c*) The Issue Department of the Indian Reserve Bank could not hold dollars without fresh legislation, though this legislation might be quite easy to obtain.

It is, however, important that India should recognise that this gold might have to be used under condition (1) above and must not be regarded as something which goes into the currency reserve but can never come out again.

V

The proposal under IV is required as well as those under III, since the effect of III by itself would not be nearly enough. But the effect of both is to deplete our gold reserves whilst allowing our dollar balances to grow. To offset this and to restore a proper balance certain other measures are advisable, such as:–

(i) We might ask Russia to pay in future wholly in gold and not in dollars. Since she has in any case to ship gold to put herself in funds and since we can accept delivery in Ottawa, there should be no difficulty about this. We could not however press Russia to pay in gold if for any reason it suits her better to pay in dollars.

(ii) We should, wherever we have the choice or can persuade the other party to agree, meet our gold liabilities in dollars instead of gold; and we should in such cases clear off such liabilities in terms of dollars by actual payment as soon as possible. This will release gold and keep our dollar balances within limits.

11 May 1943   KEYNES

The summer brought renewed American pressures to keep dollar earnings and reserve holdings down, this time in the form of a proposal to include major raw materials supplied to American government departments under reciprocal aid.

With this request came another for the presentation of figures of the volume of reciprocal aid to emphasise its importance to Congress. This led to a suggestion from Keynes that the Treasury should provide the figures in a White Paper with a summary for American use. Mr Playfair drafted a possible White Paper on 16 July; Keynes then weighed in with his own draft about 24 July. Keynes's version, with amendments, provided the basis for the White Paper which the Treasury proposed to present to Parliament on 5 August, the last day before the recess. On 2 August the U.S. State Department, Office of Lend Lease Administration and Treasury received copies of the draft White Paper, plus proposals concerning raw materials and Britain's freedom to export, which had been restricted since 1941 (above p. 201). However, Mr Morgenthau asked for postponement of the White Paper and accompanying Parliamentary statement, as he did not regard the raw materials proposals as satisfactory, particularly as Britain's reserves were growing rapidly. As a result of his opposition the White Paper and accompanying statement were suppressed, much to Mr Stettinius's disappointment.

Discussion of the outstanding lend lease and reciprocal aid matters continued during the visit to Washington of the Law[11] Mission on post-war economic collaboration, of which Keynes was a member.[12] In the course of the mission a memorandum by Keynes, 'The Overseas Assets and

[11] Richard Kidston Law (b. 1901), 1st Baron Coleraine 1954; M.P. (U.), 1931-54; Financial Secretary, War Office, 1940-1; Parliamentary Under-Secretary of State for Foreign Affairs, 1941-3; Minister of State, 1943-5; Leader, U.K. Delegation, Hot Springs Conference on Food and Agriculture, 1943.
[12] For details of other aspects of the negotiations see *JMK*, vol. xxv.

Liabilities of the United Kingdom', went to Mr Morgenthau along with a letter from the Chancellor. The course of the subsequent discussions, in so far as they concerned lend lease, are best summarised in the series of minutes of meetings and letters which follow the Keynes memorandum.[13]

THE OVERSEAS ASSETS AND LIABILITIES OF THE UNITED KINGDOM

The passage of the Lend Lease Act early in 1942 and the assistance given by Canada from 1942 onwards have dealt most liberally with the more recent financial requirements of the United Kingdom in North America. These measures are well-known and widely appreciated. But they have not much lightened the financial burden outside North America, partly for purchases elsewhere which cannot be paid for by current exports, and particularly as a result of the burden of local cash expenditures in the principal areas of hostilities ranging from North Africa through the Middle East to India and the Far East. The following is an attempt to give a complete picture, for the *confidential* information of the American Administration, covering the whole period since 1 January 1940.

The excess of the financial burden overseas beyond what could be met out of current income in the last 3½ years has been met in four ways, as follows:

[13] The short note on the balances problems provided for Mr Acheson on 27 October (below pp. 299–301) also went to Mr Roosevelt from the Prime Minister during their meeting in Cairo.

	\$ million			
	1 Jan. 1940 to 31 Dec. 1941	In 1942	1st half 1943 (approx.)*	Total, 1 Jan. 1940 to 30 June 1943
(i) *By overseas loans†*				
R.F.C. loan	345	15	−10	350
Canadian secured loan	—	635	−15	620
Sundry loans and advances	115	125	15	255
Total loan	460	775	−10	1225
(ii) *By sale of overseas investments* (including sinking funds)	1545	845	525	2925
(iii) By net increase of quick liabilities‡ (excluding those carrying a gold liability)	2575§	1220	1280	5075
(iv) By sale of gold and dollars (*net*, i.e. allowing for gold and dollar liabilities)	1950	−305	−330	1315
Grand Total	6530	2545	1465	10,540

* The figures for the second quarter of 1943 are provisional and subject to correction.
† No credit is here taken for certain loans advanced during the war to Allied Governments.
‡ I.e. banking liabilities, Crown Agents balances and currency boards.
§ The calculation of this figure requires an estimate of the quick liabilities at the commencement of the period on 1 Jan. 1940. The estimate of this assumed above is \$2,195 million approximately, and it is this figure which has to be added to the figures above to give the correct total of the quick liabilities at any subsequent date. This estimate is under further examination and may have to be raised.

The effect of these changes on the aggregate of the gold and dollar reserves has been as follows:–

	$ million (gold at $35 per fine oz.)			
	31 Dec. 1939	31 Dec. 1941	31 Dec. 1942	30 June 1943
Gross gold and dollar reserves*	2335†	500	930	1335
Less gold and dollar liabilities	—	115	240	315
	2335	385	690	1020

* Exclusive of dealers' balances.
† Including an approximate allowance for $200 million held in private accounts at
   that date, but subsequently requisitioned and added to the official balances.

It will be observed that the gold and dollar reserves, whilst they have fallen by more than half over the period as a whole, have been increasing moderately since 1942. Moreover they are likely to increase more rapidly, for reasons which are explained below, in the latter half of 1943. Since this movement has produced a misleading impression that the U.K.'s financial position has been improving, it is important to present the facts in their right perspective:–

(a) The most important consideration is the relation between the quick assets and the quick liabilities. It will be seen that, taking the war period as a whole, the net gold and dollar reserves have fallen by more than a billion dollars, whilst the quick liabilities have risen by more than five billion dollars. It is true that, taking the eighteen months since 31 December 1941, the net gold and dollar reserves have risen by about $600 million from the low point touched at the former date. But the quick liabilities have risen during the same period by about $2,500 million. To a large extent, moreover (for reasons to be explained in (b) and (c)) the increased reserves have been acquired only at the cost of a directly consequential increase in the liquid liabilities, and do not constitute new resources.

(b) The liabilities are liabilities solely of the U.K. and not of any other part of the sterling area. But the quick assets cannot be regarded as wholly available for the U.K.'s require-

279

ments. For a large part of them has been acquired under the pooling arrangements, by which any part of the sterling area (other than some of the temporary adherents) sell to the U.K. for sterling any dollars which they earn in excess of their own small direct requirements. This increases by the same amount the quick sterling liabilities of the U.K., which it has an implied obligation to turn back again into dollars when other parts of the sterling area have a legitimate need for them. The way in which this operated during the first quarter of 1943 is illustrated in detail below.

(c) The quick liabilities are the more burdensome because of the disposal of many of the more saleable capital assets, which otherwise would have served as a second line of defence. As the table above shows, the total loss of assets and increase of liabilities so far suffered by the U.K. during the war has amounted to 10½ billion dollars. It may be mentioned that only a very small proportion of this has been disposed of to neutrals. More than 90 per cent of this loss has been to the advantage of other members of the United Nations. The U.K. alone has been expected to mortgage the future on a large scale by incurring overseas liabilities. During the earlier period of the war, expenditure in North America was the main cause of the deterioration of the U.K.'s financial position. More recently her responsibility for meeting the greater part of the local cash expenditures in the whole area of hostilities from Tunis to Burma has been the main influence. At the present time the U.K.'s local cash expenditure in Egypt, the Middle East and India, over and above the supplies shipped across the seas, is amounting to some $2½ billion annually, the greater part of which has to be borrowed from the countries concerned.

Between the beginning of the war and the end of 1943, for example, it is estimated that India will have improved her position against the U.K. by some $3,750 million, of which some $1,200 million will have been used to discharge her

Government sterling debt and the balance will remain owing to her.

(*d*) In judging whether, in spite of the above considerations, the U.K. is nevertheless accumulating unnecessarily large quick reserves at someone else's expense, it is relevant to consider the relationship between the U.K.'s resources as shown above and those of other members of the United Nations. For example, the gold and dollar reserves of the U.S.S.R., which are not published, are estimated by the U.S. Treasury at $1,600 million and those of China at $750 million. U.S. official estimates put the corresponding figures of France at $2,875 million, of the Netherlands at $690 million and Belgium at $870 million. None of these countries have any significant amount of overseas quick liabilities against these reserves. The figures for the U.K. (which in respect of dollars includes the whole of the sterling area) are, as shown above, about $1,300 million with liabilities seven times this amount against them. The net gold reserves of the United States (after deducting *all* foreign balances held in U.S.) are about eighteen times those of the U.K. (after deducting only those foreign balances held in U.K. which carry a gold or dollar guarantee).

(*e*) A detailed analysis of the causes of the growth of the British gold and dollar balances in the first quarter of 1943 may help to elucidate the position.

$167 million in gold was obtained from South Africa in payment for the repatriation of South African Government sterling securities held in London. This, therefore, represented no gain of assets but an exchange. A further $39 million of South African gold was acquired at the cost of increasing South Africa's sterling balances by this amount, so that this was acquired by an increase of liabilities. The rest of the sterling area outside the U.K. earned a dollar surplus of $25 million and a further $64 million in respect of American troops, both of which amounts were sold to the U.K. for sterling balances; so that this also led to an increase of liabilities. $9 million was realised from security sales and the like in the U.S., so that this again represented an exchange of assets. These items, none of which represented a net increment of assets to the U.K., add up to $304 million. The net growth of British gold and dollar balances during the same period amounted, however, to no more than $120 million. It follows that the British current account in gold and dollars was overspent by $184 million, and the apparent improvement of $120 million was only achieved by a directly consequential deterioration of $304 million on the other side of the account.

(*f*) Apart from special capital transactions a new factor had entered into the current dollar balance of the U.K. with the arrival of large American forces in the sterling area. Practically the whole of the local requirements of these forces is now being provided with mutual aid. But it is recognised that the responsibility for their pay must remain with their own Government, just as the responsibility for the pay of the British troops abroad remains with the U.K. Government. During 1942 it is estimated that the total accrual of dollars to the U.K. on account of American troops in the British Isles and the sterling area as a whole was some $250 million. During 1943 it may amount to $600 million. This is a new source of dollar receipts which is quite unconnected with lend lease. If the resulting accrual of dollars to our reserves be taken as a reason for correspondingly reducing lend lease the effect will be to throw the whole cost of these American forces in the Empire on to the shoulders of the U.K.; for the dollars accruing to sterling area members will be sold to the U.K. for sterling, thus adding to the U.K.'s quick liabilities. So long as the dollars are retained by the U.K. a balancing asset is held against this sterling liability. But if lend lease were to be reduced in order to prevent such an increase in the U.K.'s dollar holdings, then we should be left with the liability but be deprived of the asset.

During the same quarter the U.K. had to meet a special expenditure of $150 million to cover its own needs and those of the sterling area in Canada, and it would, of course, have been possible to avoid the apparent misleading improvement of $120 million by using the increment to wipe off other liabilities or by not incurring the liabilities referred to above. But decisions whether to use assets to discharge selected liabilities obviously raise many questions of comparison and precedent, and in some respects our position may be somewhat stronger if we retain assets rather than discharge liabilities. We continue to keep this question constantly in front of us, and where it appears to be generally advantageous we shall not hesitate to use assets to discharge particular liabilities.

In the light of these figures the British Government ask the U.S. Administration to agree with them that the present arrangements are not open to criticism; and that it cannot fairly be represented by anyone acquainted with the complete facts, that the growth of balances represents a net improvement of the British position which justifies a call upon her to undertake a larger share of the common financial burden than at present. Furthermore, this will remain true if the increased expenditure on account of American troops in the sterling area leads to some further growth (as we expect it will) in the ensuing months. For there will be a further, much larger growth of liabilities during the same period; and even if there were not, an increased total of reserves is urgently needed to meet the requirements of the already existing situation. The U.K. has already handed over nearly 10 billion of gold, assets and claims to her friends and Allies for the help they have afforded to the common cause.

To SIR WILFRID EADY, *15 September 1943*

My dear Eady,

You will have had long before this letter the telegram in which I gave an account of my opening conversation with

Harry White on 13 September. There was, however, a further suggestion which he made in this conversation which I thought it better to omit from the telegram and keep strictly amongst ourselves. For although, as you will see when I mention it, the thought is a comforting one its implications require a good deal of quiet consideration before it would be safe to allow others to rely on it when considering the future. I have therefore not mentioned it outside the Treasury Delegation.

White, you will remember, indicated that he did not expect lend lease to continue after the war. At the same time he admitted that our prospective adverse balance of trade in the first year or two after the war would be out of proportion to our quota under the Stabilisation Fund and in any case it would be most inadvisable to draw on the quota to any appreciable extent to cover this early period. To cover the interval between the end of lend lease and the beginning of normality he suggested that we might contemplate raising a very substantial post-war dollar loan in U.S.A. He thought that both the Administration and the investors would welcome this. He anticipates that in U.S.A. it will be necessary to abate war taxation with very little delay. They will be on the lookout for all possible means of absorbing funds. He holds that our credit is excellent, subject only to the qualification of the exchange risk being cared for. Subject to this qualification he was of the opinion that we could without difficulty raise by instalments in the course of a year fully $1 billion at, say, 3 per cent for a fifteen-year term. Over a longer period the amount might be greater than this.

He laid stress, however, on some means being found to take care of the exchange risk. His own thought obviously was that his projected international investment institution might guarantee that.

Now obviously we have to think twice before incurring indebtedness to the U.S.A. on that sort of scale. On the other hand, it is obviously capable of enormously mitigating the acuteness of our post-war anxieties. And it would provide capital funds not only to take care of the adverse balance of trade but also at one stage removed to provide capital for reconstruction at home.

If we had lend lease not tapering off too sharply but extending *pace* White into the demobilisation period; if we were free to continue sterling area arrangements and special accounts, as White suggested, until we felt strong enough to do without them; if we had by that time accumulated quick reserves of £500 million, which is by no means out of the question; if we had the quota of the Stabilisation Fund to look forward to; and if on top of all that we could if necessary borrow in U.S.A. a billion dollars or more—then assuredly we could face our post-war problems with some confidence so far as external finance is concerned.

I should suppose, however, that the Chancellor would want to give this sort of thing and its implications a good deal of quiet reflection before even the adumbration of the idea was suitable outside the narrowest circle.

I may mention that I have reason to believe that the Dutch have already asked the U.S. Treasury if they would favour their issuing a post-war dollar loan.

Yours ever,

KEYNES

NOTE OF A CONVERSATION AT A LUNCH ON
24 SEPTEMBER 1943 IN LORD KEYNES'S ROOM AT THE
STATLER HOTEL AT WHICH WERE PRESENT:

Lord Keynes
Sir David Waley
Mr L. P. Thompson-McCausland[14]
Mr Bernhard Knollenberg[15] –Senior Deputy Administrator O.L.L.A.
Mr Charles Denby[16]   –Assistant Administrator O.L.L.A.
Dr Edward Acheson[17]   –Economist, working directly with and
                           under Mr Denby

Mr Knollenberg had told Lord Keynes that O.L.L.A. would like to discuss our balances memorandum informally. Lord Keynes therefore asked him to bring one or two assistants to lunch. The Americans explained that they had had no prior consultation among themselves and were concerned only to explain their difficulties and elicit our suggestions.

Mr Knollenberg traced the history of the dollar balances problem. He himself had joined O.L.L.A. in November 1942. At that time there was a general expectation that in view of our improved gold and dollar position Congress would raise difficulties, on the next lend lease appropriation, over the extent of lend lease to the U.K. In the event the appropriation passed through Congress with little difficulty.

The next stage came about the end of the year when the U.S. Treasury notified O.L.L.A. that our balances were increasing and seemed likely to go on increasing. In view of existing instructions, they doubted whether O.L.L.A. would be justified in continuing lend lease at the current rate. We questioned Mr Knollenberg on the nature of the instructions to which the U.S. Treasury had referred. He told us that there was no Presidential directive, but that in the early days of lend lease an agreed inter-departmental memorandum had been prepared on lend lease policy recommending that lend lease should be afforded to an extent necessary to restore our balances to a reasonable working level, which, after con-

[14] Lucius Perronet Thompson-McCausland (b. 1904); *Financial News*, 1929–34; Moody's Economic Service, 1929–39; Bank of England, 1939–65; Adviser to the Governor, 1949–65.
[15] Bernhard Knollenberg (b. 1892); consultant expert, U.S. Treasury, 1939–40; senior departmental administrator, Lend Lease Administration, 1943–4; divisional deputy, Office of Strategic Services, 1944–5.
[16] Charles Denby (b. 1901); lawyer; assistant administrator, Lend Lease Administration.
[17] Edward Campion Acheson (1902–66), economist; economic adviser on reciprocal aid, Lend Lease Administration, 1943.

sultation with H.M. Treasury, had been defined as $600 million; with latitude for some increase beyond that (interpreted as $600–$1,000 million). This interdepartmental document had been submitted to the President and approved by him. While not constituting a directive, it was undoubtedly a policy document of importance. To disregard it would be to lay the Departments open to the charge that they had altered policy approved by the President without consulting him. The position was therefore that approval must be gained for some new policy if British balances were to continue rising as at present. He added, in reply to a further question, that at no stage had any figure of $600 or $1,000 million been mentioned to Congress. The U.S. Administrator is entirely without detailed commitments so far as Congress is concerned.

The third stage arose about February, when O.E.W. foresaw the need of further appropriations for pre-emption and for certain imports. These imports included some from the sterling area and O.E.W. were unwilling to ask Congress for funds to spend on sterling area imports when Congress was well aware that billions of dollars were being expended on lend lease for the sterling area's benefit. This attitude was reflected also in letters received by O.L.L.A. and by remarks among congressmen (with whom Mr Stettinius had made it his business to maintain close contact). This was the origin of the request for reciprocal aid on commodities; the granting of that request would remove a great part of this particular difficulty.

Mr Knollenberg, having thus traced the history of the subject, said he wished to explore possible solutions. He explained that he and his colleagues in O.L.L.A. were convinced of the justice of our case, but acutely aware of the difficulty of persuading the Administration and Congress. Could we help? He suggested that we might, for example, consider leaving in the hands of individual dominions such gold and dollars as came to them. Lord Keynes answered that we had not a closed mind on this but that there were difficulties. Australia and New Zealand, which Mr Knollenberg had particularly referred to, could not absorb any important amount of dollars. But in any case would not the accumulation of dollars and gold by Australia etc. lead Congress to reduce lend lease to them? And would Congress, in any event, be prepared to accept what was obviously a subterfuge? We had, in 1941, argued for lend lease to the Dominions on the ground that the sterling area was one. Could be we now expect to succeed in reversing that argument? The Americans agreed that it would be difficult. Lord Keynes enquired whether India was in a different position. The Americans were unanimous (with perhaps some slight reserve by Mr Knollenberg) that it would be even more difficult to maintain the argument on India than on the other Dominions. However erroneously, the man-in-the-street believed that the Government of India was run by Whitehall (the man does not have to go into the street, remarked Mr Acheson, he can stay in the State Department). We could not hope to persuade Congress that dollars held by India were much different from dollars held by ourselves. It was even suggested that gold sold by us to India would be suspect. On the subject of dispersing gold and dollars over the sterling area, Sir David Waley pointed out that the interests of the American exporter were better served by centralising the area's holding so that it could be made available to those who needed it instead of being put into cold storage reserves by individual area members.

Mr Acheson then asked whether we could not use our accruing gold and dollars to pay off some of our dollar liabilities. Lord Keynes and Sir David Waley referred to the financial policy set out in section 1 of our balances memorandum, explaining that there was a certain minimum level below which we should not feel comfortable in normal times, and that level could not be put much lower than our present holding. If we were to pay off liabilities and keep balances at about the present level, we should only be relieving ourselves of about, say, a fifth of the currently accruing liabilities and would find ourselves at the end of the year with our liabilities much increased and our assets remaining at or little above the minimum comfortable level. That was not a position which we could contemplate.

Mr Acheson then asked whether our proposition was that a frontal attack should be made on the existing policy of limitation. Lord Keynes confirmed that that was our position.

Mr Denby then pointed out that our friends in the United States could not merely leave our balances to increase but were under the necessity of securing approval for a new policy. We had friends who were already convinced of our case, and there might be others who would easily come over. But Dr White of the U.S. Treasury and Mr Laughlin Currie of O.E.W. were formidable opponents with whom to argue on the sub-cabinet committee, where the subject would first of all have to be thrashed out. O.L.L.A.'s hope was that we could supply our friends with convincing arguments. How, for example, could we answer the argument that our plea was, in effect, to be allowed to increase our assets at a certain rate proportionate to the increase in our liabilities—since there was no hope in practice of their increasing at the same rate as the liabilities? Lord Keynes explained that the Americans must dismiss from their minds that any Chancellor could get up in the House of Commons and explain that we had accepted any limit to our balances. The financial sacrifices which we had made for the common cause were incomparably greater than those of any other of the United Nations and had enured very largely to the benefit of those who were fighting with us. This fact was not absent from the minds of M.P.s and publicists. To suggest that we should now accept either a flat or a moving limit to such assets as we could accumulate was simply not practical politics. Why, moreover, should the poverty test be applied to us alone? It was not applied to Russia nor, in the case of reciprocal aid, to America herself.

Mr Knollenberg then enquired what procedure we would recommend if, despite the wishes of our friends, some limit were to be placed by the Americans on our gold and dollar balances. Would we in that event prefer to increase reciprocal aid or to decrease lend lease or would we consider an arrangement whereby dollars in excess of the stipulated maximum were reimbursed to America? Lord Keynes and Sir David Waley explained that none of these courses could be accepted by us. If the American Government decided that the time had come to reduce lend lease that was a matter for them, and we could not complain of the decision. We should have to make do as well as we could. Indeed, it was clear that at some time, at any rate after the end of the war, it would be right for the American Government to take that decision, and we should in that case hope to see lend lease taper off gradually rather than to have it cut off at a single stroke. In those conditions it would be appropriate to consult together on which type of aid should be eliminated first and which last. What we could not do was to agree to consultation on means of limiting our own assets short of a point at which the increase in our assets was equivalent to the increase in our liabilities.

Mr Knollenberg enquired whether Lord Keynes would be prepared, at no very distant date, to argue our case before the sub-cabinet committee. Lord Keynes and Sir David Waley both considered that such a course would be reasonable and acceptable to H.M.G. They also considered that, for the purposes of the sub-cabinet committee, we would be prepared to give such detailed analysis of our liabilities as might be relevant to the argument, but emphasised that we would not provide statistics which were asked for merely out of curiosity. Sir David Waley asked whether, in the event of Mr Knollenberg's suggestions being followed up, it might not be wise for some preliminary conversation to be arranged with Dr White. It was agreed that this would be wise. The suggestion was also made that it would be politic to bring in Mr Morgenthau to the conversations at an early point.

To sum up. The essence of our position was that the existing situation rightly understood as explained was in no way open to criticism. We took our stand on that. Accordingly we discouraged our American friends from trying to find ways round which might indeed leave matters substantially unchanged but could be represented as subterfuges and as tacit admissions of a weakness in our case. We did not want to run away from justifying the existing position without qualification or abatement.

To SIR WILFRID EADY, *3 October 1943*

My dear Eady,

The Balances question. As you will know already, Morgy responded to the Chancellor's letter with a brief but friendly acknowledgement. Thereafter we duly pushed in the memorandum. This has been discussed with Knollenberg, the acting head of O.L.L.A. in the absence of Stettinius, and his associates. A record of the conversation has gone to you. We expect to have a further talk with Knollenberg and to learn how things are progressing on his side in the course of this week. Meanwhile, you may like to have a few preliminary impressions. As we already knew, the State Department and O.L.L.A. are entirely on our side. The difficulty comes from the Treasury. We are warned that it is the Treasury we have ultimately to square. But although we have been seeing Harry White about twice a day all the time we have been here he has not breathed a word on the subject or given any sign of having seen or studied the document or the Chancellor's letter. This may be explained by his intense preoccupation with other matters. Morgy has been entirely occupied with his War Loan Drive and with the preparation of his tax programme, and has not, I think, given the smallest thought to anything else. Harry White has been equally occupied with the currency talks and getting his investment plan through the departments. This week Morgy and White will both be largely occupied with Congress, superimposed on a continuation of the currency talks. After that it will be in accordance with Morgy's usual habits to disappear into the country for a bit, whilst, as I mentioned in another letter, Harry proposes to disappear from Washington for a fortnight. We shall seek advice from our friends whether, to avoid hopeless delays, we ought to broach the matter with the Treasury this week.

The alternative explanation is that a tacit agreement is growing up to let the controversy die a tacit death. In some ways this would suit us, but nevertheless some think it would be dangerous not to clear things up by getting a new statement of policy laid on the President's table and approved by him. The process of pigeon-holing in this country is described as 'taking a matter under advisement', which apparently means forgetting all about it. People are inclined to tell us that this particular matter has been 'taken under advisement'.

As you will have seen from our conversation with Knollenberg, we took the line of avoiding subterfuge and claimed that we must justify our policy as it stands. I am quite clear that this is right. I believe that it is quite safe to stick to that policy.

O.L.L.A.'s people seem to think that for their own purposes they must invent some kind of formula. But that is none of our business, if they do not communicate it to us officially or expect us to accept it. For example, the new statement of policy to be laid before the President might provide that there can be no objection to an increase in our balances if the rate of increase is no greater than a certain high proportion of the increase in our liabilities. In practice this would mean putting off the issue for as long as lend lease is likely to last. I should be very strongly opposed to our agreeing to any such formula, but obviously no harm in their setting-up something of that sort purely for their own guidance.

Thus you will see that we have not really made any positive progress and that the omens are obscure, but not, I think, unfavourable.

Yours ever,

[copy initialled] K

NOTE OF DISCUSSION ON U.K. DOLLAR BALANCES AND RECIPROCAL AID

1. Mr Knollenberg, Mr Ted Acheson and Mr Denby lunched with Lord Keynes and Mr Lee[18] on the 14th October. Discussion centred upon the following questions:

2. *Limitation of U.K. dollar balances*

Mr Knollenberg (who emphasised that he was talking in strict confidence) said that O.L.L.A. had recently received from Mr Harry White the draft of a letter which it was proposed should be sent by Mr Morgenthau to Mr Crowley,[19] in which the thesis sustained by the State Department and O.L.L.A. that U.K. dollar balances should not be subject to limitation was 'peremptorily' rejected and O.L.L.A. were asked forthwith to restrict lend lease aid to the U.K. with the object of reducing the U.K. balances. Mr Knollenberg went on to say that the receipt of this draft had come as a complete surprise, but that he had assumed that it followed upon full discussions between Mr Harry White and the U.K. Treasury representatives. He (Mr Knollenberg) had had a draft reply prepared (which had not yet been issued) in which the view was expressed that no decision ought to be taken on this question before there had been an opportunity of full discussion on the official inter-departmental Balances Committee (Harry White, Knollenberg, Dean Acheson, Coe, Patterson[20] or a deputy). He added that Dean Acheson and he remained fully convinced that there should be no limitation of U.K. balances; Coe was uncertain; the War Department representative did not count.

Lord Keynes explained that since his arrival there had been no discussions of any kind on this subject between Mr White and the U.K. Treasury representatives. For our part we have been content to accept the advice that the best course would be to allow the question to drift, and we had not therefore tried to initiate discussions with the U.S. Treasury. The formal position was that the Chancellor had already indicated in his letter to Mr Morgenthau the standpoint of H.M.G.: if the U.S. Government

---

[18] Frank Godbould Lee (1903-70), K.C.B. 1950; Colonial Office, 1926-40; transferred to Treasury, 1940; Treasury Delegation, Washington, 1944-6; Ministry of Supply, 1946; Deputy Secretary, 1947; Minister at Washington, 1948; Permanent Secretary, Ministry of Food, 1959-61, Board of Trade, 1951-9; Joint Permanent Secretary of Treasury, 1960-2; Master of Corpus Christi College, Cambridge, from 1962.

[19] Leo T. Crowley (d. 1972); corporation official and chairman; chairman Federal Deposit Insurance Corporation, 1934-45; alien property custodian; member of Roosevelt's cabinet, 1942-3; head of Office of Economic Warfare, 1943; of Foreign Economic Administration, 1943-5.

[20] Robert Porter Patterson (1891-1952), judge; Assistant Secretary of War, U.S.A., 1940, Under-Secretary, December 1940, Secretary of War, 1945-7.

disagreed with this standpoint the appropriate course would be for Mr Morgenthau to indicate as much in a further and full reply to the Chancellor's letter, in amplification of the interim acknowledgement sent to the Chancellor.

The information that Mr White had had no discussions on this subject with the U.K. Treasury representatives and that he was not now available for consultation obviously came as a complete surprise to Mr Knollenberg and his companions. (They were inclined to agree that in the light of circumstances, the draft letter was not perhaps a fully considered document, so much as an attempt by Mr White to 'freeze' the former position of the Treasury during his absence from Washington.) Mr Knollenberg said that he proposed to try to consult Mr Morgenthau forthwith about future procedure and that he would keep us in touch with developments. In particular he would let us know if it were considered appropriate and helpful for Lord Keynes to meet the official Balances Committee in the near future. He implied that he proposed to continue to argue strongly that the next step within the U.S. Administration was for the question to be considered by the committee in the light of the U.K. memorandum.

3. *Raw materials and Foodstuffs on reciprocal aid*
Mr Morgenthau [had] said that he understood that something like an impasse had been reached with O.E.W. on the procedure to be adopted in connection with the handling of raw materials and foodstuffs to be made available to the U.S. on reciprocal aid. O.L.L.A. were in sympathy with the U.K. insistence that certain broad principles of procedure must be adhered to in line with those adopted by O.L.L.A. in the case of lend lease supplies. But O.E.W. regarded themselves as champions of a policy of maintaining U.S. trade channels completely intact, and were therefore standing out for a system under which they would simply be put in funds to a given amount, so enabling U.S. agencies to continue to act as principals in the procurement field.

Mr Lee said that although it was necessary for the U.K. to maintain the broad principles of (i) ultimate procurement responsibility resting with the supplying Government and (ii) a measure of screening of U.S. requirements, and while we had to reserve our position as regards the policing of end-user pending a decision on the White Paper withdrawal, he did not despair of our being able to reach an agreement with O.E.W. if the authorities in that department could be convinced that in practice we should be prepared to go a long way towards meeting them as regards the handling of certain 'difficult' commodities. Mr Lee thought that broadly speaking the commodities concerned would be found to fall in three groups: (a) commodities already bought by a U.K. Government Department, and sold to the U.S. government (e.g. rubber, tea, fats, sisal, etc.). On these no constitutional difficulties would arise, the U.K. would simply cease to collect dollars from an agreed date; (b) commodities at present procured by the U.S. Government through private trade channels (e.g. chrome, burlap) in regard to which it ought to be possible to work out a procedure which would, to a large degree, be operated through existing procurement agencies while maintaining the principle that the ultimate responsibility for procurement remained with the supplying government; (c) cases in which O.E.W. might consider that for technical procurement reasons it would be better for them to decline the U.K. offer of reciprocal aid and to continue to buy for dollars. Goatskins is a probable candidate for this class. Mr Lee said that his own view was that the U.K. representatives should again make clear to Mr Scheuer[21] that while we must maintain the broad principles indicated above we were anxious to discuss individual cases of difficulty so as to be able to begin reciprocal aid on as broad a basis as possible.

The general view was expressed by the U.S. representatives that we should be on strong ground politically if the U.K. reiterated its offer to make all raw materials and food-stuffs, imported by the U.S. Government, available on reciprocal aid and then left it to O.E.W. to decline the offer in respect of a residual balance of commodities where, for technical procurement reasons, O.E.W. felt it to be undesirable to modify in any way existing channels of procurement. They expressed the view that a settlement might be facilitated if the U.K. could offer in practice, to ante-date reciprocal aid in respect of commodities falling under (a) above to the 1st July, while maintaining that the date had no particular validity in this context. It was agreed that copies of any further letter sent to Mr Scheuer in the matter should be communicated to the State Department and O.L.L.A. for information.

4. *Publication of U.K. reciprocal aid White Paper*

Mr Denby explained that a submission on this subject was just being made to Mr Hopkins and that the considered views of the State Department and O.L.L.A. could be expected within the course of a few days.

5. *Mr Stettinius's book on lend lease*[22]

It was mentioned that it was now hoped that this would appear in January. Its issue had been largely held up because of Mr Stettinius's preoccupation with other matters as a result of the recent changes.

[21] Sidney Henry Scheuer (b. 1893); executive director, Foreign Economic Administration, U.S.A., 1942–5.
[22] See *JMK*, vol. XXIV.

My dear Eady,

Thank you very much for telegram 7058 which you sent me on the 16th when the currency talks came to an end. It has indeed been a strenuous time: I don't know when I have been more occupied. What overwhelms one in Washington is the enormous amount of work, or semi-work, which one has to do at meal times. I reckon that whilst I was in Washington, including a fair number of parties which I had to give myself, I dined and lunched out 42 times. And all one's ostensible work was on top of that.

Now I am in New York for a few days to see the bankers. Yesterday was spent with groups of private bankers, today I am due to go to a long conference with the Board of the Federal Reserve Bank. There is no doubt that I am able to make a great deal more progress than Harry White could, since unquestionably anything coming from the U.S. Treasury faces a terrific load of prejudice here before it starts. It is too soon for me to put anything on paper. But I shall have some interesting things to tell the Chancellor about the attitude here towards special Anglo-American financial arrangements, as distinct from an international set-up.

I have just heard from Waley that Morgy and Harry White may very likely be in Whitehall before I am. If they are delayed, and if my Clipper keeps to its schedule without any delays, which seldom happens, I suppose I might conceivably arrive before they have left. I am rather sorry that I should not have had an opportunity of an oral explanation of the position here before the Chancellor sees them. I assume that they can scarcely get away without a proper discussion of the balances situation. You will have had before now my latest up-to-date reflections. I do not think I have learned anything here which is a reason for disturbing the present arrangements, the general principles of which you had established before we left. But perhaps it would be useful for me to recapitulate these in the light of local discussions:–

(1) We agreed that in no circumstances should we agree to any ceiling on our balances, or to any agreed arrangement on our part to limit them to any given figure. If the Americans feel, rightly or wrongly, that we are now rich enough to get along with less lend lease, then the right course is for them to pare lend lease. I fancy that this is generally accepted in Washington. If we do not persuade them that our case is good, the result will be that lend lease will be trimmed.

(2) This does not mean that we should give up efforts of our own to disperse our balances whenever we have a good occasion to do so, e.g. by returning some part of the dollar reserves to other parts of the sterling area, or handing over gold or dollars to India. I am still convinced that we should be wise to do this on as large a scale as we possibly can. There will always be a risk of discomfort here if our balances look large, however justifiable this may be in view of the under-lying circumstances. Any such dispersal of our balances, how-ever, should be entirely of our own volition and not as a result of any agreement with the Americans, though, of course, with their full knowledge.

(3) Nor does the principle in (1) preclude the Americans from having some formula in their own minds for satisfying themselves that our balances are still innocent. If they were to re-write the President's Directive to the effect that as long as our balances, or their increment, did not exceed $x\%$ of our liabilities there was no occasion for criticism, this might help them in maintaining the *status quo* of lend lease without involving us. There is all the difference in the world between their using a rough and ready formula for their own guid-ance, until the time comes to replace it by another formula, and our accepting any such formula as an *agreed* limitation of our balances.

(4) A further reason why the trimming of lend lease is the

better way out is the fact that as time goes on some trimming of the less easily defensible items is extremely likely to happen in any case. There are certain items, such as agricultural machinery and machine tools, which, if we have to give them away, may involve us in an earlier loss rather than a total loss, compared with what would happen otherwise. This does not mean that we should ever agree to trimming of lend lease, or do anything else than resist it to the last. But there is such a variety of reasons why some trimming of lend lease will come sooner or later that what we shall lose by 'sooner' may not be unduly large.

(5) I am convinced that our right course is to stand pat on our full case, and not make any gestures giving away a bit here and a bit there in the hope of creating a better atmosphere. Those things hardly count even momentarily. They certainly do not count at all when a few hours or days have passed. I saw a recent telegram in which it was suggested that we might, as a gesture, agree to antedate rubber to 31 March and collect nothing of what is owing after that date. My belief is that this would simply mean throwing away a few million pounds quite gratuitously. We must stand absolutely pat on our main thesis, and leave them to trim lend lease if they feel they must.

(6) My own belief is that they probably will not. Far from a certainty, I agree. But there are certain factors working strongly on our side:

(a) people in O.L.L.A. will not think it appropriate to trim lend lease at the very moment of our announcing a large extension of reciprocal aid in respect of war materials;

(b) nor will they want to take such a course at the moment when it might be interpreted as a concession to the five Senators, who have made them just as angry as they have made us;

(c) the principal officials of O.L.L.A. are entirely, even passionately, on our side, and would take a defeat quite seriously to heart. I believe that the State Department, though with less ardour, are also convinced of the justice of our case. Nor, I suspect, is the U.S. Treasury really as fierce as it pretends to be; they are partly concerned, I think, on getting on record for Congressional purposes; but mainly this is one more example of the extraordinary obstinacy of Morgy and Harry White—once they have taken up any attitude they simply hate to alter it.

Thus I believe extreme firmness, combined with sweet reasonableness, and an entire absence of any gesture to give oddments away, should prove successful.

Yours ever,

[copy initialled] K

To DEAN ACHESON, *27 October 1943*

My dear Dean,

When I saw you on Monday I threw out the suggestion that perhaps it might be helpful if I were to let you have a peptonised version of the British argument about balances reduced to a page or two. I have now tried my hand and enclose the result. I only venture to trouble you with this as I know how useful it sometimes turns out if a really brief statement of a case is easily available at hand.

You will see that I have *not* introduced the point that any major change of policy will involve you in asking us, directly or indirectly, to meet the pay of your troops wherever they are based on British territory. I have thought it better to leave it to you to use this point if, in the context, you think it a good one to use.

I have also passed a copy to Llewellin.[23] It is possible, I think,

---

[23] John Hesbyn Llewellin (1893–1957), 1st Baron 1945; M.P. (U.) for Uxbridge, 1929–45; Parliamentary Secretary, Ministry of Supply, 1939–40, of Aircraft Production, 1940–1, of War Transport, 1941–2; President, Board of Trade, 1942; Minister of Aircraft Production, 1942; Minister-Resident in Washington for Supply, 1942–3; Minister of Food, 1943.

that he will take an opportunity of handing it to Mr Harry Hopkins. No one else will be seeing or having a copy.

Lydia and I are off by Clipper this evening. We have greatly enjoyed this visit to Washington,—a good deal more than our rather longer visit two and a half years ago. Not the least part of our enjoyment came from our meetings with you and your family. Many thanks for your most kind hospitality. We have felt that our bonds to several of our American friends have come a great deal closer and more intimate in this visit.

Ever yours sincerely,

[copy initialled] M.K.

THE QUESTION OF THE BRITISH GOLD AND DOLLAR BALANCES

1. Some time back, in different circumstances from the present, the President approved a line of policy which would permit the British gold and dollar reserves to reach some figure between $600 million and $1,000 million. There was no agreement by the British to limit their reserves to this figure.

2. For some little time past the British reserves have exceeded $1,000 million, and may be increasing at a rate of some $600 million a year. This includes gold and represents their total resources against growing liabilities in all parts of the world, which amount to six or seven times these reserves.

3. This increase in the British reserves does not reflect an improvement in their financial position. Their quick liabilities, largely caused by heavy cash outgoings in the Middle East, are increasing at four or five times the rate at which the reserves against them have increased. Their *net* overseas position, in fact, is deteriorating at a rate of about $3 billion a year.

4. The increase in their gold holdings is due to certain

receipts from South Africa and Russia. The increase in their dollar balances is due to their receiving the dollar equivalent of the local currency provided to meet the pay of American troops within the sterling area. Indeed, if it were not for the pay of the American troops the British dollar balances would be going down.

5. Apart from certain raw materials, the British are already giving reciprocal aid to the fullest extent of American Government requirements. They have now offered raw materials purchased by the U.S. Government in Great Britain and the colonies on reciprocal aid terms. This would retard the growth of their balances by about $100 million a year, and by $200 million if India and Australia join in.

6. The British argue that some growth of their reserves is indispensable to the delicate system they are operating by which they finance the war on credit throughout a large part of the world, and that the retention of some part of the above receipts, as a support to this credit system and an offset to a much larger increase of liabilities, is not open to legitimate criticism. They point out that the Russians are believed to hold gold reserves nearly double the total reserves of the British and have no significant liabilities against them. But, in the case of Russia, it is not at present proposed to require them to surrender any part of their reserves as a condition of further lend lease assistance.

7. The British feel that they ought not to be asked to agree to a ceiling to their balances, since their reserve position must be their own concern. Nevertheless, if the British argument is accepted as valid, the position could be regularised by a new Directive, which would set up a revised formula for the guidance of American departments. If the figure given by the new formula was being approached, then the whole question could be re-opened.

8. The new formula might provide that an increase in British reserves is not unreasonable if the increase does not exceed, say, 30 per cent of the increase of British liabilities.

9. Figures furnished to Congress hitherto have not disclosed the full burden of British overseas liabilities, or their rate of growth. It might be necessary to justify the new arrangement to provide that the information given to Congress in future should be fuller, and should show in some fashion, which would not be dangerous to British credit, the growth of liabilities as well as the growth of reserves.

26 October 1943

Keynes returned to London on 29 October with news that the Americans now favoured publication of the reciprocal aid White Paper. Keynes set out the developments as follows.

1. Reasons brought forward for postponing issue of reciprocal aid White Paper were five:–

(i) Might give the Senatorial Enquiry more *pabulum* for enquiry and inquisitiveness.

(ii) Should await concurrence of India and Dominions.

(iii) Should await the solution of the deadlock over methods of procurement of raw materials, etc.

(iv) Should await final agreement as to withdrawal of Export White Paper.

(v) Should not by premature publication jeopardise policy of President's re-issuing White Paper with his own flattering introduction.

2. Different individuals attached differing degrees of importance to the five reasons. Stettinius alleged to have stated (i) though he did not even mention it with me; Acheson inclined to want prior settlement of (ii) and (iii); our technical people concerned with (iii); Llewellin mainly interested in (iv); Oscar Cox and Campbell[24] and (I should add) myself particularly anxious about getting (v). The complexity of these several issues has caused the discussions in Washington

[24] Sir Ronald Ian Campbell (b. 1890) diplomat; Minister at Washington, 1941–5; Assistant Under-Secretary of State for Foreign Affairs, 1945–6.

and the ensuing telegrams to be a bit confused and not always quite accurate in emphasis.

3. Last Monday (25 Oct.) I saw Stettinius. In a telegram drafted, but not sent, immediately afterwards I wrote:–

At interview this morning Stettinius expressed to me his personal view that it had been a tragic mistake not to publish White Paper on reciprocal aid last August, before criticism had arisen. But of course postponement then had been their fault, not ours. He went on to say that he feels in his bones that it would be a tragic mistake not to publish it now with the least possibly delay. He thinks it is up to us to give our picture to the world. He thinks it likely that if we publish White Paper in the near future the President would be prepared to communicate it to Congress with a preface of his own endorsing the value of what had been done.

He added that, whilst it would be much preferable if the raw materials offer could be settled in time for inclusion, it would be better to postpone this for the time being rather than hold up any longer our statement of what was already happening about reciprocal aid. He was anxious that the raw materials offer when made should not look like a sop to the five Senators. This was a complete reversal of the advice given by him as reported in telegram 4756 of 21 October, but, not having seen this telegram, I was not at the time aware of this. On the other hand, it was a return to the advice he had given Mr Law a fortnight previously (see Mr Law's Cabinet Memo. 478). He kept on emphasising that this was his *personal* advice not to be quoted elsewhere in the State Department, but then, after some hesitation, decided to make a clean breast of it and took me round to Dean Acheson's room and repeated the same advice in his presence. The point obviously was that this was Acheson's field of responsibility with which Stettinius did not want to interfere unduly. Acheson was less enthusiastic and preferred postponement of publication until raw materials was settled, but he acquiesced in Stettinius's advice. Neither of them laid any emphasis on waiting for the end of Senatorial Enquiry.

4. I drafted a telegram reporting this and suggested immediate publication without reference to raw material offer (which merely meant omitting §9 and a few consequential changes). Campbell and Llewellin rightly held this up with my agreement, because they were reluctant without further enquiry to give up the early publication of the raw materials offer. Mr Hopkins was not available at the moment, because, as usual, he was sharing the President's influenza.

5. Late on 27 October, just before I left Washington, a meeting of Llewellin, Campbell, Waley, Opie,[25] Archer[26] and myself agreed on the substance of a telegram recommending the publication of the White Paper exactly as drafted with only such delay as would give a reasonable chance to secure the President's approval of the proposed covering document over his signature.

6. The weighty reasons to the contrary which were discussed but eventually rejected were the following:–

(i) Senatorial Enquiry. Cox's report. Five Senators fizzling out. Committee interested in (a) our getting payment for lend lease food; (b) capital works of post-war value; (c) Iceland fish; (d) plant owned and paid for by us in U.S. No mention of balances which, said Cox, had not been before Congress for two years and had quite dropt out of mind. More testimony to be given. On the whole, enquiry going much more smoothly than anticipated.

(ii) Americans seem quite clear now that from their point of view we need not wait for India and the Dominions.

---

[25] Redvers Opie (b. 1900) economist; Counsellor and Economic Adviser, British Embassy, Washington, 1939–46; Adviser, U.K. Delegation, International Food Conference, 1943; U.K. Delegate, International Monetary and Financial Conference, 1944.

[26] George Archer (1896–1960); entered Civil Service, 1913; Under-Secretary, Ministry of Supply; Secretary-General, British Raw Materials Mission, Washington, 1942–4; Head of Mission, 1945; U.K. Secretary, Combined Raw Materials Board, 1942–5.

(iii) Complete deadlock over procurement. Currie declares that they will not go through the same hoops as ourselves in procurement, and will not agree to policing on export White Paper lines. Nevertheless, there is no reason why we should not make the offer of raw materials on the same terms as those of their supplies to us. They are free to decline it if they wish.

Nature of Currie's proposed compromise.

(iv) Withdrawal of export White Paper is almost agreed. But Llewellin was afraid of this slipping through our fingers if we make raw materials offer public before we have got it. On the other hand, it was agreed that we could not make a bargain of the one against the other.

7. The form of our draft White Paper is not bad, but is not journalistically effective and deliberately makes the least, rather than the most, of the material. For this reason an accompanying speech by the Chancellor would be very helpful. This should particularly stress that the offer of raw materials was made some months ago, and the announcement has only been delayed to allow time for staff work about details.

To SIR WILFRID EADY, *1 November 1943*

This preliminary draft of the report, which the President might make to Congress as a covering letter to our White Paper on reciprocal aid, must be read subject to the following reserves:

On my last day at Washington, 27 October, I asked to see Mr Oscar Cox in order to get the latest information about the senatorial enquiry. When he came round to see me, we dealt, not only with that, but also with the whole field. He was in favour of our publishing our White Paper as soon as possible, subject only to our giving him reasonable notice so as to allow a good chance of getting through something which he has had in mind for sometime past, namely, that when the White Paper comes out it should be forwarded to Congress by the

President as a special report under the Lend Lease Act, accompanied by a covering document. He told me that he had recently made a revise of what was intended.

It was by that time within half an hour of my having to close the sealed bag in which my private papers were to come, and I asked him if he could let me have a copy immediately. As a result of this he telephoned to his secretary, who came round with the enclosed. When it arrived it appeared that, in the hurry of the moment, she had not brought with her quite the latest version.

The first reserve is, therefore, that it is the draft of 15 October. I gather that a revise of about ten days later did not really differ very much in general impression, but that the passage dealing with that part of lend lease which cannot at present be turned into terms of money has been modified and emphasised. This is to the good, since the bit in this draft dealing with the aid we have given in North Africa, which has not been quantified, is definitely inadequate.

The second reserve is that this draft has not yet been seen by Mr Harry Hopkins or by the President. On the other hand, it has been seen by Mr Stettinius, who expressed to me the definite hope and belief that the President would agree to put it forward. Also the general idea of such a document has been approved by Mr Hopkins. I doubt if at the date when I saw Mr Cox the President had anything more than the vaguest idea about it.

It is, of course, possible, therefore, that the draft may be considerably altered, and there is no knowing but that the President, at the last moment, whilst approving the paper in every other way, may use his famous political instinct to decide that it is politically dangerous. The reason for hoping the contrary is that it makes clear how much was happening of a kind the American public would approve, but of which they had no knowledge, at dates long previous to the travels or the criticisms of the five Senators.

You will see that it is very extensive and is largely concerned with recapitulating the actual substance of our White Paper. By implication it gets a long way further back again to the idea of pooling and would obviously be of the very greatest value from every point of view if the President can be brought to issuing it. It is possible that a little encouragement from this side might be very helpful.

I should explain that Mr Oscar Cox has been concerned part time with lend lease from the very beginning. He has never been concerned with the operations end of it, but has I believe, drafted all the President's Lend Lease Reports from the very start. His official position is that of Assistant Solicitor General. Hitherto he has been sitting in the Department of Justice and has been concerned with many other matters besides lend lease. In the re-organisation announced within the last few days he has become General Counsel to Mr Crowley's new department. He told me that this would mean his giving his whole time to the Office of Foreign Economic Administration and that he would probably resign before long his position as Assistant Solicitor General. Since it was Oscar Cox, and no one else, whom Mr Crowley took with him to the senatorial investigation, and since Cox seems to be entirely in charge of that, I infer that he has won Mr Crowley's confidence. In the new American departments the position of General Counsel is exceedingly influential, and he is generally the person closest to the Administrator on all matters of high policy. If this is to be Cox's position, it is exceedingly fortunate, since he is the sole survivor of our old friends, who have been associated with lend lease for a considerable time. I saw a good deal of him last time I was in Washington and then formed a high opinion of him. This time I saw him very little, since my main job was in another direction, and my last long talk with him was really the only one I had which mattered. I again felt that he was a firm friend. Experience shows, however, that he often tells one, as though it was an accepted policy, his wishes rather than the unadorned facts.

However, there is no doubt that Stettinius is behind this and also, I think, Hopkins. Mr Ronald Campbell attaches the highest importance to getting something of this kind published and thinking that it might be the beginning of a really important diplomatic improvement on this particular front. Oscar Cox told me that he would like as long notice as possible of the exact date of publication if he was to carry this through. I should surmise that too much notice might be as dangerous as too little. Cox suggested that a week's notice would be enough and that even a little less might serve, if, from the political point of view, a week was impossible for us.

1.11.43   KEYNES

In the ensuing few days Keynes, in rare agreement with Lord Beaver-brook, revised the draft of the White Paper, shortening it considerably and giving less of an air that 'the lady doth protest too much' without altering the substance. The revised White Paper was published on 11 November.

On his return from America, Keynes also drafted two notes for his colleagues, one on the proposed lend lease cuts, the other on the new body administering lend lease.

LEND LEASE CUTS

The following is a note by Mr Grant of the lend lease aid which is in course of being removed or is in jeopardy:–

(i) O.L.L.A. have cut out anything for propaganda or entertainment (e.g. paper, non-miliary radio equipment).

(ii) From 15 November, they propose to cut out capital goods.

(iii) At present Iceland fish is paid for ⅔ in dollars, ⅓ in sterling, with the dollar part lend leased. This may well come out.

(iv) We sold back to the Americans two shipyards for $14 million in 1942. Congress has clamoured.

(v) O.L.L.A. are getting very sticky about, e.g. Indian civilian requirements.

The Americans estimate that this may cost us $150 to $200 million a year. The actual cost has not been checked with the relevant departments. But Mr Grant's own guess would put the cost at not much more than $100 million, made up as follows:– (i) $m15–20, (ii) $m40–74, (iii) $m15–20, (iv) $m14, total $m84–125.

In the main these cuts do not seem to be associated with the question of our dollar balances, though no doubt that lurks in the background as an additional reason. O.L.L.A. is mainly concerned with staking out a position against possible reactions from the Senate Enquiry. They want to be able to show that they have not been backward and have acted first.

Items (ii) and (iii) and (iv) are the three items in which the Truman Committee has been showing most interest; (i) is also included because of the action of Congress towards similar expenditure of their own O.W.I.

In talking to Cox and Acheson I have taken the line that it makes all the difference in the world to us whether this is the beginning of a series of cuts directed at our dollar balances or whether they are merely isolated items which have become difficult for political reasons. So long as the balances question is unsettled, we cannot be expected to overlook the first implications. If, on the other hand, the balances question were to be definitely settled in our favour, then, of course, we should do our utmost to fall in with their wishes on details of no great magnitude which they assured us were open to political criticism.

I also pointed out that our offer of raw materials was made on the assumption that the general principles of lend lease as administered recently would continue substantially unchanged. This applied particularly to the proposal to cut out capital goods, since capital goods happen to be one of the largest ingredients in reverse lend lease.

(i) We have, I think, already relinquished. Whether (ii), (iii) and (iv) are pressed mainly depends, I should say, on the outcome of the Congressional Enquiry; (ii) includes machine tools, and, from some points of view, we should not be entirely losers by paying cash for these.

If Congress shows extreme interest in these matters, and if the balances question is settled, the items involved are not so large that we need stand out too vehemently against acquiescence.

But we ought to protest against everything until the balances issue is settled.

1.11.43   KEYNES

THE FOREIGN ECONOMIC ADMINISTRATION

A month ago Mr Crowley was appointed to bring under a single umbrella

(*a*) the Lend Lease Administration—O.L.L.A.

(*b*) the Office of Economic Warfare—O.E.W.;

(*c*) the Office of Foreign Relief and Rehabilitation—O.F.R.R.O.;

(*d*) the Office of Foreign Economic Co-operation, hitherto in the State Department and concerned with the administration of liberated areas;

(*e*) the activities of the Commodity Credit Corporation and its subsidiaries, hitherto under Jesse Jones, in so far as they relate to the purchase of raw materials outside U.S.A.

During the first month these bodies continued as hitherto under their existing officials, and there was no attempt to amalgamate them. During my last days in Washington it was announced that all the above organisations were abolished, and a single organisation on quite new lines was established to take their place.

This has involved two main issues: (i) the nature of the new organisation; (ii) the character of the new personnel.

On both these matters details were only emerging in my

last day or two in Washington, and I was at the mercy of incomplete and not always quite consistent reports. It is very probable, therefore, that what follows may require amendment in some respects. Nevertheless, I think that the broad outline is as described below.

(i) *The nature of the new organisation*

The five bodies described above will no longer have a separate existence or separate staffing, but will be fully amalgamated. The resulting single organisation, to be known as the Foreign Economic Administration, will have to be reorganised according to two principles. The first is geographical (Bureau of Areas). For example, all matters connected with the British Empire will come, in the first instance, to what will be known as the British Empire desk; and similarly with all other geographical areas. Oscar Cox spoke as if there would be a single desk for the British Commonwealth. But he may have been simplifying. At any rate, it is to be presumed that there will be sub-desks for the different parts of the Commonwealth.

The second division of organisation will be according to commodities (Bureau of Supplies). For example, there will be a department dealing with copper. Thus, if the British Empire desk becomes concerned with an application relating to copper, it will refer this to the copper department. On the face of it, this involves some duplication with the W.P.A. and the Combined Boards. But presumably the commodity departments will keep in close touch with the departments dealing with the same commodity in W.P.A. At any rate, it can be claimed that all overseas interests are now brought together.

Whether this new classification of duties will make as much difference in practice as appears on the surface I am not sure. For example, the British Empire desk will presumably be mainly concerned with lend lease. The Italian desk will be mainly concerned with what used to be done by O.F.R.R.O. or the Office of Foreign Economic Co-operation. The Spanish desk will take over what O.E.W. used to do. On the other hand, when we come to the commodity sub-sections, no doubt there is a considerable increase of co-ordination.

The third element in the new organisation, namely financial, is still obscure. At present finance is provided through the appropriations voted to each of the previously existing separate departments. Nothing has yet been done to merge the financial appropriations. Oscar Cox told me that the unspent appropriations of all the departments together amounted to something like $4 billions. Thus, they could considerably extend their existing activities without going to Congress for new money, if they were allowed to pool their existing appropriations and have somewhat enlarged discretion as to how to apply them. His hope is that Congress will agree to something on these lines. I have, however, heard nothing about this from any other source, and it may be a possible line of policy that at present is purely personal to Oscar Cox. It is certainly the present intention of the U.S. Treasury and also of the State Department to seek a separate appropriation for relief, whereas under Cox's plan, as he explicitly explained, there would not be any request for additional sums specifically ear-marked, but only a large discretion to use for that purpose appropriations already voted.

(ii) *The character of the new personnel*

This was still somewhat obscure when I left Washington. The particulars published in the press are appended below. The general character of the change seems to have been as follows:–

Before Mr Crowley became Foreign Economic Administrator, he was in charge of the Office of Economic Warfare. In the course of the last month there had been a struggle behind

the scenes as to how far O.E.W. staff should get the big
posts together with certain new-comers, and how far those
previously holding responsible jobs in O.L.L.A. should go on
doing much the same work. It now appears that O.E.W. has
won all along the line.

The only survivor of our friends, with whom we have built
up long associations in O.L.L.A., who has a fairly important
position is Oscar Cox, who becomes General Counsel to Mr
Crowley and, therefore, stands at his right hand. Mr Lauchlin
Currie of O.E.W. is so to speak the head civil servant. Frank
Coe, also of O.E.W., seems to have improved his situation.

I understand that our friends in O.L.L.A. knew nothing
about what their personal situations were to be until the press
announcements were about to be issued. Some of them found
that their names did not appear. On their making complaint
to Mr Crowley, the usual American course was adopted, that
is to say titles were invented for them without any definite
duties attached. For example, Mr Knollenberg, who has been
running O.L.L.A. for the last month, becomes Executive
Adviser, but no-one knows what an Executive Adviser does,
if anything. Philip Young and one or two others were at the
last moment denominated Assistant Deputy Administrators,
again with no definite duties. Some of those lower down the
staff, such as Ted Acheson and Denby, with whom we have
had particularly close associations, believe that they have been
squeezed out. All the above tell us that they will attend the
office for two or three weeks to see if any duties are assigned
to them, but they expect to be resigning shortly. They were
saying to us tearfully last Tuesday that we had lost every single
one of our best friends.

Those of whom we already have experience and have
improved their positions, namely Currie and Coe, are not, I
think, fundamentally unfriendly, but they are suspicious and
difficult and almost certain, I should say, to make trouble for
us. Both are said to be ready for hostilities on the matter of

the balances. Thus, amongst the lower staff, instead of having nothing but friends, apart from the action of the Treasury, we may now find ourselves in quite a different position. (This does not apply to Oscar Cox, who is vehemently on our side in the matter of the balances, and that should count a good deal.)

Mr Schubart, whom Lord Catto and I met more than once when he was in London and thought friendly but a boob, is brought in as head of the Supplies Bureau.

Currie has survived owing to his particularly close relationship to the President (on whose personal staff he has been for some years); and Coe has survived because he is a protégé of Currie. Otherwise a clean sweep seems to have been made of the intelligentsia and the professors in favour of outside businessmen, stiffened with a few lawyers. Moreover, Mr Crowley himself is an Irish Roman Catholic, and, judging from their names, it seems that some of those he is now bringing in from outside for important positions are of the same complexion.

Those of our own staff, such as Archer, who have had dealings both with O.E.W. and with O.L.L.A., consider that the calibre of the former's personnel was much inferior to that of the latter. So it is the unfit who have survived. I can confirm this also in the case of Currie and Coe, who are by no means without capacity, but are certainly small-minded officials, decidedly of the second class.

Moreover, we shall be dealing largely with people with whom we have not yet cultivated relations and who are enormously ignorant of the historical development of the present system and how it has evolved.

No one seems to be able to give any account whatever of Mr Crowley himself. Llewellin has met him once and said that he seemed pleasant and easy to get on with. I have not met anyone else who has seen him or even anyone who knows anyone who knows him. The impression seems to be that he is a capable administrator but colourless. He is a bachelor and said to be a very pious Roman Catholic.

So far as the State Department is concerned, Dean Acheson is in charge of the policy side and the Foreign Economic Administration's contact with the State Department. And the F.E.A. is supposed to conform in policy with the wishes of the State Department, though it will be far from clear where one draws the line between policy and operations. At any rate, Dean Acheson's position seems to be improved rather than otherwise, and he will have behind him the wisdom and strong support of Stettinius. This is all to the good.

So far as the President is concerned, the link will doubtless be through Mr Harry Hopkins.

Thus it would appear that we shall receive much more consideration at the top than further down the line. It looks to me as if we shall have to rely much more than before on contacts with Mr Hopkins at the White House, Mr Dean Acheson and Mr Stettinius in the State Department and Mr Oscar Cox as an adviser of Mr Crowley in F.E.A.

Meanwhile it is easy to imagine how much confusion exists and uncertainty on future policy. Currie has made a bad start, from our point of view, in the very difficult and obstinate line he has taken over the methods of procuring raw materials given under reciprocal aid.

As regards balances, this new situation, which has developed so rapidly, is an important additional reason why we should seek a very early settlement at the highest levels. I am reporting on this separately.

1.11.43   KEYNES

P.S. Since dictating the above, I have seen Washington telegram 4895 of 30 October. This adds a few additional particulars to the above.

For the lend lease cuts and reciprocal aid additions under discussion late in 1943, the outcome was as follows: Britain agreed to the exclusion of capital goods, Icelandic fish and Caribbean sugar from lend lease and the inclusion of raw materials in reciprocal aid; the United States dropped its cuts on pulp and paper, but continued to be difficult over Indian civilian requirements and other items.

From the end of 1943, Keynes's involvement with lend lease brought a change of emphasis. Although he kept a watching brief on day-to-day lend lease problems, he became much more concerned than previously with preparations for an orderly transition from war to peace. His initiation of and involvement in these discussions and the two further rounds of Anglo-American negotiations over Stage II (the period between the defeat of Germany and that of Japan) and Stage III (the early post-war period) are the subject of volume XXIV.

Chapter 8

THE MIDDLE EAST AND INDIA, 1940–43

I

Keynes's interest in the wartime financial problems of Egypt and the Middle East would doubtless have been stimulated in any case as news of them reached the Treasury through normal channels. However, after October 1941, R. F. Kahn's position as Economic Adviser to Mr Oliver Lyttleton,[1] Minister of State in the Middle East, meant that Keynes received an additional series of letters, memoranda and the like dealing with Middle Eastern questions and administrative problems.

Kahn's arrival in Egypt coincided with a period of considerable economic difficulties in the area. During 1939, 1940 and early 1941, the decline in demand for Middle Eastern exports resulting from wartime marketing disruptions and the slow build-up of British and Commonwealth forces in the area meant that inflationary pressures had proved relatively mild. However, from the spring of 1941 the economies of the area were affected by growing military operations, mounting local military expenditures and cuts in imports. Added to these forces was a disastrously short harvest in the summer of 1941. This led to food shortages in the towns, aggravated by producers' hoarding in the expectation of higher prices, and a shortage of goods and alternative stores of wealth. The inflation that resulted from these pressures led to discontent in the towns and British fears of possible political repercussions—repercussions that looked increasingly serious as the war moved closer to the area. At the same time, the governments of the area, with full treasuries and often little interest in the war, were deaf to Allied pleas to raise taxes and float local bond issues to mop up surplus purchasing power. They were also unwilling to control prices.

Local military expenditure was financed by rising Egyptian balances in London. The scale of this expenditure rose as local prices and wages rose.

---

[1] Oliver Lyttleton (1893–1973), 1st Viscount Chandos, 1954; Controller of Non-Ferrous Metals, 1939–40; M.P. (C.) for Aldershot, 1940–54; President of Board of Trade, 1940–1; Minister of State and member of War Cabinet, 1941–2; Minister of Production and member of War Cabinet, 1942–5; President of Board of Trade and Minister of Production, May–July 1945; Secretary of State for the Colonies, 1951–4.

On top of this, restriction of imports caused by shortage of shipping resulted in an Egyptian balance of payments surplus with the sterling area which was also financed by rising sterling balances. Keynes wrote to R. F. Kahn on 31 October 1941.[2]

From a letter to R. F. KAHN, *31 October 1941*

I have been looking into the question of Egyptian balances in London and the scale on which they are increasing. I do not believe that this phenomenon has been receiving sufficient attention from those concerned. So it may be desirable that you should be aware of the broad facts and perhaps communicate them to Lyttelton and Miles Lampson. But I must add that the Bank of England attach great importance to the confidential character of these figures and emphasise the consideration that they are not entirely accurate. On the one hand, the returns from the clearing banks are not in such a form that they are necessarily comprehensive. On the other hand, they may easily include balances that more properly belong to Palestine or other parts of the Middle East, since the whole of the London balances of the Egyptian Bank are included. Subject to these reserves, the London balances in favour of Egypt amounted at the end of September to about £61 million in addition to which £34 million were held in British Government securities, making a total of £95 million. During the last year this total has been increasing at an average rate of £40 million a year. Thus, if this continues, it will not be long before our indebtedness to Egypt on short-term and in the shape of British Government securities will be approaching £150 million. Since there are various ways in which we hope to deal with similar balances in favour of India and Dominions it may well be the case that in a year or two's time the Egyptian sterling balance will be the largest of any

---

[2] The other subjects discussed in the letter included the treatment of Egyptian lend lease supplies, inefficiency in railway development and improvement in the Middle East, and French currency arrangements in the area.

part of the world, which is a bit of an anomaly. I should add that the above includes the cover held by the Issue Department of the National Bank of Egypt. My figures here are not later than the end of May 1941, when the Issue Department held the following:–

	£m.E
British Treasury bills (deposited in lieu of gold)	15.21
British Treasury bills and War Loan	19.95
	35.16

At any rate this is not consistent with the assumption too frequently made that Egypt is an impoverished country which must be assisted to finance its surpluses and must be allowed as much benefit as possible of lend lease arrangements, etc. etc. In short, we are still treating the Egyptians as impoverished connections who are entitled to call on their rich uncle for whatever costs anything. In particular, you will observe that the sums now available are very large in relation to the sums involved in financing or carrying the cotton crop.

It is, therefore, of considerable importance that any practicable steps should be taken to prevent this indebtedness from growing unreasonably. It is not at all easy to know what can be done.* At any rate not easy for us here in London. But I feel that, if those directly concerned on the spot are aware of the circumstances, they may approach day to day problems with rather a different attitude from what they may think reasonable if the facts have been withheld from them.

Kahn replied in part on 15 December with a letter concerned, as he put it, with 'providing capital assets to relieve the strain on consumable goods as a source of holding wealth'. He enclosed a memorandum, entitled 'A Gold Policy for M.E.', by Colonel R. A. Harari,[3] advocating obtaining gold

* Could we ask Egypt to pay some part of the cost of defending her?
[3] Col. R. A. Harari, Chief Economic Adviser, G.H.Q. Middle East.

on lend lease and selling it at open market prices to remove surplus purchasing power and provide an alternative to goods as a store of wealth. Kahn also enclosed a note supporting the scheme.

At the time, the Treasury did not consider the scheme practical politics and the only outcome of the resulting inter-departmental discussions of the problem was a circular letter in June 1942 to British representatives in the Middle East urging economy in expenditure. Keynes reported the position to Kahn in a letter on 11 May.

From a letter to R. F. KAHN, *11 May 1942*

I come next to the general issue how to prevent inflation in the Middle East and such proposals as Harari's. What must now be some two or three months ago we had a general conference called together by Waley to consider your letter and Harari's proposals about this. We reached the conclusion that we had nothing very useful or constructive to propose, but that it was important that all those concerned, particularly the military, should be fully alive to the nature of the problem and, in small matters if not in large, should take opportunities of acting in ways which would mitigate rather than aggravate the problem. But it is perhaps typical that when I enquired long afterwards what had happened about the memorandum I discovered that it had never been prepared or circulated and, indeed, that nothing whatever had been done.

Harari's proposal was, of course, perfectly sound in principle and in theory. So far as we are concerned it is impracticable because we cannot spare the gold and, above all, because we cannot afford to create a *precedent* for letting gold out for such purposes. But I am not at all sure that a moment might not come when it would be well worth raising it with the United States. Some of them, I know, are reaching the sensible opinion that now is the time at which the United States might put some of their redundant gold to a useful purpose, an opportunity which may never recur. There are indeed signs that they may oblige us a little in this direction

319

in the case of Persia. I should not rule out the possibility of their doing something of the sort in Egypt if it was put to them in the right way, by the right people and on the right occasion. But, like everything else, it is no-one's job in particular to do this. If it is to happen, it would have to be, I fancy, as part of a general programme by which they share with us financial responsibility in Egypt and the Middle East. If they could be persuaded to do this, the satisfaction of local demands for gold for hoarding might be a convenient technique of doing it. I shall not lose sight of this possibility. But, for the reasons given above, just the present moment, when we are hoping for rather satisfactory assistance along quite a different line, is not the right one to choose for going off on a different tack. The difficulty about other proposals is that they seem so trifling quantitatively. The main remedy is, of course, not to shell out so much money. But it seems difficult to persuade the Foreign Office and the military that mere money is not the most effective form of munitions for getting their way.

In July 1942 Kahn sent Keynes another memorandum by Harari suggesting, as Kahn had previously, that higher import prices might prove a useful method of draining away surplus purchasing power. The recommendations of the memorandum were discussed with other proposals at an Anti-Inflation Conference held in Cairo from 23–25 September. The Conference recommended several anti-inflation policies; economy in expenditure, tax increases plus government saving, increased import prices, savings schemes and gold sales. The recommendation favouring gold sales was, however, diluted with a warning that if sales took the form of coin, they might undermine confidence in the local currencies.

The authorities in London were reluctant to raise British export prices, which had remained relatively low owing to price controls and the success of the 1941 stabilisation policy, as the move might create problems in operating the price control and might distort British manufacturers' output decisions with consequential effects on the demand for labour and raw materials. In addition lend lease supplies of many inputs provided a complication, given American sensitivity regarding profiteering. As for gold sales, although Keynes advocated them at a meeting called on 15 October to discuss the Anti-Inflation Conference's recommendations, both he and the others present realised that the proposal was still academic unless America supplied the gold.

Two developments in the following months moved matters nearer a decision:

(1) The rise in Britain's gold and dollar reserves which brought the probability of consequential costs in lend lease or demands for increased reciprocal aid.

(2) The beginning of Allied military operations in Persia with their usual inflationary consequences.

The Persian inflation proved important because the country was not a member of the sterling area, with the result that a payments agreement was necessary. Under the agreement, part of Britain's adverse balance of payments was settled in gold, at first 40 and later 60 per cent. Major Illiff,[4] the local Treasury representative, suggested gold sales on the open market as a means of dealing with inflation and, in the Persian case, economising gold as the open market price was nearly double the price received in official settlements. Major Illiff repeated his proposals and asked for permission to experiment at one of the later Anti-Inflation Conferences held in London late in December 1942. He found support from Mr R. Casey, the new Minister of State,[5] and Mr Rosa, the Treasury official responsible for Syria,[6] who wished to widen the coverage of the experiment. The Bank of England opposed the extension of the scheme beyond Persia, which had a primitive monetary system with few notes and coins in circulation, owing to possible effects on the acceptability of the local currency in other areas and the size of the potential demand. The authorities agreed to the experiment within a limit of one hundred thousand gold pounds (about £119,000).

At this point, the issue of gold sales in the Middle East became involved in the question of gold sales elsewhere, particularly in India where similar problems of inflation and hoarding existed. One of the factors in broadening the discussion was a brief note by Keynes.

[4] Sir William Iliff (b. 1898); Assistant Secretary, Ministry of Labour, 1935; Permanent Secretary, Ministry of Public Security (N. Ireland), 1940–1; Finance Adviser to Governor of Legation, Teheran, 1941–4; Finance Adviser to Governor of Burma, 1944; Representative of Treasury in Middle East, 1944–8.

[5] Richard Gardiner Casey (1890–1976); Assistant Federal Treasurer, Australia, 1933–5; Federal Treasurer, 1935–9; Australia Minister to U.S.A., 1940–2; Minister of State Resident in Middle East and member of U.K. War Cabinet, 1942–3; Governor of Bengal, 1944–6.

[6] John Nogueira Rosa; Treasury representative in Syria and the Lebanon, 1941–2.

To LORD CATTO *and others, 11 February 1943*

This a very significant table [see p. 324]. It means that in all these countries the local currency, alleged to be on some sort of a gold standard, is very heavily depreciated. It looks as if, broadly speaking, gold has gone up about the same amount as prices generally. For example, the highest figure is in Turkey, which is also the case with the index number of prices. It would be a very dubious inference from this that by bringing down the price of gold we could bring down the prices of commodities generally. But I should have thought there must be a good deal of force in the conclusion that to bring down the premium on gold would have some, possibly an appreciable, influence on prices generally.

I think there is a confusion in some people's minds between currency for purposes of circulation and currency or gold for purposes of hoarding. One should be most careful not to do anything which would lead to gold being preferred to currency for circulation purposes. But there does not seem the slightest risk of this. It is only if that were to happen that one could say that the prestige of the currency was being inerfered with. On the other hand, to reduce the depreciation of the currency in terms of gold for hoarding purposes must surely improve the prestige of the currency. These high prices for gold can only indicate an acute distrust of the currency for purposes of hoarding and a belief that it will be heavily depreciated after the war in terms of gold. If people see the price of gold going down, this expectation is likely to be considerably weakened.

I notice that the price of gold is very high in Portugal, Sweden and Switzerland as well as in the Middle East countries. Surely it would pay us, in these countries at least, to sell gold bullion as a commodity as a means of meeting our expenses? I seem to have heard that there is some opposition to this in the case of countries which are neighbours of

Germany. But, if so, this can only be the result of a wild confusion of mind.

I am increasingly inclined to the conclusion that we should approach the U.S. Administration in a big way on the question of putting gold to good use for war purposes. Nor should it be only American gold. Wherever we can realise our own gold at these prices without raising local difficulties or creating dangerous precedents, surely we should do so?

11.2.43   KEYNES

One of the most complex financial problems, in both its political and economic aspects, that faced the British authorities during the war was India. The war created a 'permanent' Indian balance of payments surplus and a consequential accumulation of sterling balances.

The rate of increase of Indian sterling balances was a function of several factors, of which the following were the most important.

1. Allied expenditures on defence and military supplies.

(i) Through the Chatfield modernisation arrangements for the Indian army and supplementary arrangements announced in the House of Commons on 29 February 1940 Britain agreed to defray;

(a) the cost of the Chatfield measures for reorganising and modernising the Indian army;

(b) the wartime increase in the cost of such external defence forces as existed before the war but subsequently went abroad[7];

(c) the whole cost of forces additional to the Indian peacetime establishment which India raised for service abroad after they went abroad;

(d) the full cost of military stores supplied by India for all British forces in the Middle East (and later in the war against Japan).

(ii) American demands for supplies.

2. The rise in prices in India.

3. The Indian balance of payments position. (This was important as British and overseas exports to India declined.)

Before the war, India had a sterling debt of about £360 million. Repatriation of that debt, at some cost to Britain's post-war invisible earnings, proved the first means of dealing with the rising balances. During the summer and autumn of 1940, India repatriated £24 million of her sterling

[7] In 1940, India made a 'once-for-all' payment towards these extra costs.

323

GOLD AND SILVER PRICES—LATEST AVAILABLE FIGURES

Country	Date	Gold		Silver	
		Local quotation	Comparative price in sterling terms (calculated at middle rates)	Local quotation	Comparative price in sterling terms (calculated at middle rates)
India (free market)	26 January 1943	Rupees 66, A 9 per tola	266s. 3d. per fine oz.	Rupees 100, A 14 per 100 tolas	4s. 3d. per fine oz.
Turkey (Istanbul free market)	Average March 1942	Turkish gold pound, 3,473 piastres	£T gold = £6.13.7 sterling (= 624s. per fine oz.)	Medjidie (Turkish 20-piastre piece), 152.13 piastres	9s. per fine oz.
	November 1942 Average March 1942	£T Gold, 3,750 piastres Bar gold, 485.60 piastres per fine gram	£T Gold = £7.4.3 sterling 581s. per fine oz. N.B. Rate of conversion used is £T5.20 = £1 sterling		
Iraq (Baghdad free market)	End June 1942	I. Dinars 4.750 per sovereign	95s. per sovereign	None	
Persia (Teheran free market)	End October 1942 End October 1942	I. Dinars 4.060 per sovereign Bar Gold, 365 Rials per Miskal	81s. per sovereign 382s. per fine oz.	None	
Saudi Arabia (Jeddah free market)	End December 1942 4 November 1942 29 December 1942	668 Rials per sovereign £4.16 per sovereign U.S. $16 per sovereign	104s. 4d. per sovereign 83s.3d. per sovereign 79s. 6d. per sovereign	None	
Syria (Beirut free market)	9 January 1943	£5. 5s. per sovereign	105s. per sovereign	None	
Egypt (Alexandria free market)	23 January 1943	Bar Gold, 171 piastres per dirhem	310s. per fine oz.	None	
Portugal (export of gold coins and bars prohibited from 16 December 1942)	15 December 1942 18 December 1942	Esc. 307/310 per sovereign Bar gold, Esc. 28,131 per kilo fine (Banco de Portugal purchase at this price)	61s. 9d. per sovereign 175s. per fine oz.	None	
Sweden	December 1942	Bar gold, Sw.Kr. 5,600 per kilo fine (sellers)	206s. 2d. per fine oz.	None	
Switzerland	8 December 1942 Maximum prices—subject to licence For Central Bank transactions	Sw.Fcs: 38.45 per sovereign Bar gold, Sw.Fcs. 4.970 per kilo fine National Bank's price Sw.Fcs. 4,869.80/4,920.63 per kilo fine	44s. 4d. per sovereign 178s. 2d. per fine oz. 175s. 6d. per fine oz.	None	
Germany (official rate)	31 December 1942	Reichmarks 20.42 per sovereign		None	

debt, but nevertheless her sterling balances rose by £66 million. To discuss this rise in Indian balances a meeting was held on 15 November 1940 to which Keynes was invited.

To S. D. WALEY, *19 November 1940*

At Sir Henry Strakosch's invitation, I went to a meeting at the India Office on Friday to discuss the problems arising out of the great increase in their sterling balances. Besides Sir Henry Strakosch, Sir Findlater Stewart, Sir S. K. Brown and Mr Baxter[8] were present. Problems were discussed primarily from the point of view of what suggestions it would be advisable to make to the Government of India.

I attach a bundle of statistics which were supplied to me at the meeting.[9] The broad position could be summarised as follows.

The amount of sterling acquired since the beginning of the war up to date is very nearly £m100. The amount of sterling debt purchased out of this and cancelled amounts to about £m24. It is only practicable at present to make trifling purchases on the market so that any material further amount of repatriation requires a new vesting order.

The main problem of the Government of India arises, however, out of the fact that they have made very poor progress with their war borrowing programme. The net proceeds of Defence Bonds, Saving Certificates etc. during the current financial year (i.e. since 1 April 1940) amounts to no more than £m10 after deducting conversions. Against this

---

[8] Sir Henry Strakosch (1871–1943), company director; Adviser, 1937–42, and Honorary Financial Consultant, 1942–3, to Secretary of State for India; member, Financial Committee, League of Nations, 1920–37; member, Council of India, 1930–7.
   Sir Samuel Findlater Stewart (1879–1960); Assistant Under-Secretary of State for India, 1924–30; Permanent Under-Secretary, 1930–42.
   Sir Stuart Kelson Brown (1885–1952); Deputy Under-Secretary of State for India.
   George Herbert Baxter (1894–1962); Financial Secretary, India Office, 1933–43; Assistant Under-Secretary of State for India, 1943–7; Assistant Under-Secretary of State for Commonwealth Relations, 1947–55.
[9] Not printed.

there had been heavy withdrawals of savings from the Savings Banks and cash certificates, especially during the period between April and July, when the news was bad, total withdrawals since 1 April last approaching £m80. The outstanding volume of Treasury bills is practically unchanged, but the amount in the hands of the public is reduced by between £m1 and £m5. Thus, on balance, more loan money has been lost to the public than has been gained from it. It follows that practically the whole of the acquisition of sterling has been financed by the Issue Department out of an increase in the monetary circulation. Altogether the increase in circulation since the beginning of the war amounted to about £m80, of which a very considerable proportion is in the shape of coin.

Naturally this situation is a cause of some anxiety and clearly cannot be allowed to continue indefinitely. On the other hand there is not the slightest sign of inflation. The wholesale price index, after having risen in the first four months of the war, has now fallen back to the pre-war figure, whilst the increase in the cost of living is quite trifling. Moreover, there is quite a fair increase in the volume of business as measured by the clearings. It seems probable, therefore, that a large part of the increase in the monetary circulation is due to hoarding, the public preferring that particular form for their savings in present circumstances to Savings Bank deposits or Government loans. And so long as they are in this mood the increase in the circulation is, of course, quite harmless.

Our conversation ended in two conclusions, both of which met with general approval:–

(1) It seemed advisable to ask the Treasury to vest at an early date some substantial issue. For this purpose the India Office would prefer the 4½% Loan 1950–55. The nominal amount of this outstanding is £m39, but of this some part has already been purchased by Government of India Departments, and some part is in the hands of holders not subject to

a vesting order, leaving, it is thought, some figure rather in excess of £m30 which would fall to be vested. Since the stock stands at a price of about 107½, the amount of money involved might be £m32 or a bit more. This would be purchased by the Issue Department, cancelled and rupee Government securities substituted. The sterling holdings of the Issue Department count towards the reserve, whereas rupee securities do not. But, as a result of the heavy acquisition of sterling, the reserve stands now such a long way above the legal minimum that the Issue Department could part with the above volume of sterling without being embarrassed. In a sense this is no more than a paper transaction and leaves the main problem unsolved. But from the Indian point of view it has the great advantage of saving a very substantial amount of interest and of clearing out of the way the most troublesome of the prospective maturities.

(2) The mere process of substituting rupee securities for sterling securities in the Issue Department leaves the main problem untouched. Clearly it is important to seek new ways of obtaining loans from the public. Obviously the public is now very liquid, so that if the war news improves the background for more successful issues might be favourable. At present the borrowing programme of the Government of India has been somewhat unenterprising. It was thought that they would do well to offer some more novel and some more attractive issues. One of the troubles is that they have worked the yield on the Government stock down to a very unattractive level. For example, at the beginning of the war three months Treasury Bills were yielding about 2¾ %. They now yield only ¾ %. The Defence Bonds are unattractive compared with the longer and undated securities. I need not trouble you, however, with the details about this. The main upshot was that, having regard to the movement of prices, there was no reason to be alarmed at present at the increase in the circulation, but the Government of India would do well to get

busy with a more attractive and, if possible, more successful loan issue. This would pave the way for successive vestings of sterling securities on the above lines with the probable result that the Government of India sterling debt would be reduced to very moderate and manageable proportions by the time the war came to an end.

(3) I took the opportunity of asking what their attitude was towards the surplus commodity proposals. They were extremely unwilling to be left out of this, but recognised that surplus purchase would have no other effect than to aggravate the above problem, since the Government of India's need for rupees locally would be increased by the whole amount of such purchases. Mr Baxter at any rate was prepared to play with the idea of encouraging some rather striking scheme by which a mixed bag of commodities might be held as part of the reserve against the note issue.

[copy initialled] J. M. K.

After the meeting the Indian authorities proposed a more substantial vesting operation totalling £68 million. This was done in February 1941. The rest of 1941 saw further vestings despite the deteriorating situation in the Far East. By 1942 however, the growth of Indian sterling balances and the change in the course of the war led to pressures for a reconsideration of the 1939–40 defence sharing arrangements. At this stage Keynes made a suggestion.

THE COST OF THE INDIAN ARMY

These arrangements date substantially from 1940. At that time the use of the army outside India was primarily for the purpose of defending remoter parts of the Empire, and we were paying 42 per cent of the total cost. In 1942–43 (taking India's contribution at 100 crores) we shall be paying over 78 per cent of the cost (an increase in terms of sterling from £40 million a year to £270 million), whilst the army will be largely occupied in what has now become the defence of India herself. Clearly, therefore, there is overwhelming ground for revising the arrangements.

Such a revision could take several forms. The first step, perhaps, is to consider what form our suggestions can most prudently take. Broadly there are four alternatives:–

(1) A substantial lump sum contribution towards the costs of the war from India as after the last war. Politically this is perhaps the least easy to bring off and is not related with sufficient closeness to the actual costs of India's own war effort.

(2) A new principle of sharing which is based, not on the same sort of formula as at present, but on some very broad division, as, for example, that we meet the excess over a certain sum or that India meets the excess over a certain sum; or, much preferably, that the total costs are divided in some broad proportion such as half each. On the actual figures there is a good deal to be said for an equal division, which would still be very favourable to India. In 1940–41 we were meeting 42 per cent of the cost. If the original estimate for 1941–42 were added to the actual of 1940–41, we should have been meeting just over 50 per cent for the two years together. In fact in 1941–42 we met 68 per cent; whilst in 1942–43 (assuming India's contribution at 100 crores—the exact figure is not stated in these papers) our contribution will reach the preposterous figure of 78 per cent. An equal division in 1942–43 would mean an additional contribution by India approaching £100 million and would bring down our contribution from £270 million to £170 million.

This might be the most reasonable solution to go for. The fact that India is benefiting under lend lease could be used as an additional argument. Also, if it is correct, the fact that the equipment of the Indian army is now increasingly supplied from Indian sources. There would be a rough justice about the equal division, taking all the present circumstances into account.

(3) Another broad line of division would be that we should meet all expenses incurred outside India and that India should meet all costs incurred inside India. I have no material for estimating the outcome of this. At a guess it looks as though this would be more favourable to us than the present arrangement but not so favourable as the half-and-half division.

(4) The final alternative is to vamp up a sufficient amount of special claims where there were exceptional reasons for asking India to shoulder the burden. The papers below indicate some of the more important of these. Allowing for overlaps, which it is suggested may exist, perhaps £40 million or a little better could be obtained from this source. A further sum might be gathered by suggesting that India should lend lease to us the equivalent of the lent-leased material which we transfer to her from U.S. There is no means of estimating this accurately, but I am afraid it would not be a very substantial figure. India's total imports from U.S.A. are now running at about £30 million a year. The amount we can hope to get lent-leased on the most favourable hypothesis is not, I should think likely to exceed £20 million at the most and might be appreciably less. Thus, unless the experts can find more plausible items, it would not be easy to build up so high a total as £100 million from these miscellaneous sources, though it would be possible to build up a figure which was quite worth having.

I should have been inclined to use these miscellaneous cases as the justification for coming to the half and half division rather than as the basis of some strict accounting calculation.

I suggest that this is not a question which can easily be settled departmentally. Would it not be advisable, if the Chancellor approves an approach on any of these lines, for him to discuss the subject on very broad considerations with Mr Amery[10] in the first instance and suggest to Mr Amery that

[10] Leopold Stennett Amery (1873–1955); M.P. (U.) for Sparkbrook, Birmingham, 1911–45; Assistant Secretary, War Cabinet, and Imperial War Cabinet, 1917; on

the best way of reaching a conclusion on this side would be for the matter to be considered by the Cabinet on the basis of a memorandum by the Chancellor? It could then be put to the Government of India with much more weight than would be the case if, as a result of departmental discussions here, a summary of such discussions were merely telegraphed to India departmentally. If this subject could be taken up shortly after the Canadian arrangement has become known, this might offer a specially suitable atmosphere for a discussion.[11]

20.1.42   J.M.K.

After further discussion, the Chancellor raised the matter with Mr Amery in March with an *aide memoire*, partially drafted by Keynes, suggesting that India cover all rupee expenditure and Britain meet her foreign currency needs. To this Mr Amery replied with a defence of the existing arrangements and opposition to the division suggested by the Treasury, which he called arbitrary and unrelated to India's capacity to pay on other criteria. The Chancellor's reply, while disputing some of Mr Amery's points, agreed to let the matter drop until the exact position was clearer.

In July 1942 Sir Jeremy Raisman,[12] the Finance Member of the Viceroy's Council, visited England. As a preliminary, presumably in an attempt to

staff of War Council, Versailles, and on personal staff of Secretary of State for War, 1917–18; Parliamentary Under-Secretary of State for Colonies, 1919–21; Parliamentary and Financial Secretary to Admiralty, 1921–2; First Lord of the Admiralty, 1922–4; Secretary of State for Colonies, 1924–9, for Dominion Affairs, 1925–9, for India and Burma, 1940–5.

[11] At this stage Britain was negotiating the billion dollar gift from Canada for war expenditure during 1942 and early 1943, with its associated repatriation of $295 million of Canadian Government and Canadian National Railway securities held in Britain and the conversion of Canada's sterling balance into a dollar loan interest-free for the duration of the war. Britain also undertook to provide a collateral pledge of non-government Canadian securities against this loan if she provided other Dominions with collateral or if she extended repatriation of securities, in other than marginal cases, beyond Government securities.

[12] Sir (Abraham) Jeremy Raisman (b. 1892); joined Indian Civil Service, 1916; Joint Secretary, Commerce Department, Government of India, 1931–4; member, Central Board of Revenue, 1934; Director, Reserve Bank of India, 1938; Secretary, Finance Department, 1938–9; Finance Member, Government of India, 1939–45; Vice-President, Governor-General's Executive Council, 1944; member, International Monetary Conference, Bretton Woods, 1944.

raise the matter above its current inter-departmental level, Keynes mentioned the matter to Mr Churchill (possibly at or after the meeting of the Other Club, to which they both belonged, on 16 July). The Prime Minister then raised the matter with the Chancellor on 23 July, beginning

> Lord Keynes mentioned to me the other night that we were incurring enormous indebtedness to India and to various Dominions and Colonies.

Mr Churchill then went on to ask for the facts and for a Cabinet discussion.

Given this request and in the light of the discussions with Sir Jeremy Raisman, the Chancellor presented a memorandum to the War Cabinet on 30 July. This memorandum began with Roosevelt's interpretation of lend lease and reciprocal aid, 'that each of the United Nations should end up without a monetary war debt to any of its partners' and went on to argue in favour of the Chancellor's March proposal to Mr Amery. Amery replied in a memorandum, dated 1 August, rejecting a revision of existing arrangements. When the War Cabinet discussed the subject on 6 August, it agreed to defer a final decision until Mr Churchill, then in the Middle East and going on to Moscow, was available. However, it accepted that it was impossible to tear up the existing arrangements.

After the meeting, Mr Amery wrote to the Chancellor suggesting that in the face of either a Japanese invasion or an invasion by Germany through Persia, India would be unable to bear the burden of her own defence. He also suggested that after the war accumulated sterling balances would be 'more likely to prove a blessing than a danger' as they would facilitate the purchase of British exports, particularly capital goods.

> When Mr Waley drafted a reply, on 10 August Keynes wrote on the draft
>
> The last para of Mr Amery's letter [the one on sterling balances] indicates that he is a dangerous lunatic. I think the draft reply ought to convey some hint of this.

Keynes's proposal ran

> Your last paragraph indicates a very dangerous misapprehension about our prospective balance of payments with the rest of the world.

The sentence was included in the draft reply, which, in the end, was never sent.

The Cabinet discussed the matter again in September and agreed to send the Viceroy a cable setting out the case for a revision of the financial arrangements. At the end of October, however, given Indian reaction to the proposals, it agreed to leave the matter for the time being on the clear understanding that the Chancellor retained the right to raise the matter on some future occasion.[13] The decision followed Keynes's advice of 15 September and 8 October, which he repeated on 15 October

> that in view of the political situation in India, the whole matter should be deferred for the time being; the question of what India can properly be asked to pay for her own defence being put off until we have successfully defended her.

Throughout the rest of 1942 and most of 1943, various proposals to reduce or inhibit the growth of Indian sterling balances received a hearing. Amongst these were

(1) the redemption of various securities and annuities (about £30 million in railway annuities were taken over by Britain in September 1942);

(2) provision of reciprocal aid directly by India rather than indirectly by the United Kingdom, thus avoiding the growth of sterling balances (India agreed in December 1942 to provide reciprocal aid to American troops in India and American ships in Indian ports up to the value of lend lease facilities received by India for her own defence, but excluding facilities for the prosecution of Britain's war measures in India);

(3) the payment by India of a capital sum to the United Kingdom in consideration of a series of annual payments calculated to provide the funds for sterling pensions payable by India (about £150 million);

(4) sales of gold and silver;

(5) the tying up of some balances in an Indian reconstruction fund; and

(6) separate gold reserves for India.

Many of the strands came together in Keynes's early 1943 suggestions for a comprehensive settlement arising from the stimulus of a letter to Mr Waley from Mr Baxter dated 30 January 1943.[14]

INDIAN STERLING BALANCES

(1) I agree with Sir D. Waley that this is an interesting and constructive letter, which we should approach sympathetically. It might also be made to fit in with Lord Catto's thesis

---

[13] This decision involved refusing an Indian proposal for a partial offset to British expenditure, which, by the end of the war, would have reduced Indian sterling balances by £100 million.

[14] Baxter's 'particular proposal' concerned a development and reconstruction fund with agreed arrangements for drawings.

that we should not deal with the problem of the Indian sterling balances piecemeal but comprehensively. In the light of this letter, therefore, I should definitely put off the question of a loan to cover pensions, which, for other reasons, is difficult until after the forthcoming Indian Budget, and not attempt to get that ready hastily.

(2) We could no doubt proceed with the development of the particular proposal put to us in Mr Baxter's letter, but it would be much preferable to approach the Government of India with the alternative of either attempting a comprehensive settlement now (which we should prefer) or putting off until the end of the war any attempt to deal with the Indian sterling balances, when they would be treated as part of the general problem of indebtedness arising out of the war and dealt with according to some general formula which may be thought appropriate in those circumstances.

(3) I outline below some first thoughts (though they follow in general some suggestions I made some months ago) as to the general principles of a comprehensive settlement:–

(i) A development and reconstruction fund of £m200 to be set up on the general lines of Mr Baxter's letter. This sum to be spent, at a rate not to exceed £m20 per annum except by mutual agreement and to carry no interest meanwhile, on capital goods and equipment ordered under an agreed plan.

(ii) The proposed loan for pensions of (say) £m130 to go through on the lines already discussed, subject to an unequivocal understanding that it would be to sterling pensions that this sum is actually devoted.

(iii) A sum of £m50 in gold to be sold against sterling for the Indian Currency Reserve.

(iv) A special obligation of £m100, to be deposited with the Currency Reserve against the surrender of an equal value of balances or other sterling securities now held by the currency reserve. This special security would be kept of constant value in terms of rupees at the present rate of exchange between sterling and rupees; it would carry interest at the current British Treasury bill rate; and it would be drawn upon for the purposes of the Currency Reserve only after the £m50 of additional gold under (iii) had been employed, and *pari passu* with the further use of the gold already in the Currency Reserve.

(v) India to increase her share of war expenses sufficiently to prevent the sterling balances and investments of the Reserve Bank, Currency Reserve and other Government funds from exceeding £m50 during the war and for so long after as is required to clear up existing outstanding war expenses.

The existing arrangements with India as a member of the sterling area to continue as before; i.e. whilst we should be augmenting her existing gold reserves, we should not be putting a separate dollar reserve at her disposal, but she would turn over her dollars to us and we should remain under our present responsibility to provide her with dollars.

3.2.43   KEYNES

At this stage, the problems of India and the Middle East merged in the course of the discussions on gold sales, for India experienced the same problems of inflation and commodity hoarding. Initially, the Government of India thought such sales dangerous, as did the Treasury. Initially, the Indians demanded double the amount of gold sold in the Middle East be alloted to the Indian reserves. However, inflationary conditions in India, enthusiasm with the results of gold sales in the Middle East and the powerful support of Keynes and Lord Catto for such schemes led to the Treasury agreeing to an experiment, despite Bank of England objections, for the scheme promised to soak up excess purchasing power, finance British local expenditure and keep down Britain's reserves so as to minimise the risk of lend lease cuts. On 11 June the Minister of State in Cairo and the India Office were informed of a programme of sales of 375,000 and 750,000 ounces in the Middle East and India respectively. The result, according to the official historian of British wartime financial policy, was 'an experiment that may be claimed as one of the most successful in war finance'.[15]

[15] Sayers, *Financial Policy*, p. 270.

Between then and the end of the war sales of £11 million of gold in the Middle East and £44 million in India reduced sterling balances by £22 million and £77 million respectively.

Soon after Indian gold sales began, however, the India Office suggested that the profits from the programme should accrue to India. On this proposal Keynes wrote

INDIA AND GOLD PROFIT

1. This is not a currency transaction but the sale of a commodity. The commodity we shall be selling has not risen in price more than the commodities we are buying. We shall be bearing all costs and considerable risks, and the actual amount of profit is quite uncertain.

2. India has gold of her own which she can sell at a profit if she so wishes. But this happens to be our gold. This is not one of the purposes for which gold is available to other members of the sterling area under existing arrangements.

3. The present proposal is the uniform condition of the scheme throughout the areas in which we are selling gold, which we understood the Government of India had accepted. If the Secretary of State is successful in persuading the Government of India to change their minds, our proposal must be regarded as withdrawn, since the condition was considered absolutely vital by the Chancellor of the Exchequer in initially agreeing to the scheme at all.

4. India is already profiteering out of the war unduly. If the Secretary of State on his own initiative tries to interfere with this very mild offsetting measure, the Chancellor of the Exchequer will use his influence with the Prime Minister to have the Secretary of State hung, drawn and quartered.

7.7.43   [copy initialled]   K

Meanwhile, inflation became even more rapid in India. This inflation, plus famine conditions resulting from crop failures, wartime supply disruptions and hoarding owing to shortages of consumer goods and expectations of higher prices led to the appointment of a Ministerial Standing Committee on Indian Financial Questions under the chairmanship of the Chancellor. This Committee was to deal with both the inflationary situation and the problem of sterling balances. Keynes again attempted to push the Treasury towards a comprehensive settlement. Initially he produced an outline for a Treasury paper for the Committee, which Mr N. E. Young eventually filled out. It was not used. Later he produced his own paper for the Committee. This was circulated on 10 January 1944. These two papers appear below.

To SIR WILFRED EADY, *10 August 1943*

THE PROBLEM OF INDIA'S STERLING BALANCES

I suggest that the Treasury memorandum on this subject might be arranged somewhat as follows:–

1. A statement of what India has done on the physical and man-power plane. Her contribution is very large. It is unfair to minimise it. Unless this is made clear, there will be misunderstanding of what the criticism is about. The point to be emphasised is the contrast between the excellence of India's contribution on the above plane and the unsatisfactory character of the accompanying and consequential financial arrangements.

2. It should also be admitted freely that the scale of the financial problem which has arisen is a direct consequence of the greatness of India's contribution of men and resources.

3. The nature of the *de facto* financial arrangements should be set out in a fuller and clearer form than any statement of them I have seen yet.

4. It should be emphasised that, in the main, these arrangements were made at a time when India was not directly

337

threatened but was giving (or expected to give) valuable military aid far beyond her own frontiers, and in circumstances when the subsequent scale of the expenditure was not in the least foreseen. If these arrangements are open to criticism it is because they have been insufficiently revised to meet entirely new conditions when India herself is threatened and a large proportion of the expense incurred is a direct cost of the defence of India herself.

5. The aggregate sums which we are called on to repay to the Government of India should be roughly analysed under the following heads (or under whatever heads are most relevant to the facts):–

(i) the cost of Indian troops operating in distant theatres of war not adjoining India's own frontiers;

(ii) the cost of Indian troops operating in theatres of war adjoining India or directly concerned with the defence of India's frontiers;

(iii) contributions to the cost of equipping and training the Indian Army in India itself;

(iv) expenses of the British defence forces (including the Navy) incurred within India, exclusive of the pay of the troops;

(v) the upkeep of prisoners of war transferred to India;

(vi) the cost of munitions of war and other war stores manufactured in India and delivered abroad on our account;

(vii) the cost of raw materials purchased in India by British Government Departments;

(viii) net sterling earnings of India on account of the balance of trade (including the pay of British troops);

(ix) net dollar earnings of India on account of her balance of trade (including the pay of American troops) transferred to British account in exchange for sterling;

(x) any other items.

6. A statement of other expenses incurred in sterling by

British forces, including the Navy, concerned with the defence of India.

7. The fact that India is herself incurring a fairly substantial increase of war expenditure should be developed and figures of this increased expenditure should be given, so as to show how it compares with British expenditure on Indian Defence.

8. The above items would constitute Part I and would be concerned solely with questions of fact. Clearly it would have to be prepared in collaboration with the Indian Office, which would be in a better position over a considerable part of the field to provide the facts without undue trouble. There would then follow Part II which would propose a solution of the problem of the balances.

9. It is evident that the sterling balances cannot be made freely available without limit for purchases by India in all parts of the world in the immediate post-war period. There must, therefore, be some measure of funding, and, if possible, it should at the same time be made clear what part can be regarded and hereafter treated by India as a liquid reserve available to meet an adverse balance of trade.

10. If the availability of a substantial part of the balances is to be postponed, the question of interest arises. Here is the clue to an equitable solution. The expenditure, which gave rise to the debt, has not given rise to an interest- or profit-earning asset. It is a dead-weight debt largely incurred, directly or indirectly, for the defence of India. India is, in fact, earning (or, rather, saving) interest on that part of it which has been devoted to the discharge of existing indebtedness (which indebtedness was entirely represented by interest-earning assets such as railways and public works, the former dead-weight element in it having been discharged some years ago). It is also proposed below that interest at Treasury bill rate should be allowed on the increased quasi-permanent sterling holdings of the Currency Reserve. But as regards the

rest it is entirely inappropriate that the sum should be regarded as a proper subject for usury. (We should lay this down as a principle of all-round application in the case of all dead-weight debts arising out of the war.) We do not ask India for a lump-sum contribution to the costs of the war in spite of the original financial settlement having been so excessively in her favour. The proposal below is for a full repayment, but, as regards a part of the debt, a repayment spread over a period without interest.

11. Subject to these general principles, the outline of a settlement might be as follows. The allocation of particular sums against the several heads is based on an immediate settlement covering sterling balances estimated to stand at the end of 1943 at an aggregate of £750 million:-

(a) £100 million to be transferred in gold to the Indian Currency Reserve;

(b) £250 million to be held by the Indian Currency Reserve in sterling Treasury bills, not to be reduced below this figure until after the above £100 million gold has been exhausted in meeting an adverse balance of payments on current account (exclusive of outward capital transactions and purchases of gold and silver bullion);

(c) £200 million (or whatever is the appropriate figure) to be set aside in a Pension Fund, not carrying interest, to be applied year by year to the discharge of pensions due by the Government of India in terms of sterling;

(d) £200 million to be set aside in a Reconstruction Fund, not carrying interest, to be available at a rate not exceeding £20 million a year (except by mutual agreement) commencing three years after the end of the war for the purchase of capital goods manufactured in the U.K. in accordance with a programme to be mutually agreed.

12. These proposals would clear the position up to the end of 1943. As regards subsequent expenditure, we should invite the Government of India to consider what supplies or

local expenses she is prepared to furnish to the U.S. and U.K. Governments as reciprocal aid, the *same* general principles governing the aid so applied to the two Governments.

13. As regards the balance of the war expenditure incurred in India by the U.S. and U.K. Governments, that is to say the items of §5 above excluding (vii), (viii) and (ix), we should propose to the U.S. that it should be shared by them and by us in equal portions.

14. The increase in India's sterling balances accruing in respect of the U.K.'s half-share and for items (vii), (viii) and (ix) of 5 should then be dealt with as follows:

(*a*) the equivalent of item (ix) to be transferred to the Indian Currency Reserve in gold as an addition to the gold under 11 (*a*) above and on the same conditions, but the sale of gold in India by the U.S. and U.K. Governments on joint account should be deemed to operate so as to diminish item (ix) for the purpose of calculating the amount of gold to be transferred;

(*b*) half of the balance to be added to the Treasury bill holdings of the Indian Currency Reserve, subject to the same conditions as under 11 (*b*) above;

(*c*) the remaining half to be added to the Reconstruction Fund subject to the same conditions as under 11 (*d*) above, i.e. so operating as to extend the period of years over which the annual instalments of £20 million will be available.

10.8.43   KEYNES

THE INDIAN STERLING BALANCES

There are two problems—(1) means to retard the growth of the Indian sterling balances, and (2) means to deal with the existing accumulations. (1) is, of course, very important and desirable, but unless the war continues a long time yet (2) is likely to be the more important in absolute amount.

Taking (1) first, the chief expedients open to us are the following:–

(1) A revision of the military settlement, so that India takes over a larger share of the costs of Indian troops. In particular, the existing provision by which Indian responsibility ceases when Indian troops cross the frontier, whilst perhaps reasonable when the settlement was first made in the expectation that it would apply to Indian troops employed far afield, e.g. in Egypt, in operations only remotely concerned with the defence of India, is absurd when it is applied to troops leaving India for (e.g.) Burma.

(2) A stricter control of Indian contract prices and measures to retard the progress of inflation generally,—very desirable, but not likely to save a large sum of money in the near future. Moreover, the utmost we can hope is to retard the progress of inflation,—the general price-level can scarcely be expected to fall so long as the war lasts.

(3) The taking over by India of various miscellaneous services—e.g. the cost of prisoners, the whole cost of capital works, the whole cost of reciprocal aid to U.S. and so forth —worth considering, but, here also, it is not easy to save large sums in this way.

(4) A direct contribution of (say) £50 million a year to our general costs of defending India, including the Navy.

Why not tell the Government of India that they must relieve us of (say) £75 million a year in the aggregate under the above heads, and leave them to decide which way of attaining this result is politically easiest? It would facilitate the discussion of this question if British expenditure in India could be analysed under the heads given in the Appendix to this paper.

There are two other expedients of rather a different character:–

(5) A reduction of the sterling value of the rupee, so that a given volume of rupee expenditure costs less sterling.

(6) The issue of a British Government loan in India. This does not reduce the ultimate burden, but limits the accumulation of unfunded sterling balances.

I return to these two proposals below.

Let us turn to (2), the accumulated sterling balances. These amounted to £m655 on 30 September 1943, having increased by £m296 in the previous twelve months. It is estimated that they will amount to £m900 on 30 June 1944. This gigantic obligation is the real, major problem, and its satisfactory handling is indispensable to the solution of our post-war financial problem.

I believe, most strongly, that the key is to be found in the avoidance of interest charges and the gradual repayment of the capital sum either free of interest or chargeable at a very low rate. If repayment is spread—as will in any case be necessary—over a long period, this makes a vast difference, much greater than is easily realised before it is actually worked out. Moreover, if a rate of interest were taken corresponding to what we pay in this country on a loan of similar maturity, the effective burden is very much greater than in the case of our domestic obligations, because it would have to be paid free of income tax.

The principle of no-interest is easily explained and justified. The expenditure, which gave rise to the debt, has not provided in return a profit-earning asset. There are no earnings and there was no expectation of earnings out of which interest could be paid. It is a dead-weight debt, all incurred for the common cause, and largely, directly or indirectly, for the defence of India. The investment or lending analogy, which would call for the payment of interest to individuals, is entirely false as between Allied Governments. Moreover, India is, in fact, earning (or, rather, saving) interest on that part of her gains which has been devoted to the discharge of her pre-war indebtedness (which indebtedness was entirely represented by interest-earning assets such

343

as railways and public works, the former dead-weight element in it having been discharged some years ago). Thus the no-interest principle would be applied in part only.

From the political and public point of view, therefore, the above might be easier to justify than any alternative means of equal efficacy;—above all if we apply the same principle, as I hope we shall, to *all* obligations arising between the Allies out of the war. Could not an attempt be made to establish this between heads of Governments as a principle to be adopted and publicly announced?

Before returning to the Indian problem, it is worth while to consider some of the other possible applications of this principle. It would apply, for example, to our own loan to Russia for civilian supplies. It would apply to Canada's loan to us, which carries no interest during the war but is to carry a rate of interest to be agreed hereafter when the war comes to an end. It might apply to the loan which we shall most certainly require from the U.S., after lend lease comes to an end, to enable us to clear up our international position during the demobilisation and transitional period immediately after the war. (It is certainly advisable, so as to free us in export policy, that we should pay for raw materials from the U.S. as soon as the war is over; and very possibly for food also. The principle of relief is that it should leave no inter-Allied indebtedness behind it. To us, and to us alone, it is not proposed to apply this principle. But it might be wise and reasonable for us to claim a middle course, agreeing to repay the sums advanced but not at interest.)

The application of this principle to the Indian position might be as follows:–

(*a*) £100 million to be paid off in gold forthwith for transfer to the Indian Currency Reserve.

(*b*) £250 million to be held by the Indian Currency Reserve in Special Treasury bills carrying ½ per cent interest, these bills to be renewed and not encashed until after the above

£100 million in gold has been exhausted in meeting a balance of payments adverse to India on current account, exclusive of outward capital transactions and purchases of gold and silver bullion (these items being met either out of a current favourable balance or out of India's existing gold reserves).

(c) £250 million (or whatever is the appropriate figure) to be set aside in a Pension Fund, not carrying interest, to be applied year by year to the discharge of pensions due by the Government of India in terms of sterling to British residents.

(d) The balance, say £300 million as at 30 June 1944, but increasing so long as the war lasts, to be set aside in a Reconstruction Fund, not carrying interest, to be available at a rate not exceeding £15 million a year (except by mutual agreement) commencing three years after the end of the war, for the purchase of capital goods manufactured in the U.K. in accordance with a programme to be mutually agreed.

(e) The sums under (b) and (d) to be subject to an exchange guarantee in terms of rupees, so that they would be appropriately written up if the rupee appreciates on sterling and written down if it depreciates. This provision might be actually preferred by India, especially as regards (b), since it insures that the reserve is stable in the same money of account as that in which the corresponding liabilities are expressed. About a year ago Raisman, if I remember right, was actually asking for an exchange guarantee. From our point of view, it has the great (and just) advantage that, if, in the event, it turns out to be the case (as it well may) that the present 1s. 6d. rate at which we are incurring liabilities over-values the rupee (owing to the progress of inflation in India) and so over-charges us, this will, in the long run, be remedied at least in part. For example, if the rupee falls hereafter to 1s., this would relieve us of one-third of our sterling liabilities under (b) and (d).

In the light of the above we can now return to the two

expedients, mentioned above, of a change in the rupee exchange and the issue of British Government securities in India.

The above proposal is much preferable to a change in the rupee exchange now, because it achieves the same object more completely. For, whilst the latter would relieve our current liabilities, it might seriously aggravate the task of discharging our accumulated liabilities. Moreover, if the change were made on our initiative, it would raise political difficulties; whereas it is quite likely that it will come about hereafter on Congress initiative. Failing the above no-interest settlement, there is much to be said for a British Government loan in India on appropriate terms. But, compared with the above, it has the disadvantage of bringing in the interest element and thus further compromising the above principle.

In concentrating on the Indian problem we must not lose sight of the similar problem for the other countries of the Middle East. Our largest liabilities are as follows:–

£ million

	Liabilities on 30 Sept. 1943	Change in previous year
Egypt and A.E. Sudan	254	100
Palestine and Transjordan	79	33

We were still *subsidising* Palestine when I last heard about it. The above figures are even more out of proportion than the liabilities to India, whilst the degree of inflation in the Middle East is materially greater than in India—

Wholesale prices (1939 = 100)

Egypt	289	Syria	727
Palestine	329	Iraq	612
		Persia	449

17 December 1943   KEYNES

APPENDIX

The aggregate sums which we are called on to repay to the Government of India should be roughly analysed under the following heads (or under whatever heads are most relevant to the facts):–

(i) the cost of Indian troops operating in distant theatres of war not adjoining India's own frontiers;

(ii) the cost of Indian troops operating in theatres of war adjoining India or directly concerned with the defence of India's frontiers;

(iii) contributions to the cost of equipping and training the Indian Army in India itself;

(iv) expenses of the British defence forces (including the Navy) incurred within India, exclusive of the pay of the troops;

(v) the upkeep of prisoners of war transferred to India;

(vi) the cost of munitions of war and other war stores manufactured in India and delivered abroad on our account;

(vii) the cost of raw material purchased in India by British Government Departments;

(viii) net sterling earnings of India on account of the balance of trade (including the pay of British troops);

(ix) net dollar earnings of India on account of her balance of trade (including the pay of American troops) transferred to British account in exchange for sterling;

(x) any other items.

Neither paper nor any of the Committee's deliberations came to anything beyond the Committee's agreement to leave the problem of the sterling balances until the end of the war and meanwhile pay a low rate of interest on them. As a result, the Indian problem, despite occasional eruptions, merged into the more general problem of the appropriate overall post-war financial settlement.

DOCUMENTS REPRODUCED
IN THIS VOLUME

Where Documents come from the Public Record Office, their call numbers
appear before the date.

LIST OF DOCUMENTS REPRODUCED

LIST OF DOCUMENTS REPRODUCED

ACKNOWLEDGEMENTS

The Editors would like to thank the Controller of Her Majesty's Stationery Office for permission to reproduce Crown Copyright materials. They would also like to thank Professor R. S. Sayers for advice, Mr Walter Salant for certain documents and the Canada Council for financial assistance.

INDEX

Acheson, Dean Goodenham, Assistant Secretary of State, U.S.A.

drafts paper on 'consideration', 94; talks with JMK on, 125, 126–7, 152, 153; criticises JMK's one-sided note on, 162; discussions with President on, 163, 165–6; memorandum of conversation with JMK on, 171–2, 194; hands draft agreement to JMK, 171, 173, 194; notes JMK's objections to 'discrimination' clause, 175–7, 195; problem of Imperial Preference raised by draft, 201–2

member of Balances Committee, 292; note on balances problem for, 277 n 13, 298, 299–301; views on reciprocal aid White Paper, 301, 302–3; his position improved under new Office of Foreign Economic Administration, 314

debate with Frankfurter on declaration of war, 95–6; hospitality to JMK and Mrs Keynes, 299; gets good press, 239

letters to, 177–8, 298–9

also mentioned, 207

Acheson, Edward Campion (Ted), economic adviser on reciprocal aid: attends JMK's working lunches on dollar balances, 286, 287, 292; 'squeezed out' in new Office of Foreign Economic Administration, 312

Africa, 111; 'written off' in America, 112

North Africa, hostilities in, 277; lend lease aid for, 305

West and East Africa, under lend lease, 239

see also Egypt; South Africa

agricultural products and machinery under lend lease, 43, 76, 77, 116, 117, 123, 124, 297

tank production by tractor manufacturers, 104

aeroplanes, 244, 267

ferrying of aircraft under lend lease, 158

air contracts, 233, 238, 244

air training schemes, 158

Allies

expenditure in India, 323

financed by Britain, 29, 247, 278†, 283; loans *versus* free gifts for, 32; proposed loans without interest, 260, 343–4

transfers to, under lend lease, 171

war indebtedness among Allies, aim to avoid, 171

aluminium, 104–5

American

assets in Britain, 3–4

economists, 181–93, 208; statisticians, 157

investors, 14–15

officials, 168

in Persia, 251

public, 47, 96

subsidiaries of British businesses, 10–11, 68–9, 122 n 28. *See also* American Viscose; direct investments

see also United States of America

American Viscose Company, subsidiary of Courtaulds, 10; selected for 'show sale' of British assets in U.S.A., 52; negotiations, 56, 64–6, 72, 91, 114 n 26, 122, 150, 152; JMK believed to be in U.S.A. to prevent sale, 93, 97–9; the sale effected, 72 nn 1, 4

Amery, Leopold Stennett, M.P., Secretary of State for India and Burma, 203, 206, 330–1; policy on gold profits, 336

Anglo-American Commission for postwar cooperation, proposal for, 128, 140, 142, 153, 195

between savings and investment, 182
in U.K., achieved by shortages and rationing, 190
Europe
  exchange and import controls, 146
  post-war disarmament plans, 109; police force for, 109–10
  relief and reconstruction, 119, 139
  Roosevelt promise of American co-operation, 110
exchange control, 3
  in Egypt, 261
  loopholes, 4
  and payments agreements, 6; with neutrals, 23–4
  in post-war period, 102; in South America and Europe, 146
  under lend lease, 'discrimination' clause, 172, 175–6
  sterling area Exchange Control and dollar balances, 235, 257–8
  subject to U.S. State Department under proposed trade agreement, 145
Exchange Control Conference: JMK a member, 1; memorandum for, 2–10; meetings, 10; Greek balance at Bank of England discussed, 33; Washington Mission discussed with, 196
Exchange Equalisation Account (Fund), 215, 231; Account, 231, 245
exchange reserves, 66 n 11, 229
exchange resources reservations, for trade agreement, 143
exchange risk, 284
'Export Policy', 197–9
exports: U.K.
  export organisation in U.S.A., direct investments part of, 45, 57, 69–70
  and lend lease, 130–1, 196, 201
  to pay for war purchases, 8; to repay U.S. loans, 19–20; for necessary imports, 196; for foreign exchange, 199
  prices, 320
  to South America, 17
  visible and invisible, 2; to U.S.A., 27, 28, 52; attempts to maximise dollar export earnings, 143; American criticism of policy, 166–7
  wartime restrictions, 276
  White Paper on freedom to export, 276, 301, 304
  see also balance of trade; imports

exports: U.S.A.
  imbalance of exports and imports, 208
  see also balance of trade; imports

Federal Reserve System, Board of, 255
  JMK's conference with, 295
'Financial Deal with U.S.A.', 233–6
Food, Ministry of, 9, 145, 168
foods
  imports, 196
  under lend lease, 47, 92, 168, 169, 198, 227, 303; under reciprocal aid, 293–4
  post-war plans for, 344
  shortages in Middle East, 316
Foreign Economic Administration, U.S.A., Office of, 306, 309–14
foreign exchange: under Exchange Control Conference, 1; triangular transactions, 2; exchange regulations, 4–6; exports and, 196
  'Foreign Exchange Control and Payments Agreements', 2–10
  see also Exchange Control
Foreign Office, U.K., 9, 45, 224, 320
Foreign Secretary, see Eden, Robert Anthony
forestry products, 43
France
  assets in U.S.A., 1, 14
  fall of, 1, 4, 8
  Free French, 235, 260
  hoarding, 4
  reserves, 227, 281
Frankfurter, Felix, Supreme Court Justice, U.S.A., JMK dines with, 95
Fraser, W. L., at the Treasury, 33
free trade, 102, 139, 202; versus control mechanisms, 177, 196
freedom of the seas, 139
full employment, 181; full utilization of capacity, 184, 186

Galbraith, John Kenneth, American economist, 182
Germany
  indemnity after World War I, 20
  price of gold, 324
  Roosevelt's plan for a federal Germany, 110
  in World War II: successes in the West, 1; Einstein's advice to bomb, 113; defeat, 315
  also mentioned, 323